Silent Love

The Annotation and Interpretation of Nabokov's
The Real Life of Sebastian Knight

Silent Love

The Annotation and Interpretation of Nabokov's *The Real Life of Sebastian Knight*

GERARD DE VRIES

Boston
2016

Library of Congress Cataloging-in-Publication Data:
The bibliographic data for this title is available from the
Library of Congress.
© 2016 Academic Studies Press
All rights reserved

ISBN 978-1-61811-833-2
ISBN 978-1-61811-500-3 (electronic)

Book design by Kryon Publishing
www.kryonpublishing.com

On the cover: Portrait of R.S. Ernst, by Zinaida Serebriakova, 1921.
Reproduced by permission of the Nizhnii Novgorod State Art Museum.

Published by Academic Studies Press in 2016
28 Montfern Avenue
Brighton, MA 02135, USA
press@academicstudiespress.com
www.academicstudiespress.com

For Wytske, Julian, Olivia, and Isabel.

O learn to read what silent love has writ.

—William Shakespeare

Table of Contents

	Acknowledgments	viii
CHAPTER 1	Introduction	1
CHAPTER 2	Annotations	8
CHAPTER 3	Motifs: Narrative	76
CHAPTER 4	Motifs: Identities	109
CHAPTER 5	Motifs: Death and Beyond	161
CHAPTER 6	Conclusion	173
	Works Cited	195
	Index	213

Acknowledgments

When I first read Nabokov's novels I was so perplexed by their perfection that I had the impression that they would resist critical inspection, like a brilliant glittering so copious that it is impossible to study its facets. But I soon discovered that a large body of scholarly criticism on Nabokov's prose had been written, and these studies opened doors that I thought were not even there.

I met many authors of these admirable works during the first Nabokov Conference in Nice, held in 1991, and in subsequent years I received, although I had hardly any credentials to show, much support for my endeavors to find my own way in the labyrinth of Nabokov's art. The encouragement I received from, among others, Gennady Barabtarlo, Brian Boyd, Maurice Couturier, D. Barton Johnson, Stephen Parker, Pekka Tammi, and Leona Toker I still regard as invaluable.

For the present study I gratefully acknowledge the help I have recieved, with some queries or otherwise, from Dana Dragunoiu, Lara Delage-Toriel, Jeff Edmunds, Siggy Frank, Lev Grossman, Yuri Leving, Priscilla Meyer, Eric Naiman, Arthur Langeveld, Tatiana Ponomareva, Galina Rylkova, Stanislav Shvabrin and Susan Elizabeth Sweeney. Julian Connolly has been so kind as to read an earlier version and to send me some very welcome suggestions. His thoughtful reservation about my comments on Sebastian Knight's last letter caused many deliberations. I am also most grateful for the generous help I received from Barbara Wyllie. She pointed out many passages that needed improvement, mentioned new publications I had missed, and spotted a serious flaw in the book's composition that I eagerly have tried to mend. And I am indebted to an anonymous reader for specifying some lacunae which I hope I have remedied adequately.

I also wish to thank Quirine van Wijland-Kampman who helped me once more to transform many handwritten pages into a handsome typescript.

Finally, I wish to thank the editors at Academic Studies Press who took care of my manuscript, Meghan Vicks and Kira Nemirovsky, for their kind help in turning it into a book.

The book is dedicated to our grandchildren and I hope that their listening to my simple tales will stimulate them in the years to come to find their way to the many marvelous stories written by novelists like Vladimir Nabokov.

Introduction

CHAPTER 1

The Real Life of Sebastian Knight is a novel shaped as a biography about the novelist Sebastian Knight, written by his half-brother V. after Sebastian dies in 1936 at the age of thirty-six when V. is thirty years old. After V.'s mother (the last surviving parent) died in 1922, there were only two chance meetings between the brothers who had drifted apart. V. tries to compensate for this hiatus by writing Sebastian's biography. He discovers that Sebastian's life took a tragic turn when he left his lovely and devoted partner Clare after being caught in the web of a femme fatale, Nina, who wound up ruining his life.

Nabokov began writing this novel in December 1938 and completed it in January of the next year, while living with his wife, Véra, and their son, Dmitri, in Paris. Their apartment was on 8 Rue de Saigon, near the Place d'Étoile. Because the apartment had only one room, the bathroom served as Nabokov's study (Boyd, *VNRY* 492–496). It was the first novel Nabokov wrote in English, and it was published in the United States two years after its completion, in December 1941 (Boyd, *VNAY* 40). In England the first edition appeared in 1945 (Juliar 164–165). In the years following the writing of *Sebastian Knight* Nabokov wrote the novella *The Enchanter*, as well as the stories "Ultima Thule" and "Solus Rex," all written again in Russian. In the years preceding *Sebastian Knight*, he wrote *The Gift*, his great Russian novel, completed in 1938 (Boyd, *VNRY* 446).

Nabokov lamented the transition from the Russian to the English language until his death in 1977. Despite his excellent command of the English language—Nabokov is regarded as one of the greatest stylists of the twentieth century writing in English—the loss of his mother tongue was perhaps worse than his exile from Russian soil. But Nabokov had no choice: writing in Russian for a disintegrating émigré community had no future. As Simon Karlinsky writes, "the most important ingredient that a thriving literature needs—readers—was in short supply." And the Western world from the 1930s on "came to regard the existence of an exiled Russian literature in its midst with a mixture of hostility and studied indifference" (*Bitter Air of Exile* 6). Moreover, being married to a Jewish woman, Nabokov and his family had to leave Continental Europe and flee to the United States in the spring of 1940.

The years that preceded the writing of *Sebastian Knight* were exceedingly stressful for Nabokov. The impending war was of course a perilous threat; as a Jewess Véra Nabokov lost her job in Berlin in 1936. The following year Nabokov had an extramarital affair with Irina Guadanini, which ended only after it had culminated in a grim crisis in the Nabokovs' marriage. In 1939 his mother died, and although she was impoverished Nabokov had hardly been able to support her or even to attend her funeral in Prague.

Sebastian Knight's life shows many parallels with that of his creator. Both were born in St. Petersburg in 1899 into a wealthy, cultured, and British-oriented family. Both had a Swiss governess and both fled from revolutionary Russia. They studied at Trinity College in Cambridge, became novelists, and switched from Russian to English. They had stable relationships with their partners, which, in Nabokov's case, was severely tested and, in Sebastian's case, ended with the interference of an enchantress. Even Sebastian's first love recalls that of Nabokov. And, as will be discussed, Clare resembles Véra in many ways, while Nina shares her main quality as a femme fatale with Irina Guadanini.

Surprisingly, it was the relationship with his brother Sergey that Nabokov singled out in his autobiography *Speak, Memory*, a reference as clear as its purport was enigmatic: "For various reasons I find it inordinately hard to speak about my . . . brother [Sergey]. That twisted quest for Sebastian Knight . . . , with its gloriettes and self-made combinations, is really nothing in comparison to the task I balked in the first version of this memoir and am faced with now" (257). The two Nabokov brothers were not close (although much closer than Sebastian and V.) and Sergey's homosexuality did not help to make their contact more intimate. Perhaps the uneasiness Nabokov felt toward his brother was unduly influenced by Nabokov's inability to look at homosexuality without any disapproval.

V. frequently states that the responsibility to make his biography as scrupulously reliable as possible weighs heavily on him. Despite his efforts, he seems to be the worst biographer imaginable as far as objectivity is concerned. In *The Gift* Nabokov presented a portrait of Nikolay Chernyshevsky that differed radically from conventional biographies; a legitimate choice, Nabokov said, because "at least the plain truth of documents is on my side. That, and only that, is what I would ask of my biographer—plain facts" (*SO* 156). Documents can consist of letters, journals, diaries, archives, recorded testimonies, and interviews. In V.'s biography, only one single document is presented: Sebastian's last letter, and as this is translated by V. from Russian into English (with momentous consequences as will be discussed) it can be said that even this piece of evidence is not authentic.

As V.'s book is, rather, a report of the way he has composed the work and the efforts this entailed, it can also be regarded as V.'s autobiography. V. seems to endorse André Maurois's opinion "that the main subject of any biography is 'the medium of the biographer's own feelings'" (qtd. in Hermione Lee 134).

David Rampton has written that V. is a "somewhat pompous fool" and many of V.'s actions do not contradict this (70). According to Page Stegner he is "not only unreliable, but a little mad as well" (71). V.'s rash hunt after the femme fatale—a doubly passionate pursuit, first as a biographer but soon as a budding lover—takes much of his time but is, from V.'s point of view, rather ludicrous. V. wishes to "see her at all costs" because he "wants to ask her a certain question—one question only" (159). This question appears to be whether she knew that "Sebastian was one of the most remarkable writers of his time" (172). But all the time V. knew that the answer would be an affirmative one. During his second visit to Nina he asks her if her friend knows "that Sebastian Knight is dead? Madame Lecerf closed her dark velvety eyes in a silent 'yes'" (153). As V. suggests in the next sentence, she must have learned about Sebastian's death from the obituaries in the papers. Of course Sebastian's death could be of interest for the papers only because he is a writer, which means that the necrologies would have focused exclusively on his literary achievements. There seems to be no need at all to remind Nina of Sebastian's prestige as a novelist.

The novel has many such farcical episodes. It begins with a digression on a lady-diarist who collected the details of the day's weather and ends with the incredible story that V. travels for twenty weary hours to visit not his brother but a complete stranger.

Nabokov wrote that for the composition of his chess problems he used as a strategy "deceit, to the point of diabolism, and originality, verging upon the grotesque" (*Speak, Memory* 289). The better the spectators are diverted, the better the puppet master can plot the real story.

Despite its playfulness *Sebastian Knight* strikes the reader by its earnestness: one feels that something serious is going on which is unfathomable. This is due to the novel's unusual richness and subdued emotionality. "Never before," writes Brian Boyd, "had [Nabokov] packed such a complex structure into such a small space with such seeming ease" (*VNRY* 496). "Tightly constructed," says Charles Nicol, "*Sebastian Knight* is more congenially designed for rereading than any novel I know" (85).

If Nina ruins Sebastian's life, he, at least, recognizes her type and is aware of the misfortunes she brings about. How different is Clare's lot. She is spurned in a cruel way, without any clemency. This seems completely out of Sebastian's character, as he constantly instructs himself to pay attention to people who cannot command it: cloakroom ladies, beggars, cabmen. One can agree with Anthony Olcott that "the author, functioning behind his narrator," fashions "a more complete story than that [of which] the narrator, and the careless reader, is aware" (107). Lucy Léon Noel, with whom Nabokov discussed the text to improve the English, called this story the "true 'inner story'" that she sensed is concealed in the novel (215). This inner story may reflect in Nabokov's words "things which he really felt at the time of writing" so difficult to recognize when conveyed by a "faintly absurd character" (*Sebastian Knight* 112).

Sebastian Knight raises a number of questions so compelling that they not only demand attention but also require an answer:

Why does Sebastian's father challenge Palchin? Why should a man, happily remarried for many years and the father of two boys, fight a duel in 1913 to defend the honor of a former wife who left him in 1904 and who died in 1909?

Why do Sebastian and Clare drift apart after Sebastian's trip to Germany in 1926? (This occurs only two years after Sebastian first met Clare and three years before he is to meet Nina Rechnoy.) And why does V. discuss their sexual relationship as a reason for this enstrangement?

Why after his return from Blauberg is Sebastian called "mad," even though he is perfectly able to continue "with the writing of *Lost Property*, his easiest book"?

Why doesn't Sebastian give a proper explanation for his callous treatment of Clare and why does V. not attempt to give such an explanation?

Why did Nabokov write in *Speak, Memory* (257): "For various reasons I find it inordinately hard to speak about my other brother. That twisted quest for Sebastian Knight . . . is really nothing in comparison to the task I . . . am faced with now"?

Much of the language Nabokov used has an additional, connotative meaning due to etymological, historical, cultural, or linguistic values. Nabokov's work is also extremely rich in literary references and allusions: to authors, their works or their characters, or to well-known passages or felicitous phrases. Nabokov seldom used such references solely to adorn the text; in most cases they carry a meaning that contributes to the ideas and perspectives he wished to intimate. For this reason, the deciphering of these references seems quintessential. References that, as Barbara Wyllie writes, look "frustratingly opaque" may become "astonishingly revelationary" (150). For Brian Boyd "the real motivation to exhaustive annotation is the expectation that there will be rich interpretive payoffs" ("*Lolita*: What We Know" 215). However, among the many volumes devoted to Nabokov's work, the number of books that are predominantly annotative is still limited. Carl R. Proffer and Alfred Appel Jr. annotated *Lolita*, and Gennady Barabtarlo *Pnin*. This state of affairs is understandable, since Nabokov's wide erudition and his expert knowledge of the natural world make it very difficult to trace all his references, or to do so with confidence. (It has been said that due to the rapid increase of printed books, John Milton was one of the last men of letters who could have read all the literature of the Western world. Occasionally one gets the impression that Nabokov escapes this rule.) Brian Boyd, who published the first installment of his meticulous "Annotations to *Ada*" in 1993 in *The Nabokovian* (but at that time he already had "a copious file of glosses to *Ada*" [9]), had by 2013 proceeded halfway through the 589 pages of the Vintage edition he uses.

The Real Life of Sebastian Knight has several advantages: it is much shorter and less allusive than *Ada*. Moreover, it has already been annotated to some extent. The edition by The Library of America has notes by Brian Boyd, pages 675–680; the German Rowohlt edition is annotated by Dieter E. Zimmer, pages 282–299; and the French edition of the *Bibliothèque de la Pléiade* has annotations by Maurice Couturier, pages 1543–1559. In addition, numerous articles and book chapters have been published on *Sebastian Knight* in which many mysterious matters are clarified.

As this book was being written, there was a time when it looked as if most of the references of interest had been covered. However, after resuming the annotation, one begins to appreciate Nabokov's contention that "a book is like a trunk tightly packed with things. At the customs an official's hand plunges perfunctorily into it. But he who seeks treasures examines every thread" (*Lectures on Literature* 89). What makes a work by Nabokov so very intriguing is not only the affluent erudition hidden in references and allusions, but perhaps even more the way in which these are woven into many complex motifs, all interlaced and dovetailed. Looking at an expensive, precious carpet might give so much pleasure that one forgets to pay attention to its design, patterns, figures, ornaments, and coloration. But if one begins to study them one does not know where to begin or when to stop. One can repeat about Nabokov's work what has been said of Milton's opus, that "almost any word . . . could be shown to be a key word: it is a work of that degree of intellectual concentration" (Carey and Fowler 436).

Annotating a work by Nabokov is never simple. An exclusive reference has to be recognized as such and has to be identified. A general one, for example, a mention of *Hamlet* is not easy to evaluate because one has to find out what in *Hamlet* might justify this reference. In such cases the annotation needs interpretational guidance. Then, the annotator may be influenced by "his individual culture" and "his personal taste" (Couturier "Annotating vs. Interpreting" 11). But it would have been a grave mistake to limit the annotations to those that endorse the reading presented in chapter 6. In order to explore the referential wealth of the novel, my main aim was to annotate the text in a way that does most justice to the wide erudition and compositional craft invested in it.

In some instances the notes in chapter 2 serve only to point out a word or phrase that should not pass unnoticed; in others an explanatory or critical note is presented. In most cases, however, the reader is directed to one of the motifs discussed in chapters 3, 4, and 5. This is because many allusions recur and it would be arbitrary to tag the wider annotation to one of them, as it is their coherence that counts. Equally important, it allows a classification of the motifs according to the overarching themes of the novel: narrative strategies in chapter 3, problems of identity in chapter 4, and death and the hereafter in chapter 5. Chapter 6 argues that part of the information gained by the annotations leads to another than the usual reading of the novel, in which Sebastian is regarded as the victim of Nina's charms. Instead of this a quite different life of Sebastian is presented, a life entirely missed by V. because of his manner always to look at signs matching the prefigured image of his half-brother that V. has in mind. The chapter also discusses how the two readings, the narrator's and the one presented in chapter 6, can coexist.

Nabokov's narrators may be foolish or unreliable, but they are not withholding information. Because of their double role, as character and as the author's agent (see Tammi, *Poetics* 278), they magnaminously offer facts that are incompatible with or even counteract the story they wish to advance. The account of Humbert, *Lolita*'s protagonist, which is meant to be an apologia, provides enough damning evidence to make a prosecutor's charge utterly devastating. But such is Nabokov's rhetorical power that readers may still succumb to the narrator's seductive reading. This is true for *Lolita*, but can also be said of *Sebastian Knight*: that readers have observed the foolishness of this novel's narrator does not mean that they distance themselves from the persuasive aplomb and brio with which V. tells his story.

Annotations

CHAPTER 2

The Real Life of Sebastian Knight: See chapter 3, section 18, *The Quest for Corvo* (the relevant chapters and sections are henceforth presented by their numbers only: 3, 18).

The comments below begin with the number of the page referred to; the number after the slash indicates the line.

References are made to *The Real Life of Sebastian Knight* in the Vintage International edition (New York, 1992).

CHAPTER 1

3/ 1 **Sebastian:** 4, 25 St Sebastian.

3/ 1 **Knight:** Among its various meanings the *Merriam-Webster's Dictionary* lists "a man devoted to the service of a lady," and a chessman "having the power to make an L-shaped move" (645–646). The *Concise Oxford Dictionary* defines it as "Bachelor" or "Young knight serving under another's banner" (78, 628). 4, 11 *Jekyll and Hyde*.

3/ 20–21 **Olga Olegovna Orlova—an egg-like alliteration:** Because V. starts his biography at the very beginning, with the birth of Sebastian, the "egg-like alliteration" might be a wordplay on the literary term for such an opening: "ab ovo," a quotation from *The Art of Poetry*, meaning "from the egg." Here Horace discusses *The Iliad*, which Homer begins *in media res*, "into the midst of a story," and not with the earliest incident, the birth of Helen of Troy (Horace 402). Helen of Troy was hatched from a hyacinth-colored egg found by Leda (Graves 1: 206). With Helen of Troy the theme of the femme fatale in *The Real Life of Sebastian Knight* is introduced. The egg-like alliteration is formed by the three Os: O-O-O, which is also the chess notation for castling on the queen side (*Encyclopaedia Britannica* 5: 458). 4, 5 Chess.

Andrew Caulton mentions that "the offices of the Tsarist secret police were . . . commonly known as 'O.O.'s.'" He also refers to a Conan Doyle story about a former Russian nihilist and writes that "the nothingness of Nihilism" is suggested by "the triple 'O' of Olga's name." He then directs the reader to *Look at the Harlequins!*, "which features a KGB agent called Oleg Orlev" (124). This refers to Oleg Igorevich Orlov, "a young poet" who lived in Paris but returned to Soviet Russia where he becomes a publicist (*Look at the Harlequins!*, 216–217). In his annotating of *Sebastian Knight* Caulton sets out to show that this novel is "a narrative of espionage and totalitarian terror" (xii). He sparingly refers to the critical studies on *Sebastian Knight* because, according to Caulton, many of its readers have been "deceived" by the novel's exterior (Caulton 2). Instead there is a plethora of references to novels and stories by Agatha Christie, Arthur Conan Doyle, John Le Carré, W. Somerset Maugham, Baroness Orczy, and H. G. Wells. In order to hint at the spy story he assumes is hidden in this novel (with poor Uncle Black in the role of "arch-villain" [117]), much Procrusteanization is needed. (In the three examples presented here, three Os are reduced to two; Os are turned into 0s; and a person called a *littérateur* by Nabokov is turned into a KGB agent.) Even then Caulton has to disregard all that cannot be moulded to his end, and as such much if not all of what makes *Sebastian Knight* one of Nabokov's most moving stories gets lost.

4/ 11 **cabs:** 3, 4 Cars.

4/ 30–5/ 2 **that his father was killed in the duel he fought in 1913; as a matter of fact . . . could not cope:** For more on the duel, see the comment on 11/ 10–16. The concurrence of the bullet wound and the cold makes it difficult to say whether Sebastian's father died because of his involvement in a woman's cause (without the wound the cold could have been coped with easily) or because of his illness (without the cold he would have recovered from his wound). This forebodes the uncertainty surrounding

CHAPTER 2

10   Silent Love

Sebastian's death: that it is either due to a woman or to his heart condition.

5/ 24 train: 3, 22 Trains.

6/ 13 her cold white fingers: Madame Lecerf also has cold hands: 156/ 13 and 163/ 23.

7/ 1 umbrella: 3, 3 Canes.

7/ 2 one day it occurred to her . . . never heart from her lips: This suggests that Sebastian's mother told her husband her reason for divorcing him (although without revealing the name of her new lover). This contrasts with her son's behavior, who most likely did not offer Clare any explanation at all as he "stopped talking to" her (108).

7/ 5–7 as suddenly as a raindrop starts to slide tipwards down a syringe leaf. That upward jerk of the forsaken leaf: Cf. "the relieved leaf unbent" (*Speak, Memory* 217). See also the final lines of the poem "The Rain Has Flown": "Downward a leaf inclines its tip / and drops from its tip a pearl" (*Poems and Problems* 19). Maurice Couturier in his annotations for the Pléiade edition (1544) glosses this passage as an "*[é]cho d'un passage de* Du côté de chez Swann." See Marcel Proust's *Swann's Way* (178): "a stray drop or two, lingering in the hollow of a leaf, would run down and hang glistening from the point of it until suddenly they splashed." Cf. also "To bend as doth a slender blade of grass / Tipped with a raindrop" (William Wordsworth [*The Prelude* VIII] 705). For more drop references in *Sebastian Knight*, see the "dew-drop" (48), the "suspended raindrops" (66), the trickling "[r]ain drops" (190) and the "ghost-like snowflake" (190).

7/ 6 syringa: The common name of this plant is lilac. It is the first allusion to the color violet and its purple variants. 4, 6 Colors.

7/ 13–14 (the waxed moustache of ten minutes to two): Cf. "yet / Stands the church clock at ten to three?" ("The Old Vicarage, Granchester" by

Rupert Brooke [72]). Nabokov's moustache resembles a "V," an unusual shape for a moustache unless waxed in a Hercule Poirot or Salvador Dali style.

7/ 15–16 **window with its fuddled fly between muslin and pane:** Cf. "a stray butterfly was fluttering its wings as it struggled between the curtain and the window-pane" (Turgenev, *Smoke* 145). The butterfly's position is like that of the novel's hero, Grigory Litvinov, who is captured by his desire for Irina and bound by his engagement to marry Tatyana.

7/ 17 **blotting-pad:** More blotting-pads can be seen on the desk of Mr. Goodman and on that of the manager of the Beaumont hotel (55, 122).

8/ 5–8 **polished panels . . . embossed leather bind:** Cf. "the embossed leather lining of the compartment walls, their polished panels" (*Speak, Memory* 141).

8/ 8–9 **a man wheeling luggage, the milky globe of a lamp with a pale moth whirling around it:** Cf. "pale moths revolved about a lone lamp" (*Speak, Memory* 146). In *Glory* the protagonist Martin is spoken to by a "porter who was pushing a luggage cart" while "around a milky white arc light swirled pale midges and one ample dark moth with hoary margins" (158).

8/ 10 **the clank of an invisible hammer testing wheels:** Cf. "the tapping of a hammer upon iron" that Anna Karenina hears at a railway station (Tolstoy, *Anna Karenina* 117). Cf. also "the noise of a hammer with which a railwayman had remedied some defect on a wheel of a train" (Proust, *Remembrance of Things* Past 3: 901).

8/ 12–13 **the blue plush:** Cf. "the blue upholstery" (*Speak, Memory* 141).

8/ 25 **she put on her gloves:** Clare puts on her gloves as soon as she goes outside (71), Silbermann takes off one glove (124), but Sebastian does not take off his gloves when seeing Nina (158). In his dream V. discovers what the black glove on Sebastian's left hand hides (187). 4, 31 V.'s dream.

Silent Love

8/ 25 bad French: 3, 23 Transmigration by language.

8/ 25–29 gloves . . . sugar-coated violets: W. W. Rowe observes that when "V. meets Clare Bishop . . . there is much ado about one of her gloves and her box of candy," and that these "echoes of Sebastian's mother . . . are one suggestion that her spirit . . . helps to promote [Sebastian's] happiness with Clare" (24).

8/ 28–29 sugar-coated violets: Crystallized flowers of the sweet violet (*Viola odorata*) are used in sweets (Podlech 12). 4, 6 Colors.

9/ 2–3 she roamed all over the South of France, staying for a day or two at small hot provincial towns, rarely visited by tourists: See the comment on 18/ 7.

9/ 10 Lehmann's disease: Cf. "a rather rare variety of angina pectoris, called by some doctors 'Lehmann's disease'" (87). According to Dr. J. D. Quin, such a condition is nonexistent (41). Savely Senderovich and Yelena Shvarts, having noticed that the commentary to the Russian translation of *Sebastian Knight* points to the homophonic likeness with Lac Léman (French for Lake Geneva), use this as a starting point for discussing the many devices Nabokov borrowed from the commedia dell'arte for the composition of this novel. 3, 5 Commedia dell'arte.

11/ 10–16 The duel was fought in a snow-storm. . . . The whole beastly affair lasted three minutes.: This duel is a brief description of the one Alexander Pushkin had with d'Anthès, with one striking difference (and two minor ones, as d'Anthès is not reported to have lit a cigarette after the duel and there was no snowstorm on the afternoon of January 27, 1837, although there was a fierce wind blowing and there was so much snow in St. Petersburg that the principals used a sleigh to travel to their appointed meeting). The main difference is that Sebastian's father was wounded after "two shots were exchanged" whereas Pushkin was hit by the first shot. The first shot in the duel with Palchin was fired by Sebastian's father, who must have been faster at aiming and firing than his adversary. Most likely, Sebastian's father fired his pistol into the air, because, if he had wished to hit Palchin he would most likely have succeeded as he was not only a "fine soldier" (5) who achieved "military success" in the Japanese war (6), but also a good shot as he had been engaged in a "fox-hunt" (6) and a "bear-hunt" (8).

Sebastian's father acted according to his code of honor: the reason for an insulted gentleman, writes Nabokov, to challenge "the insulter to a duel [is] not to kill his man, but on the contrary to force him to fire at him, the insulted one. Exposing himself to the other's forced fire would . . . [wipe] away the insult" (*Lectures on Russian Literature* 174). That Sebastian's father fired into the air, knowing that Palchin was not trustworthy as a gentleman (he was a "fool and a cad" and a slanderer to boot [10]), is a heroic deed as he could well have expected that Palchin might try to kill him (as he did). The reason for this duel is extremely curious, as Sebastian's father is defending the honor of his first wife against the slander by a man whom she preferred as a partner. It looks as if he is defending a sense of honor in the woman's interest, possibly not valued by the lady herself. This serves to contrast with Sebastian's behavior many years later, when he leaves Clare without offering her the merest apology—which of course is so puzzling that it needs to be explained (see chapter 6)—although his father's act was not wasted on him as his feeling toward his father "changed into one of heroic worship when he learnt the reason of his father's fatal duel" (16).

11/ 11 **frozen brook:** Cf. "Pushkin . . . drove onto the frozen river" (Vitale 273). Most descriptions of Pushkin's last duel refer to the Commandant's dacha to indicate the exact spot of the rencontre, which was standing on the bank of the Black River, or Chernaya Rechka in Russian—a narrow water on the Viborg Side of St. Petersburg. (For a contemporary Russian drawing of the locality, see Suasso 308.) The first part of the word *rechka* and the second half of the word *chernaya* combine into *rechnaya*, a word that ominously augurs the name of Mme. Rechnoy, the black femme fatale.

11/ 12 **fell face downwards:** Cf. "*Pouchkine était blessé . . . et resta immobile la face contre la terre.*" This is a citation from a letter by Viscount d'Archiac to Prince P. A. Vyazemsky dated February 1, 1837. D'Archiac was d'Anthès's second, Konstantin Danzas Pushkin's. After a duel the seconds were supposed to write a report together, but because d'Archiac could not manage to meet Danzas, he wrote his record in a letter to Vyazemsky. This letter is quoted by Frans Suasso (307). This detail is

14 | Silent Love

not mentioned in the biographies or monographs in English on Pushkin I have consulted.

11/ 12 army-cloak: Cf. "fell on Danzas' military carrick" (Nabokov, *Eugene Onegin* 3: 50).

11/ 14 hailed the coachmen: Cf. "They ran to call the coachmen" (Vitale 273).

11/ 16 three minutes: Cf. "He [Pushkin] aimed a long time. Two minutes, they say." (Troyat 576).

11/ 21 I had been sulking all day: Cf. "'What is the matter? Why are you sulking?'" This question is asked by the father of Peter, a schoolboy in Nabokov's story "Orache" on the day Peter's father was supposed to duel. This story shares many of the details Nabokov gave in his memoirs of the duel his father could have had in 1911 with Mikhail Suvorin, whom he had called out. Suvorin, the editor of an ultraconservative newspaper, had refused to apologize for an article in which Nabokov-père had been insulted. (The duel did not take place—although it does in the story—because the apology was eventually conceded.) (*Stories* 326; *Speak, Memory* 188–193; Boyd, *VNRY* 98–99.)

11/ 26–27 my small half-brother: In chapter 6 it appears that Mr. Goodman is not aware of V.'s existence. Clearly he had not read *Lost Property* with enough attention to glean this fact.

11/ 29 *Chums*: As a boy Nabokov not only read *Chums* but the *Boy's Own Paper* and *Punch* (Boyd, *VNRY* 80).

11/ 30 yarn: See comment on lines 142/ 24–25.

12/ 2 cricket Blue: Cf. "Rugby Blue" (43/ 26).

12/ 5–6 conjurer: 3, 6 Conjurer.

12/ 6–7 A horseman leaping over a racing car: In chapter 15 Uncle Black mends a chessman, a mounted knight, and draws a racing car.

12/ 9–10 "Pythagoras' Pants": Schoolboys' name for the geometrical proof of Pythagoras's theorem (Hooper 40). "Pants" is a shortened form of pantaloon. 3, 5 Commedia dell'arte.

These "pants" might also be referencing Nabokov's reminiscences of the schoolday when he learned that his father might have a duel (*Speak, Memory* 189) and those of the last evening Nabokov spent with his father, who helped his son put his "trousers under the press" (qtd. in Boyd, *VNRY* 192).

CHAPTER 2

13/ 2 Mr. Goodman: 3, 5 Commedia dell'arte.

14/ 11–14 reds and blues . . . mixes his colours: 4, 6 Colors.

14/ 16 small birthmark: Cf. "a tiny pale birth-mark" (170).

14/ 17 diaphanous ear: Cf. "her diaphanous complexion" (163).

15/ 16–18 I once discovered where he kept the key. . . . There was the copy book: Cf. "A page from his diary that I found on his [brother Sergey's] desk and read" (*Speak, Memory* 257).

15/ 19 sister of one of his schoolmates: She is properly introduced in chapter 14 as Natasha Rosanov.

15/ 27 black chess knight: Cf. "a chessman—a black knight" (140).

16/ 17–25 her name was never mentioned . . . tongue-tied: Apparently the memory of Sebastian's mother was eradicated in Sebastian's father's house as being too embarrassing to keep alive. Although "her name was never mentioned," Sebastian's governess, who was engaged soon after his father's second marriage, remembers her as "'*cette horrible Anglaise*'" (20). In view of so much indifference it can be understood that Sebastian prefers to remain "tongue-tied." About twenty years later Sebastian exhibits the same behaviour as he "stopped talking to" Clare, and refuses to answer Sheldon's pressing question, "out with it, man" (108). The meaning of this "unknown language of silence" (48) will be discussed in the final chapter.

17/ 7–8 I went for a long walk and found a place called Roquebrune: As Sebastian stayed in Monte Carlo this is the mountain village Roquebrune, rising above the Mediterranean, now called Roquebrune-Cap-Martin, located halfway between Monte Carlo and Menton. In the spring of 1938 Nabokov "was roaming the hills between Menton and Roquebrune," writes Brian Boyd (*VNRY* 486).

During the first half of the twentieth century Dorothy Bussy, Lytton Strachey's sister and the translator of André Gide, lived with her husband in Roquebrune and their house became a pied-à-terre for all the figures of the Bloomsbury group, Virginia Woolf among them (Caws and Wright 328). Another possible link between Virginia Woolf and Virginia Knight is suggested by Siggy Frank (170). The Bussys also let their house and one of their tenants was Rudyard Kipling (Caws and Wright 330). Roquebrune is also the place where William Butler Yeats died.

17/ 11 "Les Violettes": 4, 6 Colors.

17/ 11 chauffeur: 3, 4 Cars.

17/ 11–14 "Les Violettes" . . . a pinkish villa: Sebastian walked to Roquebrune in 1922 to see this villa. In 1920 Katherine Mansfield was the guest of Sydney Schiff, an English writer, in his "Villa Violet" at Roquebrune (the same Roquebrune as visited by Sebastian) (Davenport-Hines 260).

17/ 15 a bunch of violets: 4, 6 Colors.

17/ 28 purple pansies: 4, 6 Colors.

18/ 2 An orange: According to Senderovich and Shvarts this is a scion of Carlo Gozzi's *The Love for Three Oranges* ("The Juice of Three Oranges" 104). 3, 5 Commedia dell'arte.

18/ 6–7 I had visited the place where she had died. "Oh," he said, "but that was the other Roquebrune, the one in the Var.": Cf. "you have been visiting

Monsieur Kegan" (202). The Roquebrune in the Var is Roquebrune-sur-Argens, about ten miles north of Sainte Maxime, which even today meets the description of a "small hot provincial town, rarely visited by tourists" (9).

18/ 24–25 let the door be closed leaving but a thin line of taut light underneath: Cf. "I shall leave the door open an inch" (200).

19/ 2–3 Sebastian is asleep, or at least mouse-quiet, in the next room: Cf. "His presence in the next room, the faint sound of breathing" (200).

19/ 5–7 I undertook a journey to Lausanne in order to find the old Swiss lady who had been first Sebastian's governess, then mine: Cf. "I chanced to visit Lausanne . . . so I thought I might as well look up Mademoiselle" (*Speak, Memory* 115).

20/ 21 Zelle: 3, 28 Zelle.

21/ 2 Demidov: The name of one of the wealthiest families of Imperial Russia.

21/ 14 useless pilgrimage: 3, 28 Zelle.

CHAPTER 3

23/ 25 (1936): In chapter 19 the year of publication mentioned is 1935. As V. discusses *The Doubtful Asphodel* with a businessman in Paris before Sebastian's death (see chapter 18), and refers to its reviews, 1936 must be a mistake.

25/ 1–3 the blue remembered hills and the happy highways, the hedge with its unofficial rose and the field with its rabbits, the distant spire and the near bluebell . . .: As has been identified by Brian Boyd ("Notes" 675–676) the "blue remembered hills" is borrowed from A.E. Housman's *A Shropshire Lad*, XL; the "unofficial rose" from Rupert Brooke's poem "The Old Vicarage, Granchester" and the "distant spire" from Thomas Gray's

"Ode on a Distant Prospect of Eton College." 4, 2 Brooke, Gray, Housman and Kipling.

Andrew Caulton argues that "the distant 'spire' is an allusion to Byron's poem 'L'Amitié est l'amour sans ailes' ['Friendship is love without its wings'], rather than to Gray's poem which has 'spires' an not a single one as Byron's: 'Seat of my youth! thy distant spire'" (Caulton 140; Byron 40). Gray's "spires," however, appear in the very first line of his much-anthologized poem, while Byron's poem does not stand out in his works. Moreover, the lines from Brooke, Gray, Housman and Kipling referred to, all pay tribute to the English countryside, whereas Byron's "seat" refers to Harrow's schoolbuilding as he in his poem celebrates the most affectionate friendships he had with some of his schoolfellows. (For the nature of the relationships with the various boys alluded to in this poem, see MacCarthy 40.)

25/ 22 Helsingfors: 3, 10 *Hamlet*.

26/ 1–2 tied it [Sebastian's father's wedding ring] to her own with a black thread: Cf. "fastened to hers by a bit of black thread" (*Speak, Memory* 50).

26/ 20 Alexis Pan: 4, 30 Velimir Khlebnikov. According to Omry Ronen "Alexis Pan is a punning parody of Aleksei Kruchenykh by way of '*Kruchenyi panych*' a South Russian variety of petunia" (65).

26/ 26 "submental grunt": 4, 30 Velimir Khlebnikov.

27/ 1–2 a very miracle of verbal transfusion: According to Stanislav Shvabrin this is a reflection on Nabokov's own translation of Keats's poem, which "owes more to Nabokov's desire to associate his composition with his favourite Russian paragons than with the English poet himself" ("Vladimir Nabokov's 'La Belle Dame Sans Merci'" 115, see also comment on lines 27/ 2–3). In Nabokov's expression the "miracle," seems to be confined to the "transfusion" and not to the final result as he, in 1942, called his translation "very poor" (Karlinsky, *Dear Bunny* 87).

27/ 2–3 Keats's "La Belle Dame Sans Merci.": In this poems Keats tells how a lonely and loitering "knight" is held "in thrall" by a malicious enchantress (Keats 334–336).

As a futurist Alexis Pan belongs to the Russian Silver Age and this is the major reason why Keats's poem is mentioned here. "Indeed," writes Sonia Ketchian, "Keats made his principal impact on Russian poetry at the turn of the nineteenth and the twentieth centuries at the onset of and during the Silver Age of Russian literature and a rippling one, still unparalleled for intensity, through his ballad with the French title, which must have appealed to Russian Francophilism, and to the Symbolist love of ballads, namely, 'La Belle Dame Sans Merci. A Ballad'" (*Keats and the Russian Poets*, 20). In her book Ketchian devotes two chapters to the many traces Keats's poem left in the poetry of Alexander Blok and Nikolai Gumilev (chapter 5: "Blok and Keats: 'Nightingale Garden' and 'La Belle Dame Sans Merci'"; chapter 6: "Gumilev, Keats and the Femme Fatale").

A deadly coquette emerging from the Russian Silver Age is Professor Botanik's daughter in Fyodor Sologub's story "The Poison Garden" (1908), a close replica (enchanted garden—learned and wicked botanist—beautiful daughter—poisonous flowers—youthful death) of Nathaniel Hawthorne's story "Rappaccini's Daughter" (1844) which, according to Priscilla Meyer, is an important subtext for *Sebastian Knight* (see Meyer "Life as Annotation").

Keats's poem was translated for the first time in 1911 by Leonid Andrusov; Nabokov translated it in 1921. By twice calling Keats's enchantress "*Prekrasnaia Dama*" ("beautiful lady") Nabokov distinctly invokes Alexander Blok's famous persona of his cycle *Verses on the Beautiful Lady* (Grayson, "French Connection" 635; see also Mochulsky 89). And, as Stanislav Shvabrin in his detailed study argues, by adopting meter, idiom, and imagery from poets like Nikolai Nekrasov, Aleksei Koltsov and Blok, echoing from a poem by Afanasy Fet and by calling Keats's protagonist after the title of a novella by Dmitri Grigorivich, Nabokov's translation can be regarded as an "attempt at domesticating" Keats's poem in Russian (Shvabrin, "Vladimir Nabokov's 'La Belle Dame Sans Merci'" 110–115).

One may conclude that the studies by Ketchian and Shvabrin show how Russian poets assimilated Keats's poem thoroughly. Most likely, Keats's "Belle Dame" is mentioned in *Sebastian Knight* as a window to the femmes fatales in Russian literature, who, after the nineteenth century (which offered Maria Nikolaevna Poloza in Ivan Turgenev's *Spring Torrents* and Nastasya Filipovna Barashkova in Fyodor Dostoevsky's

The Idiot) revived so energetically in the Russian Silver Age (as they did at the same time in France and England as will be discussed in chapter 6).

In view of the novel's inconclusiveness with respect to Sebastian's decline (see comment to lines 4/ 30–5/ 2 and section 3, 10 "Hamlet") it is worth noticing that in Nabokov's variant of "La Belle Dame Sans Merci" the knight's "fateful encounter with the elfin lady is profoundly ambiguous, since madness seems the only reasonable explanation for what he has allegedly experienced" (Shvabrin, "Vladimir Nabokov's 'La Belle Dame Sans Merci'" 108).

27/ 14 Marcopolian journey: 4, 30 Velimir Khlebnikov.

27/ 24–26 morning coat . . . lotus flowers: Another fellow futurist appeared during recitals in "evening dress with a painted wooden Russian spoon as a boutonniere" (Langeveld 92; translated from the Dutch). This happens to be David Burliuk, who reappears in section 4, 30.

27/ 29 a mouse engendering mountains; Brian Boyd ("Notes" 676) refers to Horace's *The Art of Poetry*: "mountains in labor and – a mouse comes out!" (Horace 402).

28/ 4 Javanese wrist-play: 4, 30 Velimir Khlebnikov.

28/ 30 a cold bath every morning: Sebastian's daily baths are also mentioned by Mr. Goodman and the manager of the Beaumont hotel.

29/ 3–4 though the Lord knows how hard I have tried to be kind to the boy: This utterance suggests that her efforts were not always quite successful. See comment on lines 137/ 2–28.

29/ 7 a canary yellow jumper: In *Speak, Memory* Nabokov recounts the attires of Cambridge students, noting that "[w]hat I suppose might be the gay set wore old pumps, very light gray flannel trousers, a bright-yellow 'jumper,' and the coat part of a good suit" (260).

29/ 13–16 He spoke Russian gingerly, lapsing into English . . . sentences: 4, 29 Uncle Ruka.

CHAPTER 4

31/ 15 But what actually did I know about Sebastian?: When they settled in Helsingfors in 1918 Sebastian was still eighteen years old, and V. "thirteen" (23). (As Sebastian is "six years" V.'s senior [14] this means that he was born in the second part of 1905.) After Sebastian left for Cambridge there were only four short meetings in 1919 or 1920, in 1922, 1924 and finally 1929.

31/ 15–32/ 11 I might devote . . . following the bends of his life.: In this passage V. lists, not without poise, the main pillars upon which to found his biography: remembrances, research, inner knowledge, intuition based on sameness of brothers and their "common rhythm."

32/ 3–4 far, far better: Michael Wood (35) compares this with Sidney Carton's exclamation "It is a far better thing that I do, than I have ever done; it is a far better rest I go to than I have ever known," a citation from Charles Dickens's *A Tale of Two Cities*.

33/ 22 Everyman: *Everyman* (c. 1500) is the best of the English morality plays. Of all his friends it is only Good Deeds who redeems Everyman in his dying hour, when his soul is liberated from his body to become "spouse to Jesu!" (Norton 1: 367). 5, 1 Donne.

34/ 15–16 imperfections . . . its own head: Cf. "With all my imperfections on my head," *Hamlet* (1.5.79) (qtd. in Boyd, "Notes" 676). 3, 10 *Hamlet*. See also chapter 6.

35/ 1 A small old oil-painting, a little cracked (muddy road, rainbow, beautiful puddles): Susan Elizabeth Sweeney ("Looking at Harlequins" 93) and Gavriel Shapiro (*The Sublime Artist's Studio* 101) suggest that this painting may be attributed to Konstantin Somov (1869–1939). Although Somov painted many pictures with rainbows, Sebastian's anglophilia, Somov's preference for watercolors and the painting's age, do not support this. Moreover, Somov's resplendent and colorful landscapes are not suggestive of "muddy roads." The many rainbows painted by J.W.M.

Turner and John Constable, all intended to glorify the arched splendour, have no muddy roads either. Because the images of rainbows and puddles have so much significance in Nabokov's oeuvre, it seems likely that this painting has no original(s). *Bend Sinister* opens with reflections on a puddle filled with water, which Nabokov compares with a "hole through which you can see the nether sky." That the puddles in Sebastian's painting are called "beautiful" probably means that they reflect the radiance coming from the sun or rainbow. See also the comments on Roy Carswell's portrait of Sebastian, attached to line 117/14. (There happens to be a painting by Willem Roelofs [1822–1897], arguably his best work, *The Rainbow* [1875] that matches the description, while some of the puddles in the very muddy road reflect the golden glow of the diffused sunlight. Fuchs [161] gives a b & w reproduction.)

35/ 11 **a Brazil nut:** 4, 15 Moon.

35/ 15 **violets:** 4, 6 Colors.

35/ 22 **a glass ashtray:** As the study with its writing desk, many bookshelves, hearth, divan and armchair(s) might have probably served as the reception room, one may wonder why the house-agent brought an ashtray into the dining-room. In chapter 17 the same happens in Lescaux where an "ashtray" is brought into the dining-room by "the blond gentleman" (165/ 10–12).

35/ 23 **Mr. McMath:** 3, 14 Mysterious Men.

36/ 7 **the note-paper was egg-shell blue:** Birds' eggs may have all sorts of colors and blue ones are not uncommon. The American Robin (*Merula migratoria*) lends its name for the color "Robin's Egg Blue," a strong greenish blue (Maerz and Paul 177). This color has been adopted by the jewellery company Tiffany & Co (established in 1837) as its trademark color. (For examples of blue stationery, see Loring [51]). 4, 20 Robinsonnade.

In his biographical sketch of Sergey Nabokov, Lev Grossman relates how Sergey used "the spare, elegant stationery of Schloss Weissenstein," the home of Sergey's partner Hermann Thieme, to describe for his brother Vladimir the funeral of their mother who died in Prague in

1939. The luxurious quality of both the paper used by Sebastian's correspondent and that used by Sergey is apparent, however their colors differ as the Weissenstein stationery used by Sergey is white or ivory, as Lev Grossman was so kind to inform me.

36/ 12–13 **blue became loose, curving backwards under the torturing flame:** The blue of the paper and the red of the flame may have resulted in a violet glow. 4, 6 Colors.

36/ 19–21 **(not that I might have expected from the flame of chance the slick intent of a novelist's plot):** A dismissively phrased message between parentheses is often a generous gesture by Nabokov to direct the reader in the right—that is reverse—track.

36/ 22 **"thy manner always to find":** the writer of the letter is questioning the addressee's constancy or perhaps even his pertinaciousness, which the sender appreciates or disapproves of. "Thy" is the possessive form of "thou," both archaic words used to stress informality, which seems unnecessary here as colored stationery is used for private correspondence only.

36/ 22 **manner:** For a discussion of the frequent recurrence of the word "manner" in *Sebastian Knight*, see Jonathan B. Sisson (640–41).

36/ 25 **that Russian woman whose letters Sebastian had kept:** The course V.'s biography takes after chapter 7—cherchez la femme—depends largely on this conjecture. That V. could see that the writing on the "burning," "curving," and "crumpling" sheet was in Cyrillic is clever enough. But what skills as a graphologist does one need to make out in a split second that the handwriting is definitely that of a woman? An interesting case of the misreading of a letter can be found in Proust's *Remembrance of Things Past*. Reflecting on the many wrong inferences of such a mistake, the narrator writes: "everything starts with an initial error; those that follow . . ., extraordinary as they may appear to a person who has not begun at the same starting point, are quite natural. A large part of what we believe true (and this even applies to our final conclusions) with an obstinacy equalled only by our good faith, springs from an original mistake in our premises" (3: 671). The identity of the sender of these letters will be discussed in chapter 6.

37/ 9–10 none of them were reviews . . . too vain to collect them: Cf. Nabokov's "almost pathological and not always justified indifference to reviews" (qtd. in Boyd, *VNRY* 121).

37/ 13 an album with cuttings: This is most likely the album mentioned by Mr. Goodman (114; see also that Sebastian "refused . . . to subscribe to the clippings" [100])

38/ 5 francs, marks, schillings, crowns: Money from France, Germany, Austria, and England, respectively. If Sebastian had gone to Italy as Sheldon suggested (109/ 9) one might expect to find some liras as well. That the currency of Austria is among Sebastian's collection of coins is conspicuous as this country is not mentioned or hinted at elsewhere in *Sebastian Knight*.

38/ 8 Oriental amethyst, unset: a purple or violet variety of quartz. Its Oriental origin must, as it is unset, refer to its faceting or its bezel.

38/ 11 Photographs: Cf. "His charming little flat was full of . . . photographs" (*Speak, Memory* 60).

38/ 12 I thought I should find lots of girls: This expectation is most likely the reason why V. has attributed the blue letters—rightly or wrongly—to a woman.

38/ 16 Mr. H.: In combination with the archaic "thy" (36) Mr. H. recalls the initial of Mr. W.H. the begetter of Shakespeare's sonnets. See the first lines of Sonnet 39, "Oh, how thy worth with manners may I sing, / When thou art all the better part of me?" See also comment on 165/2 and the discussion of Shakespeare's sonnets in chapter 6.

38/ 18 a moonfaced urchin: 4, 15 Moon.

38/ 21–22 a rather repellent bulldog type of man: Noted for his likeness to a bulldog was Sergey Diaghilev, artistic director of the Ballets Russes.

According to Bronislava Nijinska (Vaslav Nijinsky's sister) his face had an expression "like a bulldog's" (Davenport-Hines 9), a resemblance also observed by Jean Cocteau: "[h]is face was a bull dog's" (Caws, *Proust* 86) and Lady Ripon, Diaghilev's most important London patron: "Diaghilev looks like a bulldog" (Scheijen 323; translated from the Dutch). Nabokov gave Diaghilev's "physical aspect" to Prince Adulf, an imperious character in "Solus Rex," the story he wrote after having finished *Sebastian Knight* (*Stories* 654; see also Boyd, *VNRY* 520). In *Sebastian Knight*, another, older, man with a "bulldog face" is seen by V. on the day Sebastian died (195). Sebastian owned a "little black bulldog" and Nina's "black bulldog' is "frog-faced" (101, 152).

38/ 28 **bachelors**: 4, 11 *Jekyll and Hyde*.

39/ 10–11 **a Chinese . . . beheaded**: Nabokov's Cambridge acquaintance Dietrich had among his collection of photographs a "series . . . that depicted the successive stages of a routine execution in China" (*Speak, Memory* 278). 5, 2 Executions.

39/ 20 **Hamlet**: 3, 10 *Hamlet*.

39/ 20 **La morte d'Arthur**: 3, 13 *Le Morte d'Arthur*.

39/ 20–21 **The Bridge of San Luis Rey**: 3, 27 Wilder.

39/ 21 **Dr. Jekyll and Mr. Hyde**: 4, 11 *Jekyll and Hyde*.

39/ 21 **South Wind**: 4, 9 Douglas.

39/ 21–22 **The Lady with the Dog**: 3, 12 *Lady with the Dog*.

39/ 22 **Madame Bovary**: 3, 1 Boat trip.

39/ 22 **The Invisible Man**: A playful suggestion for a subtitle for V.'s biography. Wells' novel was published in 1897, eleven years after Stevenson's *Dr. Jekyll and Mr. Hyde*, which it resembles in many ways. The protagonists of the novels, Griffin and Jekyll, have made scientific discoveries enabling them to change their usual appearance. In *Ada* Wells's novel is called "one of the greatest novels of English literature" (203). In the "Notes to *Ada* by Vivian Darkbloom" a reference is made to "the h-dropping policeman in Wells's *Invisible Man*" (*Ada* 597). There is, however, no policeman in Wells's novel who drops his aitches; Vivian Darkbloom must have confused Wells's novel with Sebastian Knight's *Prismatic Bezel*.

39/ 22–23 *Le Temps Retrouvé*: 4, 18 Proust.

39/ 23 *Anglo-Persian Dictionary*: 4, 29 Uncle Ruka.

39/ 23 *The Author of Trixie*: 4, 23 Sherlock Holmes.

39/ 24 *Alice in Wonderland*: 3, 7 Elenctic.

39/ 24 *Ulysses;* 4, 28 *Ulysses*.

39/ 24 *About Buying a Horse*: 3, 21 *The Colonel*.

39/ 24–25 *King Lear*: 3, 11 *King Lear*.

40/ 9–10 **leaving out the "con" and cultivating the "radish"**: 3, 6 Conjuror. See also Eric Naiman 27.

CHAPTER 5

41/ 6 **Trinity College:** Nabokov's years at Trinity is the subject of pages 259–273 of *Speak, Memory*.

41/ 9 **Large Copper:** This butterfly, typical for the fenny areas of Cambridge, became extinct in 1851 (Stokoe 139).

42/ 4–5 **would remain as hopelessly alone as it has always been**: 3, 24 Unfinished Pictures.

42/ 8–9 **his inability to fit into a picture**: 3, 24 Unfinished Pictures.

Annotations

42/ 17 cornered part of the academical cap: Its board has four corners. Cf. 69/ 23 where Clare's "three-cornered hat" is described.

42/ 26 D. W. Gorget: A gorget is an ornamental collar, as well as a piece of armour to protect the throat. Cf. "with a brass stud at his collarless throat" (140).

42/ 29 umbrella: 3, 3 Canes.

43/ 26: he was a Rugby Blue: A "Blue" is a "sportsman who represents or has represented Oxford or Cambridge universities, and has the right to wear the university colour" (*Collins*). Cf. "Martin was proud that he ... had qualified for the title of College Blue" (*Glory* 108).

43/ 30–31 the tea things which stood humbly on the carpet: Cf. "the tea things that stood on the rug" (*Speak, Memory* 259).

43/ 31 Sebastian's spirit: 5, 5 Voices and visions.

44/ 12–13 Clad in a brown dressing gown ... carrying ... a sponge-bag: Cf. "in a thin dressing gown ... and with a cold, fat sponge-bag" (*Speak, Memory* 260). The dressing gown in which "Nabokov walked daily to the Baths at the end of Trinity Lane" was a "beautiful purple" one (Boyd, *VNRY* 169).

44/ 20 the Pitt: 4, 1 Baring.

44/ 23 fives: A ball game now called squash. Cf. "a game of badminton (or was it fives?) that he [Nabokov's father] had with H.G. Wells" (*Speak, Memory* 255).

44/ 23–26 or some other tame game, and then had had tea with two or three friends; the talk had hobbled along between crumpet and pipe: Cf. "things as the hot muffins and crumpets one had with one's tea after games" (*Speak, Memory* 269).

45/ 8–9 to the little cinema on the market place: Cf. "a small Cambridge cinema" (*Glory* 83).

45/ 27 **celadon:** 4, 4 Celadon.

46/ 26 **His "r"s, when beginning a word, rolled . . .:** Cf. "the gentlemanly St. Petersburgan burr of his r's" (*Pnin* 125; see Tammi, *Subtexts* 78).

46/ 27 **queer mistakes:** 4, 19 Queer.

46/ 31 **Socrates:** 3, 7 Elenctic.

46/ 31 **Desdemona:** 3, 16 *Othello*. 4, 17 Nesbit.

47/ 17 **a bleak day in February:** 3, 2 Calender.

48/ 2–4 **grassblade . . . dew-drop:** To accord much unexpected or hyperbolic meaning to (sometimes odd) minutiae is the forte of the metaphysical poets. Andrew Marvell wrote a poem titled "On a Drop of Dew," while a "Blade of Grass" appears in his "The Mower's Song" (48). Another "blade of grass" is mentioned in the comment on lines 7/ 5–7, where it is also suggested that the watery traces in *Sebastian Knight* (like raindrops and snowflakes) might be part of a greater coherence. This "watery imagery" is discussed in some detail by J.B. Sisson, who refers to some of Nabokov's expressions about the soul and the universe of which it is part (641–642). In "On a Drop of Dew" Marvell discusses how the short-lived existence of a drop of dew (landed on a "purple" flower), is caused by its belonging to the universe, and compares it to the sublunary sojourn of the sempiternal soul (12).

48/ 3 **the unknown language of silence:** See comment on line 16/ 17–25.

48/ 21–22 **this cat, she does not seem to know milk:** 4, 28 *Ulysses*.

48/ 25–26 **his sudden trips to London generally without the authorities' leave:** Cf. "A Complete Description of Sixty-seven Ways of Getting inside Trinity College after Closing the Gates . . . Verified many Times by the Author, who has never been Caught" (*Glory* 59).

49/ 3 **not been born in Russia really:** 3. 23 Transmigration by Language.

49/ 4–5 the delightful old man at once started to speak Bulgarian: Cf. "walked in on Harrison [Nabokov's former Cambridge tutor] . . . and he told me . . . how he was learning Bulgarian" (*Letters to Véra* 311).

49/ 21 called Sebastian's friend after me: V. is called back again by Helen Pratt (58) to whom he responded as eagerly as in this case, and once more, in a dream, by Sebastian (187) to whom he reacted so reluctantly that Sebastian could not intimate his message before the dream ended.

49/ 30–31 voice in the mist, "Who is speaking of Sebastian Knight?": This call, resounding two times more (50, 63), pointedly questioning V.'s (and Mr. Goodman's) ambition (or illusion) to become Sebastian's biographer, is soon silenced with V.'s idea that he possesses some "inner," "secret knowledge" (31, 99). 5, 5 Voices and visions.

CHAPTER 6

50/ 2–3 the easy swing of a well-oiled novel: Cf. "a novel in the old mood" (*Eugene Onegin* 1: 155; Pushkin's "old" returns in the English "oiled"). In the *Eugene Onegin* Canto 3, XIII from which this line is taken, Pushkin muses about the merit of writing a novel, which may surprise the reader as the subtitle *A Novel in Verse* indicates that he already is writing a novel. The analogy seems applicable to V.'s "biography." See also Will Norman who writes that *Sebastian Knight* "enacts the transformation" of a biography in a novel (91).

This Canto follows the one in which Pushkin discusses the seductiveness of the "British Muse" and, of course, its competition with the Russian Muse is an important motif in *Sebastian Knight* as well.

50/ 12 Voice in the Mist: 5, 5 Voices and visions.

50/ 24–51/ 1 Peering unseen over my shoulder . . . ghost: 5, 5 Voices and visions.

51/ 3 a few casual facts: See comment on 61/ 28.

51/ 8–10 At our last meeting . . . between 1930 and 1934.: In chapter 12 V. tells that it was at the beginning of 1930 that Mr. Goodman "made his appearance." The last recorded meeting V. had with Sebastian was in the summer of 1929. Because it seems unlikely that Sebastian engaged Mr. Goodman a year before his actual employment, this "last meeting" seems to be a mistake.

51/ 28 Mr. Goodman: 3, 5 Commedia dell'arte.

51/ 30–52/2 for I intended to follow his life . . . post-Cambridge period: 4, 27 *The Tragedy of Sebastian Knight*.

52/ 4 Fleet Street: The name of this street is "synonymous . . . with the British newspaper industry" (Urdang 49), a hint that Goodman is probably a mere journalist and not a literary biographer.

52/ 10–53/ 16 a certain living author . . . an influential and esteemed writer.: 4, 14 Mann.

52/ 19–21 budding author . . . into blossom: 4, 18 Proust.

52/ 29–31 *Modern Masterpieces* . . . "post-war" generation: Cf. "I find unbearable both intelligent and stupid speeches about 'modern times,' 'inquiétude,' 'religious renaissance' and really, any phrase containing the word 'post-war' . . . I wish neither to be 'anxious' nor to be reborn." (From a letter by Vladimir Nabokov to Vladislav Khodasevich, dated July 24, 1934, qtd. in Leonid Livak [164].)

53/ 8–9 a dash of Freud or "stream of consciousness" or whatnot: The possibilities of the techniques of stream of consciousness have been exploited by James Joyce more than by any other writer, and it is remarkable to see it mentioned next to Freud, whose realm is the unconscious. However, the techniques used by Joyce and Freud can also be called "free association," which annihilates the contrast (Burns 71; Cuddon 330).

53/ 10 the pretty cynics of today are Marie Correli's nieces and Mrs. Grundy's nephews: "Cynics" here denote writers who think that they are above the common standards of decency. Marie Corelli (née Mary Mackay, she took her pseudonym after the composer Arcangelo Corelli) was "the most publicized British author of the 1880s" whose fame, however, was "ephemeral" (Patricia Smith 176). Mrs. Grundy (from Thomas Morton's *Speed the Plough* [1798]) is the proverbial guardian of middle-class morality, a name often used to snub Victorian prudery. Both apply to Mann's *Death in Venice* because this story quickly became a bestseller and because the unseemly sexual obsession the protagonist feels for a child is wrapped in aestheticism to make it look respectable. Nabokov might have come across "Mrs. Grundy" in Lewis Carroll's letters, in one of the several "*Life and Letters*" biographies of which the first one (by Carroll's nephew Stuart Collingwood) appeared in 1898. Carroll repeatedly attributed the gossip aroused by the photographs he took of nude small children to a Mrs. Grundy rigidity (Carpenter 88). Nabokov was "always very fond of Carroll" and translated *Alice in Wonderland* in Russian in 1923, but was highly critical of Carroll's "perversion" (*SO* 81).

54/ 5 my point in quoting this letter: 4, 27 *The Tragedy of Sebastian Knight*.

54/ 31 A black mask: 3, 5 Commedia dell'arte. 4.27 *The Tragedy of Sebastian Knight*.

55/ 3 my name: Lara Delage-Toriel mentions five instances where V. explicitly refers to his name (*Sebastian Knight* 125, 134, 140, 202), without actually revealing it, which, she argues, is a persistent ploy to prompt the reader to find the truth the narrator conceals ("Disclosures under Seal").

55/ 27 what's done is done: Andrew Caulton has identified this phrase as coming from *Macbeth* (3.2.12). Lady Macbeth utters it after her husband has instructed the two murderers to kill Banquo.

56/ 5 *The Funny Mountain*: 4, 14 Mann.

56/ 21 lozenge: 3, 5 Commedia dell'arte.

57/ 28–29 he returned the black mask: 4, 27 *The Tragedy of Sebastian Knight*.

32 | Silent Love

58/ 22–23 **face . . . like a cow's udder:** Cf. "Face like an udder" from Nikolay Gumilev's "The Tram That Lost Its Way" (Dmitri Obolensky, *The Penguin Book of Russian Verse* 302). 3, 22 Trains. 5, 2 Executions.

CHAPTER 7

59/ 1–2 *The Tragedy of Sebastian Knight* **. . . a very good press:** 4, 27 *The Tragedy of Sebastian Knight*.

59/ 22–23 **Godfrey Goodman . . . Samuel Goodrich:** "[I]n this pair of references [Nabokov] casts a broad Anglophone net in space, time, genre, [a] web of interconnections and readership," writes Priscilla Meyer ("Anglophonia and Optimysticism" 217) and she elaborates especially on the link with James Joyce and Nathaniel Hawthorne. Nabokov might have come across Goodman's book while reading about John Milton who partook in "the great seventeenth-century debate on whether the world was getting better or worse." Goodman in his *Fall of Man* provided "the most elaborate form" to argue for the decay of nature (Daiches 19).

59/ 23 *Fall of Man*: Cf. "apple of sin" (147/ 23).

60/ 4–5 **chronometric concepts:** 4, 27 *The Tragedy of Sebastian Knight*.

61/ 28 **Mr. Goodman was no Boswell:** Nor is V. whose complete lack of interest to reveal the documents he uses, such as "Sebastian's very short letters" (51/4) is unlike Boswell's assiduity, whose records of his hero's conversations were highly praised by Dr. Johnson himself. The dates V. produces, to give another example, are highly vague or even inconsistent (see 3, 2 Calendar), while Boswell ran "half over London in order to fix a date correctly" (Boswell 2: 188 and 1: xvii).

62/ 15 **Germany:** 3, 8 Germany.

62/ 21 **Jerome K. Jerome book:** the passage described is from *Three Men on the Bummel* (132). Jerome's book recounts a jaunt on bikes by three friends through Germany, from Hanover via Dresden to the Black Forest. Its humor depends on exaggerated incidents told in a contrasting, dry, matter-of-fact style. The only reason for mentioning this novel seems that it might serve as a tag for mentioning Germany as a destination for Sebastian's travels. 3, 8 Germany.

62/ 24–26 **young student . . . student's father:** 3, 10 *Hamlet*.

62/ 30–31 **a black-robed monk moving swiftly towards him from the sky:** 3, 26 Varvara Mitrofanna.

63/ 9 **Juggernauts:** 3, 22 Trains. 5, 2 Executioners.

63/ 14–15 **a trashy concoction:** 4, 27 *The Tragedy of Sebastian Knight*.

63/ 22–24 **who . . . never quotes anything that may clash with the main idea of his fallacious work:** A well deserved comment on (at least) one of Sebastian's biographers.

64/ 15 **pantomine:** 3, 5 Commedia dell'arte.

65/ 27–29 **to see the editor . . . of my Cambridge poems:** During his years in Cambridge Nabokov published two English poems, "Home," which appeared in *Trinity Magazine,* 1920 and "Remembrance," published in *English Review.* "One can speculate," writes D. Barton Johnson, "that Nabokov's submission of this [latter] poem is echoed in Sebastian Knight's description of how the narrator of his novel, *Lost Property,* submits his poetry to a Cambridge literary magazine" ("Nabokov and de la Mare" 75 and 86 note 16).

66/ 18–19 **Kipling moods . . . Housman moods:** 4, 2 Brooke, Gray, Housman and Kipling.

66/ 22 **purple passage:** A well-known phrase from Horace's *Art of Poetry,* "to catch the eye and enhance the colour" (397).

66/ 22 **Hamlet:** 3, 10 *Hamlet*.

66/ 27 **suspended raindrops:** Cf. "dew-drop" (48).

66/ 29–30 **Hawaian:** See comment on lines 203/ 9–13.

CHAPTER 8

69/ 6 Étoile: Nabokov wrote *Sebastian Knight* in the apartment he and his wife had rented in 8, Rue de Saigon, near the Place d'Étoile (Boyd, *VNRY* 492).

69/ 23 three-cornered hat: Such a hat was common in the eighteenth Century and worn mostly by men (Laver 125 and 137).

70/ 4 handkerchief: 3, 16 *Othello*.

70/ 11 Cock Robin Hits Back: Allusion to a very old rhyme, already recorded in the fifteenth century. It has fourteen stanzas, the first being:

> Who killed Cock Robin?
> I, said the Sparrow,
> With my bow and arrow,
> I killed Cock Robin. (Opie 130–132)
>   4, 20 Robinsonnade.

70/ 20 Cock Robin is so impopular: During the Great War this rhyme was adapted to convey most macabre allusions, like the RAF-song:

> Who killed Cock Robin?
> "I," said the Hun,
> "With my machine gun
> I killed Cock Robin!"
>   (Pegler 367. See also Fussell *The Great War* [289])

71/ 9–72/ 4 gloves . . . bongs-bongs: See comment on 8/ 25–29.

72/ 5–7 I was going to the Etoile . . . Avenue Kleber: The Place d'Étoile has been renamed in 1970 in the Place Charles de Gaulle. Before reaching the Avenue Kléber and skirting "the place from the left" one has to cross the Avenue Marceau and the Avenue d'Iéna. 4, 6 Colors.

72/ 15–22 "Iris and rubber" . . . Sebastian's third book.: According to Terry Breverton the iris called "stinking gladwin" has leaves which, when crushed, "smell . . . like burning rubber" (191). This malodorous flower and the various associations in this passage are brought into a felicitous union. 3, 6 Colors. 4, 29 Uncle Ruka.

72/ 21–22 "that stone melting into wing": Cf. "on the Arc de Triomphe, a fragment of the frieze suddenly comes to life—a pigeon taking off" (*Letters to Véra* 338).

72/ 26–27 She took his arm . . . stride.: Lara Delage-Toriel ("Ultraviolet Darlings") discusses in great detail the correspondences between inter alia Clare and Mrs. Luzhin, the heroine of *The Defence*, both "spiritual companions [who] only temporarily coexist with their male companion, soon to be cast aside" (32). Like Clare, Mrs. Luzhin is "taking her husband's arm and changing step in order to match his" (Delage-Toriel 43; see also *The Defence* 203). Delage-Toriel also observes that both women, meeting their partner, went into "the wrong door" or "opened the wrong door" (*Sebastian Knight* 79; see also *The Defence* 109; Delage-Toriel 43). And how these women, sensing the end of their relationships, have the impression of being kept out of some secret, as if their companions "were hiding something from her" (Delage-Toriel 44; see also *The Defence* 222). The lack of passion in their relationships is marked by the absence of color. Mrs. Luzhin is clad "in a white dress and soundless white shoes" (*The Defence* 132). And Clare is (in a circuitous way, as will be discussed in section 4, 26) compared to a *"Women in White"* (97).

73/ 30–74/23 "because, you see, I can tell you lots myself" . . . When she had gone I wrote it all down: Unfortunately, V. decides not to convey Helen Pratt's information to the reader.

74/ 9 "When do you say it began?": This is a fine piece of rhetorical juggling. In V.'s mind "it" refers to Sebastian's love affair with the Russian woman. As is clear from Helen Pratt's answer, she refers to Sebastian's heart failures. As far as Helen Pratt is concerned the Russian woman's role may be peripheral to Sebastian's complaints, or perhaps even non-existent. Pratt dates Sebastian's illness by saying that it "must have been in twenty-seven or twenty-eight" while the "letters in Russian" arrive "[a]fter his return to London," in the summer of 1929 (109). While their conversation briefly converges during the few remarks about "that other woman" (74) V.'s and Miss Pratt's minds soon diverge onto different tracks, V. to the liaison Sebastian had with the Russian woman, Helen Pratt to her "dismal tale" (74) most likely related to Sebastian's physical deterioration and his forsaking Clare.

75/ 7 her [Clare Bishop] having married a man with the same name: Cf. "took the queen with his bishop" (141/ 4–5): 4, 5 Chess.

75/ 10 an L-shaped drawing room: A possible reference to the knight's move, see comment on line 3/ 1.

75/ 16 purple: 4, 6 Colors.

76/ 5–8 Quite recently . . . our first conversation.: Obviously V. is not willing to tell his readers how this appeasement has been effected. Doubtless, the "very sad circumstances" refer to Clare's death. This implies that this sentence has been written in May 1936 or later (see 3, 2 Calender). It is highly unlikely that Mr. Bishop took the initiative to enter into correspondence with V., as at the end of their short meeting he reproaches V. for his unannounced visit: "I do not think you should have come." The reason for this remark is clear; the callousness with which Sebastian left Clare without offering her even the slightest apology must have hurt her to such a degree that she refused "to speak of the past" (73). It is equally unlikely that what V. learns about Nina Rechnoy's character might have been considered as helpful to alleviate the impasse. How exactly V. has been able to re-open his communication with Mr. Bishop in a friendly manner remains for these reasons a rather mysterious question. This question is the more compelling as in *Speak, Memory* Nabokov mentions *Sebastian Knight*'s "self-mate combinations" (257). Self-mate is a chess problem, an end game, in which white forces black to give mate: a self-defeating winner. As V.'s succesful attempt to appease Mr Bishop is his last move, it deserves careful attention. A possible solution is presented in chapter 6.

76/ 14 past friendships: This is the denominator Mr. Bishop uses to classify the relationship between Clare and Sebastian.

CHAPTER 9

79/ 18 into the wrong room: In view of the often exultant phrases V. uses to portray Clare's relationship with Sebastian, the adjective "wrong" deserves attention. It could easily have been avoided by, for example, "someone's else," which, moreover, would have discriminated better with "one's own." See also comment on lines 72/ 26–27.

80/ 3–5 marriage . . . it did not enter their heads: A rather euphemistic apology, as very few couples at that time simply forget to get married. See also comment on 109/ 15.

80/ 21 the old sophism: This refers to the philosophical question as to whether something of which all the component parts have been successively replaced, can still be called the same thing. In Nabokov's example the "handle" and the "blade" refers to one of its variants, as Robert Graves does: "[a]s the proverb says: 'This is my grandfather's axe: my father fitted it with a new stock, and I have fitted it with a new head" (*Hercules* 442).

81/ 18 violet: 4, 6 Colors.

81/ 21 he did not merely dictate; Cf. "She [Véra Nabokov] worked from his dictation" (Schiff 52).

82/ 9–10 the thought which only seemed naked was but pleading for the clothes: Cf. "Expression is the *Dress* of *Thought*" (Pope [*Essay on Criticism*] 153).

82/ 19–25 And Clare, who . . . ideal line of expression.: According to Stacy Schiff this passage "truly conjures up Véra" (53).

83/ 8 a letter: The only letter from Sebastian that V. reproduces, see 183/ 19–184/ 21.

83/ 25–26 if you think bad grammar won't hurt: Cf. "he [Nabokov] 'was very absentminded in what concerned grammar'" (Schiff 52).

83/ 29 *The Prismatic Bezel*: According to *Webster's Second* a bezel is the upper part of a ring of metal in which a jewel is set; or the slanting facets of a cut jewel; or the bevel of a cutting jewel. "Prismatic" refers to the working of a prism: refracting a ray of white light into colors. A jewel is cut and faceted in order to add to its brilliancy the lights reflected by the facets. A prismatic bezel, though not feasible, seems to suggest the union of refraction and reflection, as it fragments and integrates its surrounding lights. It might be regarded as the embodiment of the artistic creed proposed by Nabokov: to "dismember a familiar world . . . and to create a new one as harmonious as the old" (*Lectures on Literature* 377).

84/ 30–31 **a remarkably handsome young man wearing a luxurious turban:** 3, 25 Valentino.

85/ 15 **lavender:** 4, 6 Colors.

85/ 24 **German seaside resort:** 3, 8 Germany.

85/ 26 **an unknown destination:** What would have been the problem for Sebastian, if indeed he intended to go "to Berlin" (see 87), to tell this to the staff of the hotel, especially as he was expecting Clare's arrival?

86/ 4–5 **a beech wood, deep and dark with no undergrowth except bindwood:** Andrew Caulton (174) refers to a similar passage in *Speak, Memory* (86): "one of those eerily dense European beechwoods, where the only undergrowth is bindwood and the only sound one's thumping heart."

86/ 5 **bindwood:** In contrast with the white, common Hedge Bindwood (*Calystegia sepium*) the Sea Bindwood (*Calystegia soldanella*) has pink flowers (Lippert and Podlech 132 and 200). 4, 6 Colors

86/ 8 **red-capped German gnome:** 4, 20 Robinsonnade.

86/ 13 **Donne:** 5, 1 Donne.

86/ 18 **averted his face:** This indicates that something has happened that Sebastian does not wish to discuss with Clare.

86/ 19–21 **come across a man . . . the man's car:** 3, 4 Cars. 3, 9 Germany. 3, 14 Mysterious Men.

87/ 4–5 **mysterious and dull suspense:** Cf. "something dreary and dull" (167).

87/ 7 **brownie:** 4, 20 Robinsonnade.

87/ 16 **dash to Berlin:** see comment on line 85/ 26.

87/ 18 **coronary arteries . . . sinuses of Salva:** "Probably the sinus of Valsalva" (Boyd, "Notes" 677). With these medical terms Sebastian wishes to show Clare that he has discussed them with a Berlin doctor, although he might have been familiar with them as he probably "already knew from what exact heart disease he was suffering" (87). This makes one wonder why Sebastian is so reluctant to inform Clare about his more recent heart complaints. Surely, he would have informed her about the earlier troubles? Perhaps Sebastian's inaccurate "Salva" indicates that he did not have heard the correct "Valsalva" that recently.

87/ 24 **angina pectoris:** The cause of Uncle Ruka's death (*Speak, Memory* 71). 4, 29 Uncle Ruka.

87/ 27–28 **a queer twinge as of inner itch in his left arm:** 4, 19 Queer. Cf. "left hand" (186).

88/ 11 **spread-eagled:** The way Uncle Ruka found relief for his seizures (*Speak, Memory* 71). 4, 29 Uncle Ruka.

88/ 14 **Leslie:** 3, 14 Mysterious Men.

CHAPTER 10

89/ 9 **a clown developing wings:** 3, 6 Conjuror.

89/ 24 **'penny dreadfuls':** A cheap boy's paper (Brewer's 818).

Silent Love

90/ 8–10 the fashionable trick of grouping a medley of people in a limited space (a hotel, an island, a street): A hotel: Thomas Mann, *The Magic Mountain*; an island: Norman Douglas, *South Wind*; a street: Louis Golding, *Magnolia Street*. The setting of Sebastian Knight's *Prismatic Bezel* is a country house, like the locale of Aldous Huxley's *Crome Yellow*, for which the country house satires by Thomas Love Peacock (1785–1866) may have served as examples. (In 1939 Nabokov wrote from London to his wife Véra that he had met "the amiable but supremely ungifted author of 'Magnolia Street'" [*Letters to Véra* 426].)

91/ 1 old Nosebag: Cf. "Nosebag time" (Joyce 78). 4, 28 *Ulysses*.

91/ 20–21 moonfaced person: 4, 14 Moon.

92/ 15 drops his h's: Cf. "Dropped his 'h's'" (Burnand, *The Colonel*). 3, 21 *The Colonel*.

92/ 16–18 not a parody of the Sherlock Holmes vogue but a parody of the modern reaction from it.: The plot of *The Prismatic Bezel* as summarized by V. has a number of glaring similarities with Agatha Christie's *Murder on the Orient Express* (1934). Its setting is as confined as possible, not an isolated boarding house, but a train marooned in a snowdrift. A passenger is murdered in his compartment and the perpetrator must be one of the twelve travelers from the same coach, the same number as that of the guests staying in the boarding house in *The Prismatic Bezel*. Like these guests, who have all their own rooms, the passengers have their individual compartments. Although their antecedents differ even more widely than those of the guests, it turns out that they somehow are all connected to the same (Armstrong) family, just as the lodgers appear to be all related to the old lady of room No. 3. In both cases the family is headed by a colonel.

This "metamorphosis" of visitors turning into members of one family, is indeed so remarkable that the reader might feel "baffled" by it, as V. rightly apprehends. And this should make the reader of *Sebastian Knight* wonder what kind of ties might possibly connect the chance visitors of the Beaumont Hotel. (For more on this question, see section 3, 9 Guests.)

Although Nabokov dubbed Agatha Christie "unreadable," he mentions her and her novel *A Murder Is Announced* (1950) in *Lolita*

(Karlinsky, *Dear Bunny* 159; *Lolita* 31.) See also Catharine Theimer Nepomnyashchy who discusses traces Agatha Christie left in *Lolita, Sebastian Knight* and *Despair,* and mentions *The Prismatic Bezel* as it "seems to invoke" two of Christie's novels, *Murder on the Orient Express* and *And Then There Were None* (164). An additional interesting detail is the confusion caused by the mingling of the Cyrillic and Roman alphabets, see comment on lines 184/ 6–8. In Christie's novel much importance is attached to a lady's handkerchief, found in the compartment of the murdered man. It has an embroidered "H," and is for this reason mistakenly attributed to Countess Andrenyi because of her Christian name, Helena. But it belongs to Princess Dragomiroff, whose first name is Natalia, and, as it is explained, "'H' is 'N' in Russian" (Christie 165).

92/ 17 Sherlock Holmes: 4, 23 Sherlock Holmes.

92/ 25 'ow about Hart?: Cf. "we should have heard nothing about Art. / The Colonel: No—he'd have called it Hart." (Burnand, *The Colonel*). 3, 21 *The Colonel*.

93/ 12–15 It is as if a painter . . . different way of painting a certain landscape.: The comparison with the pictorial arts in order to elucidate the process of artistic composition is much to the point as studies by painters are often preserved, while literary drafts are usually discarded by their authors. The importance of pictorial studies can be illustrated by the many preliminary sketches and preparatory studies by Leonardo for his *Last Supper*, as commentaries on this work are always grounded on a scrupulous investigation of these drawings.

Sebastian seems to be strongly opposed to the idea of showing the reader something else than "the perfect achievement: the printed book" (34). It was also Sebastian's habit to destroy "rough drafts" (34). The recommendation to do the opposite and give priority to drafts above the final result, has been formulated by André Gide in his *Counterfeiters* (1925): "Just think how interesting . . .—the story of the work—of its gestation! How thrilling it would be . . . more interesting than the work itself" (189). Sebastian dismisses "this or that literary experiment" by "putting [them] to the *ad absurdum* test," and *The Prismatic Bezel* shows how unworkable such an approach would be. As the idea of the family ties in this novel, which connects all its twelve characters, must have been preconceived, it would be ludicrous, once this idea has been revealed, to present these people as complete strangers. Staging close members of one family as nomadic individuals who happen to be stranded in a chance boarding house would indeed be hilarious. (See also Leonid Livak who devotes a chapter of his book *How It Was Done in Paris* to discuss how Nabokov in *The Gift* uses *The Counterfeiters* "as a spring board in refining his novelistic esthetics, which he opposed to the writings of his Parisian peers" [166].)

93/ 24 the methods of human fate: In *Speak, Memory* Nabokov follows the same procedure as Sebastian in *Success*: using his art to ascertain the main patterns dominating his life, as he has explained in "Chapter Sixteen," a pseudo-review of his autobiography, written in 1950 and posthumously published. It is primarily a creative process in which "all the magic and force of . . . art are summoned" (*Sebastian Knight* 94) to achieve "the blissful anastomosis provided jointly by art and fate" ("Chapter Sixteen" 241). In V.'s synopsis of Sebastian's novel, "fate" is mentioned six times but this "fate" is not the expression of fatality, but the sublunary manifestation of a higher reality, which can be thwarted by numerous contingencies, the actions resulting from man's autonomy among them, as is dicussed in the lines 95/ 20–26, a passage regarded by Dana Dragunoiu as the one in which "Nabokov's attempt to reconcile the competing claims of fate and free will is most elaborately described" (70).

94/ 1 quest: a search for an object or a journey toward a goal. As the way toward the end may be long, the experiences during the pursuit itself may become the main objective. The oldest, mythological quests are in search of the Holy Grail. 3, 13 *La morte d'Arthur*.

94/ 4–5 Percival Q.: Cf. the hero of Chrétien de Troyes' *Perceval ou le Conte du Graal (Percival, the Story of the Grail)* (ca. 1185). Sir Percival Glyde is a main character in Wilkie Collins' *The Woman in White*. 4, 32 *Woman in White*.

94/ 6 a conjuror's assistant: Cf. "zany" (97), which according to the *Webster's Collegiate* has as it first mentioned meaning "a subordinate clown or acrobat."

94/ 7–8 both happen to use the same car belonging to an amiable stranger: Cf. "had come across a man he had known ages ago, in Russia, and they had gone in the man's car" (86).

95/ 4 Anne: Anne (Catherick) happens to be the name of Sir Percival Glyde's wife's half-sister. See comment on line 94/ 4–5.

95/ 14–15 two occasions in these two people's life when unknowingly to one another they all but met: In the synopsis V. gives of *Success* it appears that before fate finally brings Percival and Anne together, there were two earlier occasions when "they all but met." In *The Gift* a similar summary is presented when Fyodor recounts how fate has carefully arranged attempts to unite Zina and Fyodor, but that it was only fate's third try that was successful (363). Brian Boyd, having told how Nabokov and his future wife had a near meeting in a Berlin office, also mentions related similarities with *Bend Sinister* and *Look at the Harlequins!* (VNRY 212).

96/ 12–98/ 22 Sebastian's inner life . . . The conjuror began to snore.: 4, 26 *Success.*

96/ 12–13 Sebastian's life at the time of the completing of the last chapters: Knight wrote Success in "July, 1925–April, 1927" (79), which means that the reference to Sebastian's inner life must concern the period after the visit to Germany in the summer of 1926 and well before his stay in the Beaumony Hotel in 1929. 4, 26 *Success.*

96/ 21 willow: 4, 26 *Success.*

97/ 9–10 The Woman in White: 4, 32 Woman in White. See also comment on line 72/ 26–27.

97/ 13 Coates (the doctor): Cf. "Dr. Oates" (104).

97/ 19 conjuror: 3, 6 Conjuror.

97/ 26–27 lost hair, fingernails: Cf. "Of nails and hairs, . . ." and "In nails, and hairs, . . .," *Of the Progress of the Soul. The Second Anniversary*, lines 278 and 337 (Donne 294 and 296). 5, 1 Donne.

98/ 12 **forbidden bliss:** 4, 26 *Success*.

98/ 12 **laundry:** According to *The Oxford English Dictionary* "laundry" is an "[a]ltered form of lavendry" (VII: 703). 4, 6 Colors.

CHAPTER 11

99/ 12 **Sebastian's shade:** 5, 5 Voices and visions.

99/ 13 **P.G.:** Some male characters of *Sebastian Knight* are conspicuously equipped with two initials as is Stainton (H.F.), Gorget (D.W.), Coleman (J.L.), and Sheldon. For females the given name of Helen(e) appears to be contagious, as the name is shared by the ladies Pratt, Grinstein, and Von Graun.

99/ 13 **Sheldon:** As a child Nabokov had a governess, or nanny, called Sheldon, and a governess of the same name appears in Nabokov's story "Orache" (Boyd, *VNRY* 47; *Stories* 325). Sheldon seems to be Sebastian's and Clare's closest friend, see "Not even Sheldon" (118). 4, 1 Baring.

101/ 11 **meek little man:** Cf. "meek little man" (101/ 30). 3, 14 Mysterious Men.

101/ 28–29 ***The Back of the Moon*:** Cf. "You can't see de odder side of the moon." 130/ 29–30.

101/ 30 **little man:** Cf. "little man" (124).

102/ 1 **Mr. Siller:** Cf. "My name is Silbermann" (125). 4, 14 Mann.

102/ 7–13 **Mr. Siller makes his bow, . . . the Adam's apple . . . "arrased eavesdropper" . . . lost his hump:** In an attractive quest for the literary origins of the name "Robin," Jansy Berndt de Souza Mello discusses "Adam de la Halle (1230–1288), a poet and musician from Arras" (33). De la Halle is the author of *Le Jeu de Robin and Marion,* and is also called "'Adan d'Arras' or 'Adan le Bossu,' i.e. a hunchback" (36). These names link the "Adam," "arras" and the "hump" in the quotation V. gives from *The Back of the Moon,* while the "Robin" in the title of De la Halle's work connects Mr. Siller's "bow" with the "bow and arrow" used to kill Cock Robin (34).

102/ 10 **Adam's apple:** Not only prominent in Mr. Siller's appearance but also in Mr. Silbermann's, see 125.

102/ 10–11 **arrased eavesdropper:** Reference to *Hamlet* (3.3.28), see Brian Boyd ("Notes" 677). 3, 10 *Hamlet.*

103/ 7–27 **Naturally, I cannot touch . . . mere repetition":** 4, 22 Sexuality.

103/ 18 **the whole sea, from its moon to its serpent:** 4, 24 Snake.

103/ 18–20 **moon . . . *Moon*:** 4, 15 Moon.

103/ 19 **diamond-rippled road to Cathay:** "The Road to Cathay" is the title of the second chapter of Marco Polo's *Travels*. The mercantile approach of Polo's voyage explains his emphasis "on precious gems" because of their "high value in proportion to their bulk" (Latham 19). Despite Polo's commercial interests, he often discusses sexual customs and connubial arrangements of the people in the various countries, which is probably the reason for Knight's reference, to show that sexuality cannot be divorced from common life.

103/ 21–22 **Physical love is but another way of saying the same thing and not a special sexophone note, . . . :** A very similar dictum as the one in the "love letter" in chapter 12 where it is said that the love of a human being cannot be split into physical and spiritual love, see comment on lines 111/ 22–25.

104/ 3 **the colour of his romance:** 4, 6 Colors.

104/ 16 **Clare . . . dropped her . . . handkerchief:** Cf. "She [Desdemona] let it [her handkerchief] drop" (*Othello* 3.3.311). 3, 16 *Othello.*

104/ 18–19 **he [Sebastian] never wore a wristwatch himself:** 3, 10 *Hamlet.*

104/ 25 **his meals:** Sebastian and Clare, who do not share a home (see comment on line 109/ 15), do not even dine together. It seems that these details have been overlooked by Michael Long when he writes that Sebastian "sets up house with Clare" (122).

105/ 5 **to my place, pack a thing or two:** Cf. "her lodgings" (109).

106/ 2 **We're sort of married.:** See comment on line 104/ 25 and on line 109/ 15.

106/ 4 **"pelmenies":** Like *piroshki* (eaten by Fyodor, see *The Gift* 30) and *blini* (served in the Larins household, see *Eugene Onegin* 2: 299) the name of this Russian dish is *pelmeni*. 3, 23 Transmigration by Languages.

106/ 28–107/ 14 **the woman who had handed us our hats . . . I have cut a beggar:** Sebastian's commiseration with the slight ailments of the cloakroom attendant, taxi driver, and chocolate-girl become more pronounced when Sebastian expresses his regret for not having alleviated the predicaments of an "ugly woman" or an "old street violinist" (174). V. offers no explanation, although the contrast with the callousness Sebastian shows when separating from Clare is too strong to neglect.

107/ 28–29 **Sebastian looked queer. But he had looked queer before:** 4, 19 Queer.

108/ 2 **Sebastian has gone mad:** 3, 10 *Hamlet*.

108/ 10 **lost soul:** Cf "souls lost" (109).

CHAPTER 12

109/ 15 **her lodgings:** That Sebastian and Clare do not live together contradicts the suggestion that they are "sort of married" (106). Clare has not even enough clothes ("a thing or two") at Sebastian's place to pack her bag for a short stay abroad.

109/ 24–110/ 1 the clinking sound of unsaddled horses browsing in the dark; the glow of a camp fire; stars overhead: The evocation of a scenic camp of riders in the evening enjoying the serenity of a camp fire under a clear sky is a surprising image to illustrate the impression *Lost Property* makes on V., who is as much an urbanite as Sebastian. But they are bookish as well and will certainly have read Leo Tolstoy's novels with its camp fires surrounded by riders and their horses, as in *War and Peace* (1137) and *The Cossacks* (205–206).

110/ 1–6 an aeroplane crash . . . misery and pain: 4, 29 Uncle Ruka.

110/ 7 toothache: Cf. "toothache" (38).

110/ 20–21 milk-puddingy: The innocence and purity suggested by the milk (see the next comment) is sugared for the pudding in order to hide the bitterness of the "consolation" offered. The "milk-pudding" prefigures another lacteal dessert, the "curds" (sort of quark or cottage cheese), spilled by Nina Rechnoy, who, despite her pretence of innocence, does not tell the truth about her identity (171).

110/ 20–23 milk-puddingy . . . doves and lilies: Doves and lilies are used by the writer of the love letter to exemplify the "lovely" relationship he has had with the addressee. Doves and lilies are images heavily charged with symbolic meanings. A dove symbolizes "from antiquity," "love and constancy and thus a dove or a pair of doves is one of the chief attributes of Venus" (Hall 109) and are represented in Renaissance paintings as white birds (Impelluso 323–329). The lily, with its color as immaculate as milk, denotes purity.

110/ 23–25 that soft pink "v" . . . the long, lingering "l": 4, 13 "L" and "V."

110/ 25 Our life together was alliterative: The "lovely" that qualifies this relationship is spelled out by its vowels, the "l" and the "v." In so far the "l" and the "v" connote the masculinity and the femininity of the respective lovers, this seems to be annihilated by making this relationship "alliterative."

111/1 Lily-livered: an adjective coined by Shakespeare in *Macbeth* (5.3.15) and meaning "cowardly" (*Oxford English Dictionary* VIII: 955). As a "liver" is blood-colored, a pale liver suggests the lack of blood or cowardice. But "liver" is also regarded as "the seat of emotion" ("hot-liver" equals a "passionate or amorous temperament") (*Concise Oxford Dictionary* 699). Shakespeare employs both meanings: "lily-livered," "pigeon-livered," and "milk-livered," as well as "the ardour of my liver" (spoken by Ferdinand to express his love for Miranda in *The Tempest*); "liver, brain, and heart" (which Orsino wishes to see filled with love thoughts for him by Olivia in *Twelfth Night*) or the "motion of the liver" (by which Orsino indicates the very strong passion possessing him) (*Macbeth* 5.3.15; *Hamlet* 2.2.613; *King Lear* 4.2.50; *Tempest* 4.1.55; *Twelfth Night* 1.1.37 and 2.4.100, respectively). Because in the letter "lilies" are singled out to mark the loveliness of a relationship, it might be that the reader is expected to attach another meaning to "lily-livered" than cowardice, and to regard "liver' in this collocation as the seat of emotion rather than of (the lack of) combativeness, in which case "lily-livered" would mean that one's passion has paled. This of course would contradict that he is possessed by another woman, in which case passion would be diverted or rekindled rather than paled.

111/ 22–25 It would be absurd . . . comedy of the flesh. All is flesh and all is purity.: Here the possible distinction between "pure love" on the one hand and "a passion" is dismissed as "absurd." Yet it was this very idea that was pursued by André Gide in his letters and life. He wished to prove the feasibility of his desire "to dissociate pleasure and love" by having a *mariage blanc* with his cousin Madeleine Rondeaux (*If It Die* 240). He married her in 1895 after having spent a long time in Algeria in the company of various (quite) young male prostitutes as he tells in his autobiography, because he preferred to be "indecent" rather than "dishonest" (*If It Die* 250). The idea that a person can have two separate identities, body, and soul, is the main theme of his semi-autobiographical *The Notebooks of André Walter* (1891), a collection of esoteric diary fragments. Its keywords are "soul," "body," "passion," "purity" and "flesh." In the lines from *Sebastian Knight* discussed here, "love," "pure," and "passion" reappear and twice the word "flesh" is used, a word with biblical and surgical connotations, seldom used by Nabokov to indicate sensual or sexual animation. The reason why Nabokov refers to Gide's *Notebooks* is discussed in chapter 6. It is very likely that Nabokov is responding to Gide, and again in a rather derogatory way (see comment on lines 93/ 12–15).

André Gide was one of the most important authors in the first half of the twentieth century in France. In the Russian émigré circles, writes Leonid Livak, "Gide was the most discussed French writer after Proust" (116). Many critics have drawn attention to Nabokov's frequent use of the device that, after Gide, is called mise-en-abyme, telling a story in the same story in miniature. As an illustration Gide mentions the little convex mirrors in the paintings of Hans Memling and Quentin Matsys (see Livak [265, note 21] who reproduces the relevant passage from Gide's *Journal*). In *Pnin* these fifteenth-century mirrors are discussed as well, especially those painted by "Van Eyck and Petrus Christus and Memling" (97). One can regard the love letter written by L. also as an example of the mise-en-abyme technique as it synopsizes the novel of which it forms a part.

Nabokov refers to Gide in *Lolita* and *Pale Fire* because of his homosexuality. He ranks high in Nabokov's list of bêtes noires. *The Wellesley College News* introduced Nabokov in 1947 by writing that "Pushkin, Shakespeare and himself constitute his three favorite writers, Mann, Faulkner and André Gide receive the doubtful honor of being the three writers he most detests" (Boyd, *VNAY* 122). (This was published on October 9. Within a few weeks, on November 13 of that year, Gide was awarded the Nobel Prize for Literature.) One can think of several reasons why Nabokov, despite Gide's artful style and his erudition, despised him: his candid display of his homosexuality (not all the passages in *If It Die* and *The Immoralist* are the most palatable ones); his justification of it (Gide's *Corydon* is about a work in progress by the eponymous writer, called *In Defence of Pederasty*); his courting of the USSR; his interest in the nature of pure evil (the subject of *The Caves of the Vatican*; a novel which Nabokov qualified as "terrible nonsense, but well-written in places" [*Letters to Véra* 165]); his regard for Freud and his keen interest in psychoanalysis; and his admiration for Dostoevsky. See also Galina Rylkova who, starting from the sunbathing-scenes in *The Gift* and *The Immoralist* raises the question as to whether his "mysterious disease" might be an indication that Sebastian Knight is a homosexual, because in *The Immoralist* the protagonist regards sunbathing as a remedy against his TB, the disease that "was an outward manifestation of his inner suppression of homosexual desires" (57).

112/ 14 L.: 4, 13 'L' and 'V'.

112/ 12–14 "to a satisfactory close" . . . **"L.":** That "L." and his business partner did not finish their meeting satisfactorily foreshadows the identical situation at the end of chapter 18 where V. admits that his negotiation did not end "successful[ly]" (180). There is, however, a difference. V. has, since the age of thirteen, lived for twenty years in France and may for this reason pass as a Frenchman. Mr. Mortimer, L.'s partner, has a surname with a French origin, Mortemar, a place in Seine-Maritime (Cottle 262). So in L.'s letter it is an Englishman who reports about his talk with a Frenchman, while in chapter 18 it is a Frenchman who relates his negotiations with an Englishman. It can also be observed that the messenger's signature is "L.," one of the two letters juxtaposed in its text: the "v" and the "l." This turns "L." into the opposite number of "V." And perhaps more striking than this mirrored situation is that the first talk (between "L." and Mortimer) is part of *Lost Property*, while the second one (between "V." and his business partner) is about *Lost Property*.

It is inconceivable that Sebastian, while composing *Lost Property*, could have predicted with so many accurate details events five years ahead of him. It seems somewhat less fantastic to assume that both mimicked versions are written by the same author, that is that either Sebastian or V. has written *Sebastian Knight* and Sebastian's novels. An exponent of this one-author theory is Gennady Barabtarlo who regards the name "Sebastian Knight" as the key to the novel, because of its near-anagram "Knight Is Absent" and argues that Sebastian's "'real life' has been invented by V., the only writer of the book" (*Aerial View* 215–16). This option, the selection of a single author, has often been proposed in order to account for the many echoes between Sebastian's novels and V.'s quest (see Julian Connolly's short survey in "The Challenge of Interpreting and Decoding Nabokov" 160–161). This proposition resembles the well-known Shade-Kinbote controversy: who invented the other? Such a reading may imply, for example, that Sebastian staged his own death. In this way anything could be thought of, and many of the novel's fascinating details would be outlawed and lose their contextual attraction. As David Lodge writes, it would "drastically impoverish the meaning and beauty of the text" (163). The correspondences and the inverted doublings should rather be understood as belonging to a pattern that links the lives of Sebastian and his half-brother. As D. Barton Johnson has explained, "the webs of coincidences that pervade the world of characters, are but an imperfect mirroring of events on a second, controlling world" the latter world being that of the "author-persona" (*Worlds in Regression* 1). It is not the correspondences but the plan behind the correspondences that the reader should focus on.

An extraordinary aspect of "L."'s letter is that it belongs to a "short chapter dealing with an aeroplane crash." But how can this chapter fit into *Lost Property*, Sebastian's "most autobiographical work" as is mentioned twice by V.? Apart from this letter, six quotations of *Lost Property* are presented; they all have to do with Sebastian's life, his family, his feelings and recollections. Doubtless, the crash is fictitious; one cannot relate a real disaster in such a farcical way. And telling the real reason for his separation from Clare in this circuitous manner would of course be self-defeating: making public what is too sensitive for telling in private does not make sense. Still the letter tells the same story as V. does. Are we as readers expected to conjecture that V.'s account is equally ill-assorted and equally fictitious as this capricious short chapter?

114/ 8–30 **"I usually found him . . . the perfect 'poseur.'"**: 4, 28 *The Tragedy of Sebastian Knight*.

114/ 10–11 **Little Red Riding Hood**: 4, 20 Robinsonnade.

114/ 13–14 **M. Proust, whom Knight consciously or subconsciously copied**: Cf. "Mme. Melnikov-Papoushek . . . writes . . . that I imitate Proust" (Melnikov-Papoushek wrote this in her review of *Mary* for the May 1926 issue of *Volya Rossi* [*Letters to Véra* 70 and 566]): 4, 18 Proust.

114/ 22 **pasting cuttings, most likely . . . his books**: Cf. "he refused either to subscribe to the clippings or thank the kindly critics" (100). See also 37/ 9–10.

114/ 28 **Byronic languor**: 4, 3 Byron's "Dream."

115/ 11–29 **burning problems . . . on a window sill**: John Burt Foster Jr., who has identified this reference, writes that "at this point Goodman oddly recalls H. G. Wells lamenting the meager content of a Henry James novel" (168). Foster mentions Wells' novel *Boon* in which its author "likens the Jamesion novel to a hippopotamus determined to pick up a pea or to an altar on which has been placed, 'intensely there, . . . a dead kitten, an egg-shell, a bit of string'" (248). Although Nabokov had "the deepest admiration" for Wells and disliked James "intensely" (*SO* 175, 64) he of course could not have endorsed Wells' opinion that fiction is "an instrument to be used for social reform" (qtd. in Seymour *A Ring of Conspirators* 264) which explains why Knight in this controverse sides with James and not with Wells.

116/ 2–3 He confused solitude with altitude and the Latin for sun.: To the question "What is your position in the world of letters?" Nabokov answered, "Jolly good view from up here." And in a 1968 interview he stresses his preference to compose "in glacial solitude" (*SO* 181, 117).

117/ 14 in such a manner as to convey the impression: This suggests that the artist has used an artifice to render the impression, not more. However, the "slight ripple on the hollow cheek, owing to the presence of a water-spider" (116) shows that Sebastian's portrait is actually painted as a reflection in water. The "glint of humid sunshine" (117) caught by Sebastian's temple is another reflection, and the "mysterious blueness" (117) is the mirrored sky. The art of painting objects as seen through their reflections in water was about the turn of the nineteenth century developed by Claude Monet. In Carswell's case, as in Monet's, there seems to exist "an equivalence between the surface of the water and the surface of the canvases" (Bowness 30). (Monet's *The Cloud* [1903] is not even named after the reflecting medium, a pond with water lilies, but after the reflected sky. Proust might have had this painting in mind when he noted "a clear . . . blue that was almost violet" in the "depths" of the water of the Vivonne. [*Swann's Way* 200; see Chernowitz 75].) In this way Sebastian is not only looking at his own mirror image, but at the reflected sunlight and the mysterious blueness of the nether sky as well.

117/ 18–19 Withered leaf . . . on the reflected brow: Cf. the third stanza of Keats's "La Belle Dame sans Merci"

> I see a lily on thy brow
> With anguish moist and fever dew,

And on thy cheeks a fading rose
Fast withered too.

117/ 30 "I wanted to hint at a woman": Roy Carswell painted Sebastian's portrait in 1933. The letter that Sebastian wrote to Carswell in 1934 shows that they are kind of friends. For this reason, when Carswell refers to a woman, he might well have Clare in mind. Of course, for V. any reference to a woman applies to the woman who wrote letters in Russian to Sebastian.

117/ 31 the shadow of a hand: 4, 31 V.'s dream.

118/ 4 "She smashed his life": Sounds rather speculative as this follows immediately after V.'s remark that "nobody seems to know anything about her" (118).

118/ 6 incomplete as your picture: 3, 24 Unfinished Pictures.

118/ 8 club-footed shadow: This image is by no means suggestive of a clear delineation of such a shadow. This is doubtless a reference to Lord Byron who had a clubfoot (Marchand 9). Cf. "Dora turns out," writes Lucy Maddox (147), "to have a club foot, and for those who might miss that clue she mentions in the course of the conversation that 'as a girl I dreamt of becoming a female clown, "Madame Byron," or "Trek, Trek"'" (Maddox quotes *Look at the Harlequins!* 213).

CHAPTER 13

119/ 2 quest: 3, 13 *La morte d'Arthur*.

120/ 14 a bath every morning: This reminiscence of the hotel manager tallies well with the "morning bath" Sebastian used to have according to his stepmother and to Mr. Goodman's biography (30, 114). Cf. "Martin could not manage without his morning bath" (*Glory* 182. See also Brian Boyd, *VNRY* 182).

54   Silent Love

120/ 17 **"Oh, I think he was here with his father"**: Although the hotel manager has stated quite positively that he remembered "the Englishman" (120/ 13), V., tenaciously in search of a woman, ignores this information.

121/ 7 **elenctic:** 3, 7 Elenctic.

122/ 2 **Colonel Samain:** The name recalls the symbolist poet Albert Samain. And it might perhaps be a contraction of the well known Russian name Samarin. 3, 14 Mysterious Men.

122/ 18 **Swiss couple:** Cf. "Professor Nussbaum, a Swiss scientist, shoots his young mistress and himself" (173). 4, 29 Uncle Ruka.

123/7 **An unfinished picture:** 3, 24 Unfinished Picture.

123/ 8 **the martyr with the arrows in his side:** 4, 25 St Sebastian.

123/ 19 **Switzerland:** Apart from the Swiss couple, this is the only reference to this country.

124/ 15 **factory. Paper.:** Cf. "factories and paper" (Doyle 7). 4, 23 Sherlock Holmes.

125/ 1 **robinsonnada:** "The word Robinsonade," writes Andrew Caulton, "is a German term referring to a full-length diving save in football and derives from the name of the English goalkeeper Jack Robinson (1870–1931) who was reputedly the first exponent of this technique. Silbermann misapplies the term to the scoring of a goal rather than the saving of one" (191). This inversion is interesting as David H. J. Larmour in his article "Getting Past the Goalkeeper" discusses the soccer match in *Glory* in detail, especially the protagonist's role as a goalkeeper, and shows that "sporting prowess" and "sexual desire" are associated with each other (66). 4, 20 Robinsonnada. (A Robinsonade is also the "German term for stories which derived from Defoe's *The Life and Strange and Surprising Adventures of Robinson Crusoe*" [Cuddon 756].)

125/ 12–13 **Now I sell ledder . . .:** Cf. "Starkaus, *cuirs, peaux*" (Starkaus, leathers, hides) (194).

Annotations | 55

126/ 2 **a private detective:** 4, 23 Sherlock Holmes.

126/ 5 **Braht, millee braht—dear brodder:** Vladimir Alexandrov comments that this "sounds uncannily like a veiled appeal or greeting to V. from Sebastian" (156).

127/ 20–21 **a delightful silver pencil:** Cf. "a silver pencil-holder" and "a little silver pencil" (Mann, *Magic Mountain* 123 and 332). 4, 14 Mann.

128/ 5 **I had, have all the hotel-gentlemans here:** One may wonder why Mr. Silbermann has prepared this list. Clearly, he has foreseen V.'s request, but not V.'s fixation on women.

CHAPTER 14

129/ 1–21 **So this was ... Non-Russian.:** The hotel guests consist of 8 couples, 13 single men, and 13 single women, amounting to 42 guests. (Single means here unmarried or unaccompanied.)

129/ 12 **Rasine:** Recalls the name of the French playwright Jean Racine and the Russian rebel Stenka Razin.

130/ 9 **The name was Jewish:** See comment on lines 132/ 20.

130/ 18 **a splendid contralto:** Cf. "Contralto" (Doyle 11). A contralto, a female voice covering the same range as a male countertenor, has for this reason been attributed with a connotation of sexual ambiguity, as in Théophile Gautier's "Contralto" in which he calls this the "[h]ermaphrodite de la voix," "homme et femme à la fois" (see Burgin 194).

130/ 25–26 **mouse-grey spats:** Cf. "mouse-gray spats" (*Speak, Memory* 257).

130/ 29–30 **You can't see de odder side of de moon.:** Mr. Silbermann is right. There is only one "planet in the solar system which is tilted 'on its side'" (Holmes 102), and this planet is not the moon. 4, 15 Moon. 4, 20 Robinsonnade.

131/21 **twenty franc coin**: Cf. "twenty franc coin" (199).

132/ 11–12 **Passauer Strasse**: In 1926 Nabokov moved to rooms in the Passauer Strasse 12 where he lived for two years (Boyd, *VNRY* 263).

132/ 20 **A silent boy**: 3, 9 Guests.

132/ 20–134/ 31 **A silent boy ... toward the hall.**: "From his post-*Kristallnacht* vantage point," writes Andrea Pitzer, "Nabokov presents a loving, idealized Jewish family from two years earlier, a portrait clearly defying the real-world German propaganda of the day" (149).

135/ 13 **pages of Sebastian's life**: See comment on 173/ 13.

135/ 28–136/ 14 **The lights go out ... Slides into the rushes.**: The "dragonflies," "waterlilies," "reeds," and the "names" and "dates" in the "red" riverbank seem to have been borrowed from what Ganin and Mary see from their rowboat in *Mary* (57–58). The trip also recalls as well those in *Madame Bovary* and Axel Munthe's *Story of San Michele*. 3, 1 Boat trip. 4, 3 Byron's "Dream."

135/ 28–29 **the curtain rises and a Russian summer landscape is disclosed**: Cf. "The curtain rises, revealing a view of the lake" (Chekhov *The Seagull* 35). 3, 15 Nina Zarechny.

136/ 7 **a mere outline**: 3, 24 Unfinished Pictures.

136/ 8–10 **Dark blue dragonflies ... waterlily leaves.**: Cf. "on the leaf of a water-lily an insect with fine legs crawled or rested" (Flaubert, *Madame Bovary* 101).

136/ 15 **cox**: 4, 7 Cox.

136/ 20–21 **the aspen leaves ... Judas**: According to popular Russian folklore Judas hanged himself on a aspen, which originated the Russian saying "tremble like an aspen" (Barabtarlo, see Couturier 1556).

137/ 1 **Byron's dream**: 4, 3 Byron's "Dream."

137/ 2–28 Years later ... to make it gentler: As Andrew Caulton has observed (194–195) this passage contains no less than four phenomena which in ancient times were used to prophesy coming events, to which the stars can be added:

- "the sky ... alive with stars"
- "the bowels of a ripped up beast"
- "a ... flight of migrating cranes"
- "a felled tree"
- "a ... hand" which "writes ..."

Caulton also mentions "an owl hooting" as an "evil portent" and refers to *Julius Caesar* (1.3.26–28). Augurs, however, attach no meaning to owls when they hoot at night as they are wont to do, but only when their cry is heard during the day. In Shakespeare's play the hooting is heard "at noon-day," while "[i]t is night" in the scene described by V.

The first three of these phenomena need interpretation by soothsayers to decide whether they signify good or evil. The last two are ill-omened. (In the *Bible* King Belshazzar saw only "the fingers" of a man's hand writing [355], just as only Natasha's "arm and thin brown hand" is seen.) What might these forebodings mean? They can hardly be a means of dramatazing the end of the romance with Natasha, as this is what often happens with youthful attachments. Nor can there have been much disappointment on Sebastian's side as Natasha only confirms what he already suspects. As Sebastian's "next summer was mainly devoted to the futurist Pan," it is unlikely that any pain inflicted by Natasha's preferring another boy, lasted long. The bad omens also cannot apply to Sebastian's other liaisons with girls, as the end of the relationship with Clare was his own making, while any affair that there might have been with a fickle demimondaine as Nina Rechnoy was bound to be short-lived. Perhaps these five omens simply emphasize that all five relationships Sebastian had with women (his mother, his stepmother, Natasha, Clare, Nina) were all without future.

137/ 8 an owl hooting: Cf. "An owl hooted ..." (Munthe 75).

137/ 17–18 A Camberwell Beauty: Cf. "Camberwell Beauties" (*Speak, Memory* 231).

138/ 6 Pan: 4, 3 Byron's "Dream."

CHAPTER 15

139/ 0 **[Chapter] 15**: Of all the surprising chapters of *Sebastian Knight* this chapter might amaze the reader more than others. Seen from the point of view of V., who is going to meet Nina Rechnoy in the next two chapters, the second-hand information he acquires about her in this chapter, coming from a vindictive former husband, will soon be superseded by fresher impressions. Why has V. included this chapter at all, one may wonder? According to Shlomith Rimmon, this chapter is merely a "delay," postponing the denouement at the end of chapter 17 (118). But in the present reading this chapter (and not chapter 16 or 17) is essential in identifying Sebastian's lover as will be discussed in chapter 6.

140/ 13 **Pahl Pahlich**: "'Pavel Pavlovich,' . . . when casually interpellated is made to sound like 'Pahlpahlych'" (*Look at the Harlequins!* 249).

140/ 16–17 **a sewing machine . . . ribbon-and-linen**: See comment on lines 142/ 24–25.

140/ 21 **cigarette holder**: Cf. "cigarette holder" (148).

140/ 27 **Black**: 4, 5 Chess.

140/ 28–29 **red-and-blue pencil**: 4, 6 Colors.

141/ 3 **thimble**: Cf. "a thimble" (187).

141/ 10–16 **Imperial Family . . . Gogol's *Dead Souls***: 4, 8 *Dead Souls*.

141/ 22–23 **German friends**: The reference to Germany is so obstinately repeated (see also lines 142/ 28, 142/ 29, and 145/ 1) that it should not be disregarded. 3, 8 Germany.

142/ 7–13 **artist . . . ordinary hand**: 3, 6 Conjuror.

142/ 24–25 **"Does your wife sew?" . . . "Oh, yes, she has taken up dressmaking"**: After the details about the sewing machine, the resumption of this subject looks as if these remarks are tailormade. What relevance may the occupation of Pahl Pahlich's second wife have for the unfolding of *Sebastian Knight*? Its repeated call (V. first notices the sewing machine before he learns that Varvara Mitrofanna is indeed the one who uses it) seems to demand some attention. A possible clue may be found in *The Gift*. In the comment on lines 95/ 14–15 it has been noted that V.'s summary of *Success* resembles what Fyodor tells Zina in the very last pages of *The Gift*: both accounts relate the manœuvers fate uses to bring together "two lines of life" (94). As *The Gift* was completed in the same year that *Sebastian Knight* was begun, it might be that some of the former's rich imagery has been reworked for the latter.

In *The Gift* Fyodor finally meets Zina when he becomes a lodger in the apartment where she lives. Although the room seems at first sight "repellent" to him, he is encouraged to accept it because he sees a "gauze dress" in the room of the landlord's daughter (143–144). It appears that this dress is not Zina's; rather, her "cousin Raissa's" left it for Zina "to take something off or sew something on" (364). This dress, as fate's last recourse, is a remarkable choice. When Fyodor is "pondering . . . fate's methods" "he finally found a certain thread" (362–363). This "thread," like that of the ancient Parcae, is part of an elaborate pattern of coherent images related to fabrics, knitting, lining, garments and carpets (see Dolinin 158; Berdjis 305–311; and for fate's ploys in *The Gift*, Boyd, *VNRY* 471–478). As for the retracing of fate's steps "all the magic and force of [one's] art" is required, it is quite unique that the dress that fate uses to converge the future lovers' lives is found in the room of Fyodor's muse, Zina, the prompter of his art. Thus fate and art merge in this dress.

Like Zina, Varvara Mitrofanna is used to "sewing" and engaged in making or mending dresses. The hyphenated "ribbon-and-linen" suggests that a long string is joined with linen to make a cloth. This may signal that fate's attempts two join "two lines of life" has been successful, and that V. could find Sebastian's new lover in the circle of people one meets in chapter 15 and that V.'s pursuit beyond this point is futile.

143/ 2 **Varvara Mitrofanna**: 3, 26 Varvara Mitrofanna.

143/ 25 **Mata Hari**: 3, 28 Zelle.

143/ 28 She sucked me dry: This is the way spiders devour their prey, and also the way vampires kill their victims. Femmes fatales are often compared to vampires ("vamp" is short for "vampire") as in Baudelaire's *"Les Metamorphoses du Vampire"*; *"elle eut de mes os sucé toute la moelle"* ("she had sucked all the marrow from my bones") and in Walter Pater's description of Leonardo's *Mona Lisa* (Baudelaire 197; Pater 123).

143/ 30 Anatole: Anatole Deibler (1863–1939), France's best known executioner. 5, 2 Executions.

144/ 12 she thought the maid had stolen: Cf. "a Polish woman who had attempted to steal" (8).

145/ 12–13 Nirvana ... Lhassa: Nirvana is the term for a state of being, supposedly blissful, akin to self-obliteration, attained by practising extreme degrees of ascetism and stoicism. It is the objective of the way of life of Buddhist lamas in Tibet, spending their time as hermits in barren regions. It seems a very ambitious goal for the capricious and mondaine Nina. In *Lolita* "Nirwana" is referred to in a distinctly ironical way (293, 210). Tibet and Lhasa, long forbidden to strangers to enter, were regarded as possessing the most pure forms of religion, not contaminated by the vices of civilization.

145/ 15 Nina: 3, 15 Nina Zarechny.

145/ 15 Toorovetz: 4, 5 Chess.

146/ 15 Once upon a time: Cf. "Once upon a time" (169).

CHAPTER 16

148/ 14 Lecerf: 3, 19 Staghunt.

151/ 3 Bohemsky: 4, 23 Sherlock Holmes.

151/ 10 Sherlock Holmes stratagem: In *The Hound of Baskervilles* Holmes does the same; trying to elicit a correct description by giving some, at random, information about, in this case, a Mr. Johnson: "'A lawyer, is he not, gray-headed and walks with a limp?' 'No, sir, this is Mr. Johnson, the coal-owner, a very active gentleman, not older than yourself'" (37). 4, 23 Sherlock Holmes.

151/ 13 **Santé prison**: For the executions of prisoners sentenced to death, a guillotine was erected outside the prison, at the corner of the Rue de la Santé and the Boulevard Aragon. Dietrich, a Cambridge acquaintance of Nabokov's, attended a "*guillotinade* . . . on the Boulevard Aragon" (*Speak, Memory* 278–279). 4, 23 Sherlock Holmes.

151/ 31 **Dr. Axel Munthe's *San Michele***: 3, 1 Boat trip.

151/ 31–152/ 1 **carnations**: Cf. "pinks" (164). 4, 25 St Sebastian.

152/ 14–24 **"Remember my sapphire," she said giving me her little cold hand . . . close-fitting velvet**: Mme. Lecerf's small hand and protruding ring and her tight dress is remindful of the mysterious lady in Alexander Blok's poem "The Strange Lady" with her "taut silks" and her "slender bejeweled hand" (translated by Nabokov, see Boyd and Shvabrin 325). 3, 5 Commedia dell'arte.

153/ 17–18 **I thought her transparent skin and dark hair quite attractive**: This is the first time V. deviates from his quest to confide his enthrallment by Mme. Lecerf to the reader. He is so instantly captivated by her that he even loses his sense of decency, see line 156/ 17.

154/ 1 **when the news of his death was in the papers**: See comment on lines 172/ 1–5.

155/ 17–18 **She was a Jewess? Adorable!**: As anti-Semitism in France in 1936 was no less powerful than in Germany (see Pitzer 140 and 174), Mme. Lecerf's gleeful comments cannot have gone unnoticed by V. who had just visited the Grinstein family in Berlin. The next time Jews are mentioned (195/ 29–30) is in an anti-Semitic context.

156/ 9 **quest**: 3, 13 *La morte d'Arthur*.

156/ 17 **I looked . . . down**: See comment on lines 153/ 17–18.

156/ 19 No, not that: V.'s aversion to music contrasts with Sebastian's frequenting "concerts" (182).

157/ 2–3 brainy fellow suddenly go on all fours and wag his tail: Circe, the enchantress in Homer's *Odyssey*, "bewitched" wild animals "with her magic drugs. They did not attack my [Odysseus's] men, but rose on their hind legs to fawn on them, with much wagging of their long tails" (148).

157/ 23–24 the dreams in the dreams of his dreams: In Mikhail Lermontov's "The Dream" the poet dreams that he is dying from a wound and in his "death's sleep" begins dreaming about a young woman who in her turn has a dream very much like the poet's initial dream. Nabokov calls this "a dream within a dream within a dream" (Lermontov vii–viii).

158/ 8 his hands on the knob of a cane: Both Nabokov and his brother Sergey had a pommeled cane (*Speak, Memory* 243; Noel 212). 3, 3 Canes.

158/ 9 She got friendly with another man soon: This does not suggest that the liaison with Sebastian was an affair of some duration.

158/ 22–23 the colour of time: Cf. "the very colour of time" (*Lectures on Literature* 241). 4, 6 Colors.

159/ 6–7 He did not send her any more of his usual entreating letters, which she never read, anyway.: This makes it very unlikely that she wrote so many letters to Sebastian that he could collect them in a "bundle" (36).

160/ 1–2 *Une femme fatale?*: One of Nabokov's friends during his Western European years, Mark Aldanov, called Irina Guadanini, with whom Nabokov had an affair, "the femme fatale, the breaker of hearts" (qtd. in Schiff [87]).

CHAPTER 17

161/ 24 Lescaux: Cf. Manon Lescaut, the heroine of the eponymous novel by l'Abbé Prévost (1696–1763), a bewitching courtesan. The name

Lescaux also recalls the Caves de Lascaux, famous for its drawings of stags. 3, 19 Staghunt.

162/ 12–13 St. Damier: The French *damier* means "draughtboard." It is also the name of a butterfly, also called "checkerspot" (Zimmer, *Guide* 212).

162/ 24–25 ballet-girls waiting in the wings: Almost identical to the title of a pastel by Edgar Degas, *Ballet Dancers in the Wings* (*Danseuses dans les coulisses*, c. 1890–1900, St. Louis Art Museum).

162/ 26–27 house was large . . . old tree represented the park: 3, 1 Boat trip.

163/ 22–23 "Isn't it cold," . . . Feel my hands.: Cf. "her cold white fingers" (6).

164/ 12 pinks and daffodils: 3, 17 Pink and Narcissus.

164/ 15–16 Persian Princess . . . She blighted the Palace Gardens: 4, 21 *Rubáiyát*.

165/ 2 rather handsome man in plus-fours: 3, 14 Mysterious Men. The identity of this man will be discussed in chapter 6.

165/ 12 an ashtray: See comment on line 35/ 22.

166/ 9 Arles: "L'Arlésienne" (The girl from Arles) is the title of a short story by Alphonse Daudet (1840–1897) about a love affair ending with the man's suicide.

166/ 22 Sebastian's ghost: 5, 5 Voices and visions.

166/ 23 dreary and dull: See comment on 87/ 4–5.

167/ 30–31 your half-brother, . . . How did he die? Suicide?: A remarkable question, as Mme. Lecerf must have learnt of Sebastian's "death" from obituaries in the papers (154).

168/ 29 captured my prey: 3, 19 Staghunt.

64 Silent Love

169/ 2 a changeling, a trembling oaf: An oaf is an "[e]lf's child, a changeling" (*Concise Oxford Dictionary*). 4, 20 Robinsonnade.

169/ 3 Would I return to-night?: There is a great discrepancy in the manner both half-brothers respond to the charms of the femme fatale. V. is so enraptured by Nina that he incessantly comments on her physical attractiveness: "her thin girlish back," "her lips," "her diaphanous complexion," "her small hard bosom," and "her pale girlish neck." How different is Sebastian's reaction, which seems to have been mainly oratorical, and who, instead of telling her courtesies, overwhelms her invariably with prolix speeches on tedious thoughts and tremendous trifles.

169/ 4 Maupassant story: 3, 20 "That Pig of a Morin."

169/ 22 scrawled lines on the ground with the stick: Cf. "writes on the soft earth" (137).

169/ 30 violet: 4, 6 Colors.

170/ 3 dull whiteness of her throat: "This motif always signifies a fatal temptation, a mortal danger," write Savely Senderovich and Yelena Shvarts ("The Ghost in the Novel" 506).

171/ 6 fumbled with his watch: Cf. "fumbled at my wrist" (106).

171/ 25 curds and whey: A line from "Little Miss Muffet," a very old English nursery rhyme (Opie 323). 4, 20 Robinsonnade.

171/ 27 write upside down: A dexterity as rare as Leonardo's "mirror-writing" (Nicholl 57).

CHAPTER 18

172/ 1–5 That question . . . writers of his time: A most puzzling issue because it is hard to see how the answer (whatever it may be) might contribute to the biography of Sebastian Knight. Moreover V. already knows that Nina knows about Sebastian's career as she has learned this from the obituaries. Is V. so affected by Nina that he fervently wishes to rehabilitate his half-brother who made such a disastrous impression on her?

172/ 12–13 **bat . . . swallow:** See the section on "Swallows/Swifts and Bats" in Akiko Nakata's article "A Failed Reader Redeemed."

172/ 15 **The Doubtful Asphodel:** 3, 17 Pinks and Daffodils. For a short literary history of the asphodel, see Robert Graves, "The Common Asphodel" (*The Crowning Privilege* 344–347).

172/ 21 **Cannes:** It was in Cannes that the affair between Nabokov and Irina Guadanini was ended. Cannes is a homophone of *canne* (French for "stick") that is instrumental in terminating V.'s incipient romance with Nina and Sebastian's romance with Natasha.

172/ 21 **Juan:** Juan-les-Pins.

173/ 13 **The man is the book:** See comment on line 202/ 20. For the metaphor of "the book of life" see Jürgen Bodenstein, "The Book of Life" (441–450). 5, 1 Donne.

173/ 18 **eyed wings:** Many butterflies have wings with eye spots.

173/ 19–31 **We follow . . . in the morning:** 3, 19 Guests.

173/ 28–29 **Nussbaum, a Swiss:** 4, 29 Uncle Ruka.

174/ 11 **Tarsienlu:** Cf. "Tatlien-su" (*The Gift* 122).

174/ 14–19 **not having laughed at the poor little joke of a shy ugly woman . . . not having handed the penny . . . street violinist:** See comment on lines 106/ 28–107/ 14.

174/ 20 **juggling with themes:** 3, 6 Conjuror.

175/ 6 **Dean Park:** 5, 1 Donne.

176/ 1–2 a wave of light . . . as if somebody had flung open the door: Cf. "that death is but a groom,/ Which brings a taper to the outward room" (*Of the Progress of the Soul. The Second Anniversary*, Donne 289). 5, 1 Donne.

176/ 13–14 The hardest knot . . . the finger nails: Cf. "Because such fingers need to knit/ That subtle knot," ("The Ecstacy," Donne 55).

177/ 28–29 the world yielded its sense to the soul: 5, 1 Donne.

178/ 13–14 The asphodel on the other shore: 5, 3 *The Doubtful Asphodel*.

178/ 16–17 "absolute solution": In many novels and stories by Nabokov one may come across the promise or the prospect of a unique solution which might enable the reader to master the secretiveness of his magical prose. Indeed, Nabokov's references offer many clarifying insights, but, alas, there are so many (new) ambiguieties that in the end the reader is left without definitive answers. Nabokov's prose is as complex as he sees life, that is, to use a phrase from Brian Boyd, "splendidly overstocked" (*VNRY* 458). See also chapter 6.

179/ 27–28 without telling his partners his rules: According to Vladislav Khodasevich Nabokov "does not hide his devices . . . but . . . places them in full view like a magician who, having amazed his audience, reveals on the very spot the laboratory of his miracles" (97). This sounds as the opposite of what the Englishman says of Knight's art. However, the contrast is very vaporous because Nabokov's showing the mechanics of his verbal magic does little to lessen the marvel and amazement of his readers.

180/ 2–3 It did not prove as successful as my firm had expected: See comment on lines 112/ 12–14.

180/ 8–9 as if *they* knew certain sad dreary things about the author: A doubly puzzling remark. Is "they" italicized to stress the inferiority or to emphasize the superiority of the knowledge they claim to possess? And if V. finds the allegations too unreliable to give them further notice, why does he mention them at all?

CHAPTER 19

181/ 2–3 **He died in the beginning of 1936:** 3, 2 Calendar.

181/ 22–23 **a scarf . . . dining room:** Cf. "Proust was the only man he [the Earl of Derby] knew who wore a fur coat during meals" (Davenport-Hines 112). 4, 18 Proust.

182/ 9–10 **to swindle him at a game of poker:** 4, 29 Uncle Ruka.

182/ 16–17 **milk . . . stalls with taxi drivers:** Cf. "the cabman's shelter . . . where they might hit upon . . . milk" (Joyce 533). 4, 28 *Ulysses*.

182/ 13 **three times to see the same film:** In Rudyard Kipling's story "Mrs. Bathurst" the admirer of the heroine sees "for five consecutive nights" the same film to catch "perhaps forty-five seconds o' Mrs. B. walking" (Kipling 87). 4, 16 "Mrs. Bathurst."

182/ 19 ***The Enchanted Garden***: 4, 10 Enchanted garden.

183/ 4 **Prattle:** Cf. *Tatler*, a glossy magazine for the upperclass, founded in 1901 and named after the journal Richard Steele started in 1709. Both are noted for their attention to gossip.

183/ 16–17 **In the middle of January, 1936:** 3, 2 Calendar.

183/ 18–184/ 21 **written in Russian."I am, as you see, . . . which I see from my window:** Like Tatiana's letter to Eugene Onegin, Sebastian's letter needs translation as it is written in a different language; Tatiana's in French, Sebastian's in Russian. In his *Commentary* Nabokov even gives a "literal French translation" to approach Tatiana's original version as close as possible (*Eugene Onegin* 2: 387–389). V., who presents Sebastian's letter in English, gives only six words from the original Russian version. As long as written literature exists, letters have been used for plot twists; their contents, senders, and recipients can be misinterpretated, they can be detained, falsified and purloined, and anonymous letters can reveal startling secrets. The epistolary strategy employed here seems a novelty: its first part was initially written for someone else to read.

By readressing a letter one can convey a message without doing so directly. This seems to apply to Sebastian's letter. The part of the letter that addresses "quite a different person" consists of three sentences. In the first sentence Sebastian reports that he is in Paris, not a very indispensable notice as the letter is sent after Sebastian has moved to St. Damier. The third sentence is a rather vague one, and, being of a contemplative nature, lacks urgency. Therefore it must be the second sentence Sebastian desires to keep: the intimation that he wishes to be visited. Sebastian had "invited [V.] once or twice" before (193), but to no avail, which makes it understandable that Sebastian used this circumvention for yet another invitation. (But even now V. is not prompted into action, despite Sebastian's serious illness, as he decides to inform his half-brother only two days later that he will come.)

To whom had these three sentences been written? V. wishes his readers to believe that it is Nina, because just before recording this letter, he suggests that Sebastian might have "had any definite plan about trying to meet Nina again." For various reasons Nina can however be eliminated as Sebastian's intended recipient of these lines:

- Sebastian's letters to Nina were "usual[ly] entreating" (159) while the first sentences have a rather casual tone, not to say chatty.
- If Nina would have been invited to see Sebastian, he would certainly have proposed to visit her, and not have asked her to come to his place. That Nina does not wish "to see him ever again" and longs "to be rid of him for ever" (159, 181) makes her calling on him inconceivable.
- The second sentence refers to the (in)convenience of coming, which presupposes the willingness to make a visit. This obviously cannot apply to Nina.
- The third sentence is illustrative of Sebastian's preference for "some long and obscure speech" (158) so intensely detested by Nina that it would be the best way thinkable to rekindle her deep aversion to him and to frighten her away.

Who, then, is this Russian person Sebastian wishes to see? Given V.'s preoccupation with women ("I thought I should see lots of girls"

[38]) he would certainly have been pleased if this person is a woman. And he would certainly have tried to find her (he made an "enervating" and "long journey" to meet Helene Grinstein whom he also could have consulted by letter [132]). And even when he would not be able to find her, V. could have heralded her proudly as a much more worthy successor to Clare than Nina, because the first two sentences seem to be directed to a well-disposed friend, who is supposed to be willing to see Sebastian if not detained from doing so. V. then could even have effaced Nina's existence, thus abating his embarrassment in his half-brother surrendering to "a whimsical wanton that ruins a foolish man's life" (147).

But V. never alludes to this mysterious intended recipient of Sebastian's letter. The most likely explanation for V.'s reticence is that he has discovered that it was a man. Perhaps it was the letter's salutation that revealed this. It could not have contained a first name: that must have been crossed out and then V. would have known from the beginning that the letter was intended for someone else. A salutation like "Dear friend" would have manifested the addressee's gender. If for example the greeting "Dear friend" had originally been written in French, V. must have seen "Cher ami," (and not "Chère amie"). And the use of Russian has the same impact, as the Russian word for "friend" varies with the gender of the person concerned.

Another possibility that might have occasioned V.'s learning the gender of this mysterious person has been pointed out by Siggy Frank. She explains how the second sentence, because of the past tense form used in it, "require[s] the speaker to specify the . . . gender of the addressee" (168). "The switch from a female to a male addressee," she writes, "which is unproblematic in English, would not be possible in Russian" (169). She, however, also notes that in the Russian translation of *Sebastian Knight* by I. Gorianin and M. Meilakh "the switch in gender is avoided by opting for an impersonal construction," and that "a similar strategy" is used in the translation by Sergei Il'in (169). This inevitably raises the question why Nabokov, if he had wished to avoid the past tense form in a back-translation, did not avoid it in the English version.

It is remarkable that during the night after V. has received Sebastian's letter he has a dream, in which Sebastian most urgently wishes to say "something very important" to him. But V., "eager to escape," does not listen to Sebastian, and when he awakes out of his dream "the garbled translation of a striking disclosure" sings in his head (188). Is this a veiled admission that in V.'s English translation of Sebastian's letter "something very important" has been evaded?

183/ 24 **snake-skins:** 4, 24 Snake.

184/ 6–8 **they have heard voices in . . .** *Dot chetu?*: The letter is written in Russian and includes the passage "they have heard voices in Domremy." Domremy is the birthplace of Jeanne d'Arc where in 1425, at the age of twelve or thirteen, she heard voices. Sebastian used Roman letters for Domremy, but V. took them for Cyrillic and, not understanding the word, transliterated them. "Domremy" in handwritten Cyrillic yields "Dotchetu" in Roman. (See Boyd "Notes" 679). 4, 12 Joan of Arc. 5, 5 Voices and Visions.

185/ 13–188/ 7 **And that night I dreamt . . . half out of my dream already:** 4, 31 V.'s dream.

186/ 1-3 **picture of a steamer . . . caterpillars:** Perhaps Nabokov had a particular picture in mind. Famous seascape painters like Ivan Aivazovsky, Caspar Friedrich, and J. M. W. Turner have painted many (wild) seas, but (always) with sailing boats. Turner's famous *The Fighting Temeraire* however, has a prominent steamer (prominent because the steamer is painted in much darker colors than the Temeraire she is tugging. For a reproduction, see Reynolds 176–177. This Turner belongs to the National Gallery, where Nabokov might have seen it. Asked which artists meant most to him, Nabokov mentions one single name, that of Turner [see *Strong Opinions* 167]). With its waxing moon, and the sprayed ripples in the water stirred by the tug's bow that resemble hoary caterpillars, this painting could be a companion piece of the image pictured by Sebastian in *The Back of the Moon,* with "the whole sea, . . . its moon" and "its serpent." Like a snake a caterpillar sheds its skin several times until it is full grown (and passes to the chrysalis stage before turning into a butterfly or moth). Because of this skin-shedding V.'s dreamlike caterpillars fit well in linking the "serpent" of *The Back of the Moon* with the "shed snake-skins" of Sebastian's last letter. 4, 22 Sexuality. 4, 24 Snake. 4, 31 V.'s dream.

186/ 2–3 like a procession of caterpillars: This suggests a pattern made by processionary caterpillars, belonging to the family Thaumetopoeidae (see also Zimmer, *A Guide to Nabokov's Butterflies and Moths* 269).

186/ 26 left hand: Cf. "left arm" (87).

188/ 13–14 the garbled translation of a striking disclosure: See comment on lines 183/ 18–184/ 21.

188/ 31 Sevastian: 3, 23 Transmigration by Languages.

CHAPTER 20

190/ 1–203/ 20 The . . . knows.: This chapter covers the day after Sebastian's death, although V. learns of his death only at the end of the day. Most of the chapter's pages deal with the travels V. undertakes to reach his half-brother. He leaves Marseilles on the 0:02 train bound for Paris, where he arrives at a quarter to four. It is January, which means that sunrise is about nine and sunset about five o'clock. It is after five that V. resumes his journey from Paris to St. Damier, where he arrives at half past nine. This means that V. traveled for thirteen hours in the dark, a real night journey, of which the "last phase" was the "darkest" (197). This trip is reminscent of the night journey Nabokov made with his mother on March 28, 1922, from their home to the Philharmonia Hall in Berlin, where his father had just been shot dead. In his diary Nabokov recorded this journey in great detail and this passage has been preserved, because his mother transcribed it, and it is in this way that it survives. It is reproduced in the first volume of Brian Boyd's biography (*VNRY* 191–193). Nabokov experienced the journey by car as "monstrously slow" and "the route" as "long, long" (the distance between their house in the Sächsische Strasse and the Philharmonia is about three miles). In his recollection many lights are mentioned, "lights swimming past," "streetlights," "lights" that were "shining," and "amber lights." During his journey V., who frequently complains about the slowness of the the train ("Faster, please faster!") and the cab ("the taxi was positively crawling"), notices a "yellowish light" a "bundle of light," a "brightly lit" corridor, and "lighted windows."

Finally V. reaches St. Damier and is allowed to sit in a hospital room next to the one in which he thinks his half-brother is lying. The door is "standing slightly ajar . . . the best link imaginable." Nabokov's last communication with his father had a comparable setting. The night before the fatal day Nabokov had talked with his father about a variety of subjects, such as the "strange, abnormal inclinations" of Sergey and the opera *Boris Godunov*. Then they went to their bedrooms, and Nabokov asked his father for the newspaper, "he passed them through the slit of the parted doors."

Having reached their destination, St. Damier and the Philharmonia respectively, V.'s "teeth chattered," while Nabokov observed, upon seeing his father's friends who had witnessed the assault, that "[t]heir teeth [were] chatter[ing]."

But the similarities cease to exist altogether when the travelers meet their relatives. During his trip V. feels miserable, physically and mentally; his "spine aches[s]," his bones are "leaden," he is "much too sick in mind to go down to the train," and suddenly he is even reduced to "scrambl[ing]," unable to walk. But as soon he is setting next to the dying man, he becomes entirely cheerful: "[i]f I could have smoked, my happiness would have been perfect." Learning that Sebastian had died the day before his arrival does not affect his high spirits. He imagines himself on a "lighted stage," surrounded by Sebastian's friends "paying their graceful tribute."

As this last chapter deals exclusively with V. himself, his excursion and his thoughts, he in effect abandons the biography of his half-brother. The fact that V. during the last part of his trip in the taxi is "travelling on the very road that he passed on the train," as Caulton has convincingly argued (227), emphasizes that it is the journey and not the destination that matters. The quest for Sebastian has become a search for V.'s self, and somehow this spiritual journey brings him closer to his half-brother. This unexpected dialectic evolvement is comparable to the developments in *The Gift*. Fyodor also abandons the writing of a biography (of his father), because he realizes that he cannot penetrate the recluse recesses of his father's mind, although, at the same time, his awareness of his father's presence grows steadily (see Boyd's discussion of *The Gift* in his *VNRY* 447–478, esp. 459 and 472, note).

190/ 4–5 **violet-blue:** 4, 6 Colors.

190/ 24 **ghost-like snowflake:** See comment on line 48/ 2–4.

192/ 22 **E pericoloso**: *E pericoloso sporgersi* (It is dangerous to lean out [of the window]).

191/ 3–4 **stared at me like a Cyclopean eye:** Cf. "pierced the little red eye: *L'oeil regardait Caïn*" (*The Gift* 158). The French is a quotation from Victor Hugo's poem "*La conscience*," in which Caïn's guilt manifests itself as a haunting single eye (Conder 178–180).

192/ 8 **some ballet dancer:** 3, 5 Commedia dell'arte.

193/ 2 **it began with an "M.":** 4, 29 Uncle Ruka.

194/ 12–14 **A road . . . a bicycle wobbled among snow:** By meandering on a road, both wheels of a bicycle makes different waves in the snow, which by intersection form a pattern of a series of lemniscates, or elongated eights, the figure that recurs so frequently in Nabokov's novels. Bicycles weaving eights are also at work in *The Gift* and *Pale Fire*, see Yuri Leving (209).

194/ 19 **strapontin:** small collapsible seat fixed with hinges to the carriage wall.

194/ 30 **jongleur**: juggler. 3, 6 Conjuror.

195/ 6 **donne, donne, donne:** 5, 1 Donne.

195/ 13–14 **When I got to my office:** 3, 2 Calendar.

195/ 29–30 **"Death to the Jews" or "Vive la front populaire"**: The *Front Populaire* is the name of the alliance of left parties formed by Léon Blum for the French elections in the spring of 1936. In June 1936 Blum became the first socialist president of France. His Jewish descent lead to often vehement anti-Semitism (see Pitzer 140 and 149).

196/ 1 *Schachbrett*: A chessboard. This is the second German word in the novel, the first is "Schwartz." 3, 8 Germany.

196/ 1 *damier*: A draughtboard or checkerboard. (The French for chessboard is *echiquier*.) The interesting point is that a draughtboard has one hundred squares, a chessboard only sixty-four, the difference being thirty-six, the figure which serves as a numerical counterpoint for Sebastian's life and death.

198/ 24 Foreign names ought to be replaced by numbers: This reflection seems a bit too highbrow for this badly shod old man who is disrupted in his sleep. It can be related to a statement by Ludwig Wittgenstein that "the concept of a number is analogous to the concept of a proposition" (qtd. in *Philosophische Grammatik* by Fogelin [134]). A proposition in Wittgenstein's context is a verbal expression like a self-contained sentence (Kenny 19). *Philosophische Gramatik*, although written between 1930 and 1933, was published only in 1969, but, because Wittgenstein after the publication of his main opus *Tractatus Logico-Philosophicus* in 1922 by Kegan Paul became world famous, his ideas might have become widespread. The various references in *Transparent Things* to Wittgenstein, as has been discussed by Akiko Nakata, are connected with the riddle of being and survival after death, the same questions V. is trying to grapple with in the pages following the hospital porter's remark.

199/ 8–9 nightporter: In September 1941 Wittgenstein started his work as a porter in Guy's Hospital in London (Monk 431–432). Nabokov, who was proofreading *Sebastian Knight* in October of that year, might have heard about this, although it seems unlikely. Asked about Wittgenstein's work in an interview in 1967, Nabokov answered: "I am completely ignorant of his work, and the first time I heard his name must have been in the fifties" (*SO* 70).

199/ 9–10 pointed at me. "Number thirty-six," he said: By pointing at him, V. now shares Sebastian's numerical code, 36.

200/ 15 blue-shaded: 4, 6 Colors.

202/ 20 **Kegan:** An anagram of the Russian word for book (Barabtarlo "The Man Is the Book" 101). 5, 1 Donne.

202/ 26–27 **Whatever his secret was, I have learned one secret too:** 3, 13 *La morte d´Arthur*.

202/ 28 **any soul may be yours:** 5, 1 Donne.

203/ 1 **I am Sebastian:** Shared experiences or shared consciousness have sometimes found expression in a comparable way. Gustave Flaubert (who as an author is as invisible as V. is obtrusive) said that he himself was "the origin of Emma": "Madame Bovary, *c'est moi!*" (Russell 8). In Leo Tolstoy's *Master and Man* the sentiment of sharing one another's fate causes the merchant Vasily Andreyevich Brekhunov (while protecting his coachman Nikita from freezing to death) to believe that "he is Nikita, and Nikita is he" (80). In Nabokov's oeuvre characters often have shared experiences; "each brother suffers or enjoys the other's fate," notices Susan Elizabeth Sweeney with respect to Nabokov's *Doppelgänger* fictions (208), or even "exchange places" (Olcott 113). And Leona Toker, discussing Nabokov's metaphysics, suggests another origin for shared experiences: the intersubjectivity of "interpenetrating states of consciousness" ("Worldview" 241).

203/ 2 **on a lighted stage:** 3, 5 Commedia dell'arte.

203/ 9–13 **They move around Sebastian . . . painted palm:** V. envisages a *tableau de la troupe* of all the main characters with the exception of "the old conjuror" and "Nina" who are not participating in the turmoil on the stage. The old conjuror "waits in the wings"; clearly his part has not ended. And Nina is sitting on a table as if no chair is available for her. (The palm might be of Hawaiian origin, see 66/ 29–30.)

203/ 12 **fuchsined:** A brilliant bluish red. 4, 6 Colors.

Motifs: Narrative

CHAPTER 3

CONTENTS

1. Boat trip 77
2. Calender 78
3. Canes 83
4. Cars 84
5. Commedia dell'arte and Alexander Blok 84
6. Conjurers 87
7. Elenctic 88
8. Germany 88
9. Guests at the Beaumont Hotel 89
10. *Hamlet* 92
11. *King Lear* 93
12. *The Lady with the Dog* 94
13. *La morte d'Arthur* 94
14. Mysterious Men 95
15. Nina Zarechny 97
16. *Othello* 98
17. Pinks and Daffodils 98
18. *The Quest for Corvo* 99
19. Stag Hunt 100
20. "That Pig of a Morin" 101
21. *The Colonel* 102
22. Trains 104
23. Transmigration by Language 104

24. Unfinished Pictures 105
25. Valentino 106
26. Varvara 107
27. Wilder 107
28. Zelle 108

1. BOAT TRIP

V. introduces the story he has heard from Natasha Rosanov in a rather theatrical way. He claims to have collected "one of the most precious pages of Sebastian's life." And he notices a "strange harmony" as he hears about Sebastian's "first adolescent romance" at a time when "the echoes of his last dark love" are still audible. V. alludes to the coincidence that Sebastian has twice been spurned (also coincidental is that Natasha Rosanov and Nina Rechnoy share the same initials). After V.'s introductory remarks the real spectacle begins: "[t]he lights go out, the curtain rises." This opening suggests that there may have been rehearsals. Indeed one of the novels on Sebastian's bookshelves, *Madame Bovary*, and the novel V. saw while waiting for Madame Lecerf, *The Story of San Michele*, have a similar scene with two lovers in a rowboat. In *Madame Bovary* Emma and Léon hire a boat as they wish to dine on an island on the Seine "like two Robinsons." When they return at night she is painfully reminded of Rodolphe, her former lover, who left her (Flaubert 272–274).

Emma used to meet her lovers at the same spot near the river, where, one evening, the poplars screened the moon "like a black curtain" and where "sometimes at the top of the reeds or on the leaf of a water-lily an insect with fine legs crawled or rested" (209, 101).

In Axel Munthe's novel the narrator is invited to visit a countess in the country. The visit is comparable to V.'s visit to Lescaut: the much older husband is ignored and the young male visitors are reviewed in their capacity as possible lovers. The countess' guest is allowed to row "her slowly across the shining lake" (Munthe 74). In *The Real Life of Sebastian Knight* three more scenes are enacted after the boat trip: Sebastian's riparian reading of his poems to Natasha who sits beside him on a bench, a walk under a sky full of stars and an autumnal last meeting. In *The Story of San Michele*, a comparable sequence is presented; rowing, sitting on a bench while reciting poetry, and a nocturnal walk abruptly ending when, as in the case of Sebastian and Natasha, an owl is heard hooting.

The point is that, despite its romantic glamour, the lovers in the rowboat are not really in love. Léon (and Rodolphe as well) enjoys intimacy with the frantic Emma no longer than the liaison excites him as a novelty. And the narrator in Munthe knows that he will make a fool of himself if he tries to make advances to the countess. The same lack of uninhibited love can be observed in the romance between Sebastian and Natasha as the reference to Judas betrays. Anyway, their courtship is never cheerful; what is quoted from their conversation sounds rather sad: a mild reproof; two questions, "Must you go?" and "Is this the end?" and finally a written word which finishes all.

2. CALENDAR

1890–1895 .
Sebastian's father courts Virginia Knight.

1899
On December 31, Sebastian is born to the married couple.

1902–1903
Clare Bishop born.

1904
Virginia leaves her husband and her son.

1905
V. born after Sebastian's father has married V.'s mother.

1907–1908
Nina Tooveretz born.

1908
Virginia visits her son Sebastian in St Petersburg.

1909
Virginia dies of heart-failure in Roquebrune.

1913
In January Sebastian's father fights a duel with Pahlchin. He dies a month later.

1916
Sebastian has an adolescent romance with Natasha Rosanov.

1917
Sebastian accompanies Alexis Pan on his travels.

1918–1919
V.'s mother, Sebastian and V. flee from Bolshevik Russia. They live for some time in Helsingfors. Sebastian leaves for Cambridge, V. and his mother settle in Paris.

1920
Sebastian visits his stepmother and half-brother in Paris.

1921–1922
Sebastian goes to Germany for a short vacation.

1922
V.'s mother has her last, fatal operation. Sebastian comes to Paris to attend her funeral.

He makes a trip to the Continent and visits Monte Carlo and nearby Roquebrune. He settles in London at 36 Oak Park Gardens.

1924
Sebastian meets Clare. In the autumn Clare stays in Paris where she is visited by Sebastian several times. In November or December V. meets Sebastian and Clare during one of Sebastian's visits to Paris. Sebastian composes *The Prismatic Bezel*.

1925
Sebastian starts composing *Success* in July. *The Prismatic Bezel* is published in March.

1926

Sebastian goes to Germany and comes "across a man he had known ages ago in Russia." In April *Success* is published.

1927

Pahl Pahlich Rechnoy meets Nina Tooveretz, at that time "another's fellow's mistress," and eventually marries her.

1927–1929

Sebastian shows "dreadfull fits of temper" he never had before. Clare is "left behind," and feels that something is "awry."

1927–1930

Sebastian writes three stories: *The Funny Mountain, Albinos in Black* and *The Back of the Moon.*

1929

Sebastian is advised by Dr. Oates to go to an Alsace kurort to receive a "certain treatment." In June Sebastian leaves for Blauberg and Clare is not allowed to join him. Before returning to England Sebastian spends a week in Paris where he invites V. for dinner. Back in London he stops talking to Clare, who thinks that he has "gone mad." Sebastian starts receiving letters in Russian from a woman he had met in Blauberg. In September he leaves England. Clare changes her lodgings. Sebastian begins writing *Lost Property*. Pahl Pahlich Rechnoy divorces Nina Tooveretz.

1930

Sebastian returns to England, where he engages Goodman as his secretary. Continues to work on *Lost Property*.

1932

Sebastian's three stories are republished in one volume, *The Funny Mountain*.

1933–1934

Clare marries Mr. Bishop.

1933–1935

Sebastian writes *The Doubtful Asphodel.*

1934

Sebastian dismisses Goodman and writes to Carswell from Cannes.

1935

Colonel Samain sojourns in the Beaumont Hotel. *The Doubtful Asphodel* is published. Mr. H. is "standing happily near a brand-new car." Nina marries Monsieur Lecerf. Sebastian meets Helen Pratt in London, visits a house in the country and has a lunch with Sheldon.

1936

V.'s visit to Madame Lecerf's country house marks the climax of his quest and ends the research for his biography. This visit happens "two months" after Sebastian's death "in the very beginning of 1936" (162, 181). In March, however, V. was still in London visiting Mr. Goodman. The talks with Miss Pratt, Mr. Bishop (and the meeting with Clare), P. G. Sheldon and Roy Carswell follow V.'s visit to Mr. Goodman. It seems unlikely that V. then travels to Blauberg and to Berlin to see Helene Grinstein and the Rosanovs, completes his round of visits in Paris, and then travels to Lescaux in the middle of March, especially not since the company that employs V. becomes increasingly critical about his absences (160, 166). This is not the only flaw in V.'s calendar. Even more serious is the mist that envelops the date of Sebastian's death. That he "died in the very beginning of 1936" has to be compared with the letter that V. receives in "the middle of January 1936," since Sebastian dies a day after its arrival (181, 183).

If one follows the events in the final chapters it appears that V. receives Sebastian's letter on a Thursday and finds Doctor Starov's telegram on "Friday" (188).

He leaves Marseilles with the 0.02 train for Paris where he arrives at a quarter to four, on the same day, Saturday. He then goes to his office where his presence is met with surprise and where he talks with his chief. This is most puzzling as offices in Paris in 1936 were normally closed on Saturday afternoon. In St. Damier he learns that Sebastian died the day before his arrival, which would be Friday.

Instead of Friday, January 17 (which matches with "the middle of January"), Thursday, January 9, 1936 (9-1-1936) as the day of Sebastian's death would fit with the "occult resemblance between a man and the date of his death ... 1936" and with Doctor Starov's telephone number "Jasmin 61–93." V.'s visit to his Paris office should than be dated January 10, a feasible Friday.

According to the Gregorian calender Pushkin died on February 10, 1837 (10-2-1837), which means that Sebastian died one day, one month, and one year earlier than the date of Pushkin's death a century earlier. (See also section 4. 24.)

The main events in 1936 are as follows:

January

In the first half of this month V. receives a letter from Sebastian. The next day Sebastian dies, and the following day V. arrives in St. Damier.

February

V. visits Sebastian's Cambridge friend.

March

On the first of this month V. visits Mr. Goodman in London. A few days later he talks with Miss Pratt. Probably quite soon after this meeting, V. visits Mr. Bishop, and two days after this he has his brief encounter with Clare. "[S]oon after [this] strange half-meeting" he talks with P.G. Sheldon (99). During V.'s "month's stay in England" he probably also speaks with Roy Carswell (119). After returning to the continent V. travels to Blauberg to question the manager of the Beaumont Hotel, and on the same day he happens to meet Mr. Silbermann, whom he sees again the following Friday.

March–April

V. visits Mrs. Helene Grinstein in Berlin and meets that same day Natasha Rosanov and her brother. Back in Paris V. has his conversation with Pahl Pahlich Rechnoy, and on the same day his first talk with Madame Lecerf as well as his call on Lydia Bohemsky. The next day the discussion with Madame Lecerf is resumed, and the following Sunday they have their final rendezvous in Lescaux.

April

V. visits Sebastian's governess in Lausanne.

May

Sheldon informs V. that Clare has died, and V. somehow manages to recommence his communication with Mr. Bishop in a friendly manner by exchanging letters.

3. CANES

Canes and sticks have many roles to play in Nabokov's novels. In *The Eye* Kashmarin's bright-knobbed black cane proves almost fatal for Smurov, the main protagonist. In *Pnin* the thumping of Hagen's cane announces Pnin's dismissal from his university. In *Despair* it is Felix's stick that destroys Hermann's dream. But in *The Defence* and *Pale Fire* canes are supportive of their owners. And in the story "Lips to Lips" a cane performs as a catalyst "to link the protagonist with the world after death" and the reunion with his deceased wife (Akikusa 115). In *The Real Life of Sebastian Knight* sticks are used twice to write in the earth, to deliver telling messages. The first is the "names" and "dates" visible in the "red clay" of a steep river bank, a rather ominous message, as the next words written in the earth are Natasha's, with which she breaks off her juvenile romance with Sebastian (136). The writing on the wall V. sees when he travels by train to the dying Sebastian are also ominous: "*Il est dangereux*" and "Death to the Jews" (192, 195). Also written in sand are the lines V. scrawls, which eventually lead to the revelation of Madame Lecerf's Russian origin. V. writes these lines with a cane left by someone on a bench in the park of Madame Lecerf's country house. And in Madame Lecerf's account of the love affair her friend is supposed to have had with a young man, this man is seen "with his hands on the knob of a cane" (158).

Was Sebastian the owner of the lost cane, or of the knobbed cane? Some of Sebastian's garments are detailed; his brown coat, his white scarf, his hats and even his bedroom slippers but a cane is not mentioned at all, while the carrying of umbrellas is discussed rather excessively. For this reason the canes mentioned might well belong to someone else.

4. CARS

In *The Real Life of Sebastian Knight* about twenty-five cabs, cars, and taxis are mentioned. Most of them are used by Sebastian or appear in his novels, and only a few are connected with V. There is a distinct difference in their attitudes toward taxi drivers. Sebastian acknowledges their presence, and likes to occasionally spend time with them. In his last letter Sebastian writes that he was forced to take a rest "on the running-board of somebody's parked car." The indication that the car is owned by someone is as superfluous as it is surprising. How different is V.'s demeanor. He hails "a passing taxicab. Would he take me [V.] to St. Damier?" (196). Of course one cannot talk to a taxicab but in V.'s view its driver is just a mere annex to it. When Sebastian sees a car, he imagines its owner; when V. talks to a driver, he sees the car.

The numerous cars in the novel suggest that they function somehow as fate's medium to bring into contact the lines of two separate lives. This is the subject of Sebastian's *Success*: the reconstruction of the ways fate fails and finally succeeds in such an achievement. In *The Gift* a comparable analysis is presented when Fyodor recounts the attempts fate made to bring Fyodor and Zina together (363–364). To this end fate uses people as a medium. In its first attempt fate employs Lorentz's wife and Romanov, in the second Charski and in the last successful attempt Alexandra Yakovlevna Chernyshevski. In *The Real Life of Sebastian Knight* its role is performed by cars. The "stranger's car" from *Success* recalls the "man's car" with whom Sebastian spends a couple of days on the German coast (94, 86). This subject is further discussed in chapter 6.

5. COMMEDIA DELL'ARTE AND ALEXANDER BLOK

Commedia dell'arte is the name for theatrical productions that originated in Italy in the eighteenth century. The performances were based on stock characters and stock plots that served as a mainstay for improvisations. To enliven the action it was interspersed by sequences of acrobatics, juggling, and ballet. The main characters are Pantalone, Pierrot, Harlequin, Columbine, and Pulchinella, sometimes masked. The genre branched out into new forms such as pantomime, and its most caricatural roles survive in puppet shows like Punch and Judy. A more artistic offshoot was Carlo Gozzi's play *The Love for Three Oranges* (1761).

The more simpler forms of entertainment mentioned above were well practiced in St. Petersburg in the nineteenth century (Senderovich and Shvartz, "The Juice of Three Oranges" 77). But far more artistic achievements were inspired by the commedia dell'arte during the Russian Silver Age, all well known to Nabokov (see Stephanie Merkel; Senderovich and Shvartz; and Susan Elizabeth Sweeney "Looking at Harlequins"). The many fairy-like Harlequin paintings by Konstantin Somov, with their luminous ethereal colors, illustrate the impact of the commedia dell'arte on artists of the Silver Age. The influence of Gozzi's play was so widespread that Senderovich and Shvartz write that Nabokov "found in the orange motif a major symbol for his adored Silver Age" (83). The commedia dell'arte has permeated Nabokov's work in many ways but with respect to *The Real Life of Sebastian Knight* (Mr. Goodman, for example, with his mocking cognomen and his mask, consumes lozenges which resemble the diamond pattern of the typical Harlequin costume) one particular aspect deserves attention.

In his "Introduction" to *The Annotated* Lolita, "Nabokov's Puppet Show," Alfred Appel writes that there are "at least two 'plots' in all of Nabokov's fiction: the characters in the book, and the consciousness of the creator above it—the 'real plot' which is visible in the 'gaps' and 'holes' in the narrative" (xxvi). This "real plot," the "riddles" Nabokov has composed with its "elegant solutions" have to be executed by the characters as well (*Strong Opinions*, 16). This is especially significant for *The Real Life of Sebastian Knight* with its "true 'inside' story" as Lucie Léon Noel mentions (she worked for many hours with Nabokov to prevent the novel's English from sounding "foreign") (215). As Siggy Frank puts it "[t]he tension between the seeming autonomy of the performing object which seems to have a life of its own and the tight control of the puppeteer over the performing object is exploited throughout Nabokov's work" (132). Or should one compare Nabokov's "galley slaves" not with puppets on a string, but with chess pieces which have such very different qualities but are for their movements entirely dependent on the chess player (*SO* 95)?

Alexander Blok's adoption of the traditions of the commedia dell'arte may be of particular interest for *Sebastian Knight*. Nabokov has often expressed his great esteem for the art of Alexander Blok, the greatest poet of Russia's Silver Age. (See Boyd, *VNRY* 93–94; Boyd and Shvabrin 320–321; Karlinsky, *Dear Bunny* 103.) Despite his lifelong regard for Blok's work, his admiration was not without reservations as Nabokov did not share Blok's despondency and presentiment of apocalyptic doom (see Alexandrov 216, and Bethea, who elaborates on an earlier article by Dolinin in Russian, 378–381). This dichotomous appreciation is obvious in the references to Blok in Nabokov's autobiography, *Speak, Memory*. One can read these as a poetical garland that links Nabokov's love for his parents with his first love, Tamara (49, 224, 229). At the same time these references can be considered as harbingers of doom: the murder of his father, the Russian Revolution and the loss of his first love (*Speak, Memory* 49, 229, 241). Blok's despondency, the "gloom and despair" according to D. S. Mirsky, are characteristic of Blok's later work (459).

To Blok's early poetry belong his *Verses on the Beautiful Lady* (1904), much admired by Nabokov (as well as by his father, see Boyd, *VNRY* 186). The poetry's many "chivalric codes" reveal the extent to which the poet considered himself as the "Knight of the Beautiful Lady" (Bethea 379; Mochulsky 69). In 1906 Blok composed his famous poem "The Strange Lady," who shares her small bejeweled hand and close fitting attire with Nina Rechnoy (see comment on lines 152/ 14–15 and 24). In the same year Blok's lyrical drama *Balaganchik* appeared (translated as *The Puppet Show* or, more literally, *The Fairground Booth*). Its dramatis personae are Pierrot, Harlequin, and Columbine; its theme "Rivalry, deceit and inconstancy of love" (Senderovich and Shvarts, "The Juice" 80). The ominous heroine, Columbine, is claimed by Pierrot as his bride, and although he knows that she will poison him, he "follows her along a sinister road" (Mochulsky 124). Konstantin Mochulsky, focusing on the autobiographical sides of Blok's poetry, suggests that it was because of the unfaithfulness of Blok's wife, Lyubov, that "the Beautiful Lady ... changed into a Columbine," unsatisfied by the "knight's chaste adoration" (304, 152). The knight changes as well. Savely Senderovich and Yelena Shvarts, who paraphrase Andrei Bely's 1922 memorial speech on Blok, write that the poet's obsession turned away from the Beautiful Lady to Columbine, thus changing the Lady's "Knight" into a Harlequin (87).

The parallels with *Sebastian Knight* can easily be noticed: despite the extreme difference between the sweet and gentle Clare and the baleful Nina, Sebastian cannot withstand the latter's delirious-making charms.

6. CONJURORS

Most of the entertainers mentioned in *The Real Life of Sebastian Knight*—conjurors, clowns, jugglers—are associated with Sebastian; either they appear in his novels or he is compared to them. In *Lost Property* Sebastian recalls how he enjoyed reading in the boys' paper *Chums* about inter alia a conjuror. As a writer he is compared to someone "juggling with themes" and his style to "a clown developing wings." He is censured for being "conradish" and advised to cultivate the "radish." The word "con" has the same root as "can" and "cunning," words suggesting, according to the *Merriam Webster*'s "wiliness and trickery," skills not unlike those of conjurors. The radish, a down to earth plant, may indicate the contrary.

A rabbit, the most familiar element of a conjuror's tools, is seen four times. The first time, "the field with its rabbits," is interfused between two citations from poems by Rupert Brooke and Thomas Gray. The second rabbit will—when necessary—be hired by the old conjuror from Sebastian's novel, *Success*, which means that it will be well looked after. Quite different is the rabbit's future once owned by Madame Lecerf as it will end as a dish for a Sunday luncheon. Finally, as may be expected, the old conjuror's rabbit turns up on the novel's last page, alive and well. The conjurer par excellence seems to be Uncle Black as "he can play the violin standing upon his head, and he can multiply one telephone number by another in three seconds." That he is a real magician, however, is because he can conjure up an animal ("a little squirrel") by words alone. Uncle Black is a Russian and it is interesting to note that the conjuror from *Success*, as has been discerned by Rory Bradley, is also "not a native speaker" (22).

7. ELENCTIC

"Elenctic" means "given to refutation or cross-examination." In *Alice's Adventures in Wonderland*, the Caterpillar harangues Alice with endless questions and retorts. But "elenctic" has another meaning, as it has the same Greek root as "elenchus," which suggests the Socratic mode of eliciting the truth. (Maurice Couturier translated "elenctic" into the French "socratique" for the second volume of Nabokov's novels in the *Bibliothéque de la Pléiade*.) The nagging the interrogated person experiences is one aspect of this, that the questioner tries to share his knowledge, the other. In Alice's *Adventures* she is asked "Repeat '*you are old, Father William*,'" which she does, but when she has finished the poem she is chided by the Caterpillar that it is "wrong from beginning to end." What Alice's recites begins:

> "You are old, Father William," the young man said,
> "And your hair has become very white;
> And yet you incessantly stand on your head—
> Do you think, at your age, it is right?"

The poem has seven more stanzas, but it has, apart from the first line, nothing in common with the original poem on Father William by Robert Southey, "The Old Man's Comforts, and How he Gained Them" (Southey 124). The Caterpillar seems to make sense with his stern rebukes. By analogy the hotel-manager who, after seven years remembers so well the bath Sebastian took every morning, might well be right about the sort of companion Sebastian had in the hotel.

8. GERMANY

In 1921 or 1922 Sebastian has a short vacation in Germany. In 1926 Sebastian decides to take a month's holiday at the German seaside. When Clare arrives some two weeks later Sebastian is not there because "he had come across a man he had known ages ago, in Russia, and they had gone in the man's car to . . . a place on the coast some miles away." (The second explanation Sebastian gives for his absence, the visit to "a doctor," is questionable, see comments on lines 85/ 26 and 87/ 18.) Then, in *The Doubtful Asphodel*, a "gentle old chess player" has a German surname, "Schwarz." And somehow V., writing in English, and living in France for almost two decades, notices "a chess board, ein Schachbrett," rather conspicuously as this is the only German word in *The Real Life of Sebastian Knight*. As the German 'schwarz' means 'black' in English, it seems most likely that the "chess player Schwarz" and the chess player Uncle Black, the one called "gentle" the other behaving gently, are one and the same and that this is the man Sebastian has met in Russia and Germany.

9. GUESTS AT THE BEAUMONT HOTEL

In *The Doubtful Asphodel* Sebastian mentions ten people all of whom the reader might more or less vaguely recognize from V.'s report. The question of where Sebastian has met them can be answered as well and will be discussed in this section. Sebastian's list comprises:

- the gentle old chess player Schwarz
- an orphan boy
- the fat Bohemian woman with . . . cheaply dyed hair
- [a noisily denouncing] pale wretch
- an attentive plainclothes man
- the lovely tall prima donna
- an old man [who] sobs
- a soft-lipped girl in mourning
- Professor Nussbaum, a Swiss
- his young mistress (173)

The "chess player Schwartz" is (see section 3. 8) Uncle Black; the fat Bohemian woman is Lydia Bohemsky with her "orange hair"; the clamorous pale wretch is Pahl Pahlich who "cried" and "shouted"; the attentive plainclothes man is Mr. Silbermann who was so eager to tell that he was not a mere policeman, but "[p]lain clothes"; the prima donna is the contralto Helene von Graun; and professor Nussbaum and his mistress the "Swiss couple [who] committed suicide" in Blauberg in 1919.

Mr. Silbermann is the same as Mr. Siller, the "delightful character' from *The Back of the Moon* (see comments on lines 101/ 11–102/ 10–11). Sebastian visits Blauberg in June 1929. In the "summer" of that year he finished *The Back of the Moon*, the story in the collection *The Funny Mountain* (79). One may therefore conclude that Sebastian has met Mr. Silbermann in Blauberg, probably in the Beaumont Hotel as he is on such excellent terms with the hotel-manager that he can provide V. with numerous details about its guests.

The people who figure in *The Doubtful Asphodel* and were also on Silbermann's list of guests of the Beaumont Hotel are Lydia Bohemsky and Helene von Graun. Mr. Silbermann can also be numbered as a guest, while Professor Nussbaum and his mistress, although not actually staying at The Beaumont, were also in Blauberg at "the hotel around the corner" (122).

Not mentioned by Sebastian among the ten persons he describes in *The Doubtful Asphodel* are two hotel guests: Nina Rechnoy and Helene Grinstein, who are, however, indispensible in explaining the rest of Sebastian's list.

Uncle Black is the cousin of Pahl Pahlich who was still married to Nina Rechnoy during her stay at the Beaumont Hotel in June 1929.

The remaining three, the orphan boy, the old sobbing man and the soft-lipped girl, seem to belong to the mourners in Helene Grinstein's house at the funeral of her brother-in-law: the orphan boy is probably the "silent boy in a black tie with a pale swollen face," the old sobbing man the "old man" Helene Grinstein is consoling, and the girl probably one of the two young girls, most likely close family to Helene Grinstein, who has "tender trembling lips."

One can conclude that all ten persons mentioned by Sebastian were staying in Blauberg in 1929 or are related to those staying in the hotel. For this reason the hypothesis that Sebastian might have met all these ten characters in Blauberg deserves to be investigated.

Uncle Black/Schwarz and his cousin Pahl Pahlich Rechnoy might have been in the hotel if they brought Rechnoy's then wife Nina by car (Schwarz is a taxi driver) and stayed a few days before returning. The orphan boy, the old man and the girl who are among Mme. Grinstein's funeral guests, probably accompanied her to Blauberg as can be inferred from the account of V.'s Berlin visit.

Small boys have sometimes important, albeit seemingly inconspicuous, roles. In James Joyce's *Ulysses* Bloom recalls his dead son in only a few lines; some 500 pages later the reader is informed that the boy died "aged 11 days" and then it is revealed by Molly Bloom how his death wrecked their marriage (90, 657, 700). Humbert does a cruel disservice to Charlotte in his description of her character by skipping all that she wrote in her "confession" about "Lolita's brother who died at 2 when she was 4" (*Lolita* 67–68).

The boy in Mrs. Grinstein's Berlin house wears a "black tie" and has "a pale swollen face," showing that he is deeply affected by the death of Mme. Grinstein's brother-in-law, who must for this reason have been a near-relative, probably his father. V. sees the boy frequently during his short visit. The boy shows him in, he is seen "carrying a glass of water," he brings V. to his aunt and he answers the telephone. Like the sweet and undaunted Petrushka in Andrei Platonov's *The Return*, this boy runs the household now that his aunt is engaged in more urgent matters related to the death of her relative. That he acts as her host and answers the telephone indicates that he is familiar with his aunt's home and her relations, most likely because he lives there. Why does he not live with his father? Most likely because his mother is no longer alive. He might as well have lived with his father at his aunt's as the funeral guests are received at her place.

That Helene Grinstein's sister died might have been the reason for her visit to Blauberg in 1929. Pahl Pahlich described the Beaumont Hotel as a "famous kurort," which sounds like a *Kurhaus* in an expensive spa such as Baden-Baden or Karlsbad. But Blauberg was also recommended to Sebastian because it could provide "a certain treatment" for serious heart-ailments. This might explain why "people often die in Blauberg" (129). Staying in the Beaumont Hotel might have its recreational as well as its grim sides. The clientele of the hotel seem to belong to the higher classes of society, such as "a Strassbourg banker," "Professor Ott and wife," "Colonel Samain" and mondaine ladies such as Mme. Rechnoy and the "ravishing" Helene von Graun. Having a "splendid contralto" Helene von Graun entertained the guests several times during her stay with her songs. Somehow Mrs. Grinstein did not partake in such convivialities, as she "did not know anyone at the hotel." Clearly, she had more serious affairs to attend to.

Could it be that her sister was taken care of in the hotel, and treated for critical heart disease, like Sebastian? And if Helene Grinstein visited her together with her father and (two of) her sister's children, it might explain how Sebastian got to know them. Her brother-in-law might have been absent due to the demands of his job or because he was unaware of the acuteness of the situation. His absence might have given Sebastian the impression that the boy became an orphan after his mother's death. As Mme. Grinstein's party consisted of Russians, their mixing with their compatriot Uncle Black is easy to imagine. Knowing his kindness to small children he might by all means have tried to teach the boy how to play chess as a distraction.

If this is a true reconstruction of what happened at the hotel when Sebastian stayed there, it is equally likely that Mrs. Grinstein's brother-in-law is the boy's father as this might explain his distress as well as his familiarity with the daily routine in his aunt's home. In this way it might be explained that Sebastian saw everyone on his list of ten persons in Blauberg, and most of them probably at the Beaumont Hotel

It should be noticed, however, that although Sebastian mentions so many people staying in Blauberg, Nina Rechnoy is not among the guests selected by Sebastian to feature in *The Doubtful Asphodel*.

10. HAMLET

In *The Real Life of Sebastian Knight* many passages refer to various episodes in *Hamlet*. The scene of action of Shakespeare's drama is the Danish royal castle at Elsinore, or Helsingor in Danish. This castle stood at the narrowest part of the Sound, opposite the Swedish town of Helsingborg. When they fled from Russia, Sebastian, V. and his mother lived for some time in Helsingfors, which is the Swedish name for Helsinki, but preferred, one may assume, for its likeness with the name of the locale of *Hamlet*.

The play opens with the apparition of the ghost of Hamlet's father, who relates how he is killed by his brother who poured poison in his ears, hence the "ear-specialist" (62). Hamlet's father's spirit also complaints that his sudden death took him "in the blossom of [his] sin," with "all [his] imperfections on [his] head" (1.5.76 and 1.5.79). The request of his father's ghost to avenge him, but to leave his mother "to heaven," leads Hamlet's philosophical mind to a much agitated derangement; he complains about "the slings and arrows of outrageous fortune" and the "pangs of despised love" (1.5.86, 3.1.58, and 3.1.72) and treats Ophelia unduly harshly.

A point is made of Sebastian's dislike of watches and his using those of others. In *Bend Sinister* Nabokov attributes the same preference to Hamlet, "never using a watch, relying on Horatio's timepiece" (112; see *Hamlet* 1.4.3), probably to stress his desultoriness.

Why these references? It could be said that Sebastian's father, like Hamlet's, is killed by his mother's lover, but this seems not to be the ruling burden of his life (although it is for Hamlet). More important is that, until Hamlet let the players show (Act 3) that the murder of the King is no longer a secret, there is much debate about the causes of Hamlet unaccountable behavior. Hamlet's mother tells her husband that it can be explained by "[h]is father's death, and our o'erhasty Marriage" (2.2.57).

But Polonius, Ophelia's father, thinks otherwise. He has denied Ophelia contact with Hamlet and he is convinced that this is the reason why Hamlet, "repulsed . . . fell into . . . madness" (2.2.146–150). And indeed, Hamlet admits that the arduous relationship with Ophelia "hath made [him] mad" (3.1.146).

In *The Real Life of Sebastian Knight* the crisis in Sebastian's life seems comparable: he too "has gone mad. Quite mad" (108). And as much as Polonius is convinced that he knows why, V. is certain that Sebastian's problems are caused by his hapless love affair with the Russian lady. To prove that he is right Polonius arranges a meeting between Hamlet and his mother in her room, which he will overhear hidden "behind the arras" (3.3.28). It is to this "arrased eavesdropper" that in *The Real Life of Sebastian Knight* Mr. Siller's Adam's apple is compared, the prominence of which is also observed in Mr. Silbermann. Like Polonius (called Polonius-Pantolonius in *Bend Sinister* [116]) who protracts his search to prove his deluded idea, it is Mr. Silbermann whose list of female hotel guests enables V. to prolong his quest. Is V.'s quest a deluded one as well?

11. KING LEAR

Shakespeare opens *King Lear* with a dialogue between Kent and Gloucester in which the latter tells that he has two sons, two half-brothers in fact, as Edmund is a bastard and Edgar the legitimate and elder son. Eventually it is Edmund who is responsible for Cordelia's death (5.3.254–255). Despite his adulterated birth and his minority Edmund manages to displace Edgar as their father's heir. This he arranges by means of a counterfeited letter, supposedly written by Edgar, in which it is proposed to kill their father in order to inherit his possessions. Gloucester asks Edmund whether he recognizes his brother's handwriting; Edmund lies, claiming he does (1.2.66–1.2.71). The parallel with *The Real Life of Sebastian Knight* seems obvious: in Nabokov's novel it is the content of the blue burned letter that causes V. to succeed Sebastian (in falling in love with Nina Rechnoy). The next question is whether V., in attributing the letter to a Russian lady, is as equally misleading as Gloucester.

12. LADY WITH THE DOG

In this story Anton Chekhov tells how Gurov, a married Moscovite trained as a philologist but aspiring to a career as an opera-singer, is having an affair with Anna Sergeevna in Yalta where they are sojourning.

Chekhov tells how the incident, initially as vapid as other affairs begun for divertissement, turns into a genuine and unique mutual love, something they have not experienced before. Gurov, tells Chekhov, then "had two lives: one open, which everybody who needed to could see and know about . . . the other passing in secret. And . . . everything that was important, interesting, and essential to him, . . . everything that formed the kernel of his existence, went on in secret" (Chekhov, *Selected Stories* 289). That secret lives are not easily divulged also seems applicable to V.'s biography, unless the defaming story Nina Rechnoy tells about "the man you [V.] wrongly suppose to have been your brother" is (notwithstanding this repeated disclaimer) indeed about Sebastian. And even then it is only through a glimpse of an inimical informant that the reader learns about Sebastian's secret love.

13. LA MORTE D'ARTHUR

The history of King Arthur's life and times is mainly known through the work of Sir Thomas Malory of which two versions survive, both titled *Le Morte D'Arthur*. Malory's sources were several Norman-French romances in which "Knights forever jousted, succoured damsels, and slew monsters" (Graves xi). The title Nabokov uses—*La morte d'Arthur*—has the proper, current French feminine article but retains the archaic 'e' in 'morte,' and lacks the capitalization of the English title, suggesting that he might have a French version in mind. The great merit of Malory is giving his materials a sequence and a coherence by making the love story of Sir Lancelot and Queen Guinevere its *pièce de résistance*, and making "little trouble with the quest of the Holy Grail" (Graves xix; see also Lawler xiv). This may be the precise aspect relevant to *The Real Life of Sebastian Knight* as V. forgets his main objective, or "quest" as he calls it twice, the writing of the biography of his half-brother, as soon as he hears about Sebastian's love affair with an enchantress.

As has been noted in the comment on line 94/ 1 a quest might be so demanding and lasting that in the end it is not the initial objective, but the experiences and attainments acquired during the quest, that become its final goal. V. seems to have gained such an advancement as he, at the very end of his work, writes that "[w]hatever his [Sebastian's] secret was, I have learned a secret too" (202).

14. MYSTERIOUS MEN

V. makes a disdainful remark about Mr. Goodman by saying that he is "no Boswell" (61). Neither is V. Had Boswell acted as V., half of the biography of Dr. Johnson would have been spent on Johnson's relationship with Mrs. Thrale after the death of Henry Thrale. As Johnson loved her, he started to claim the object of his love as much as Nina's lover did, while Mrs. Thrale, like Nina, grew to detest her admirer strongly. As it is, Boswell did not devote half of his work to this episode, although it was one of the most emotional events of Johnson's life, but only half a page.

Limiting his quality as a biographer is also V.'s unfavorable disposition toward men. Although he endures Sebastian's cat-loving Cambridge friend, until his somewhat pressed retreat, V. seems hostile to most of the men he meets: Mr. Goodman, Mr. Bishop; the hotel-manager in Blauberg; Natasha Rosanov's brother; his chief in his Paris office, the bulldog faced man he quarrels with, the taxi driver who takes him from Paris to St. Damier and the nightporter of the hospital. Chatting with Helen Pratt, Helene Grinstein, Natasha Rozanov, and Nina Rechnoy is what V. really likes. Consequently, it is only a tiny bit of the information from P.G. Sheldon that V. passes on, although the poet "was kindly willing to tell [V.] anything he might know" (99). And it seems that V. has made no attempt at all to obtain or procure any information about the men (apart from Sheldon and Carswell) who were acquainted with Sebastian:

- "Mr. McMath, house agent" (35).
- Mr. H., the "brand-new car" owner whose many photographs Sebastian planned to use for a novel (38).
- The "mutual friend" who had "literary plans" (66).
- The man with the car Sebastian met in Germany and whom "he had known ages ago, in Russia" (86).

- Leslie, apparently such a good friend that Sebastian did not mind finding him "lying spread-eagled on the floor of his study" (88).
- Sebastian's editor at his new publishing firm "Bronson" (89).
- "The meek little man" with whom Sebastian had an appointment one day between 1927 and 1930 (101).
- Sebastian's older companion in Blauberg whom the hotel-manager thought was "his father" (120).
- The handsome "Russian" in Lescaut whom Sebastian possibly might have met when seeing Nina (170).

Lucy Maddox writes that V.'s "attitude toward women raises the suspicion that he may be homosexual" (164). According to her reading V. "characterizes all the women he meets as types," but gives only one, far from convincing, example, to support her statement.

V. associates quite easily with all the women he meets, even the woman sitting next to him on the train to Paris. She is initially, because V.'s sickness has impaired his vocabulary, dubbed as a "bulky monster," but is soon seen with so much benevolence that he accepts her invitation to share her coffee, which she handles "with a kind of maternal love" (193–194). And it would be atypical for a homosexual to feel a prolonged "horrible tingle" in his hand because "it had touched [the] sleeve" of a soldier who "brushed past" him (192). It is a reaction that illustrates V.'s misandry, which has such a disastrous impact on his quest.

Maddox's opinion probably stems from a misreading of passages in *Look at the Harlequins!*, which leads her to see V. and Kinbote as doubles.

15. NINA ZARECHNY

Nina Zarechny (this is Nabokov's rendering of her name, "Zarechnaya" is another often used transliteration) is the heroine of Anton Chekhov's play *The Seagull*. In this play almost all the characters are in love, but all these loves remain unrequited. How to cope (or not to cope) with the unhappiness this causes is at the heart of Chekhov's play: "what really matters is . . . knowing how to endure things. How to bear one's cross and have faith" (Chekhov, *Seagull* 87).

Nina is in love with the famous author Boris Trigorin. They live together briefly until Trigorin "went back to his former attachments" (77). Nina is also loved by Konstantin Trepliov, a young man aspiring to become a writer, and his love for Nina eventually proves to be fatal.

The strong similarity between the surnames of both Ninas, Rechnoy and Zarechny, has invited a "careful scrutiny" of the respective works. Emily Emery, following the meandering and inimitable steps of Herlman Chaplinsky, thinks that *The Real Life of Sebastian Knight* is an "intricate recapitulation of *Seagull*" (Emery 25). Despite Nabokov's great affinity with Chekhov's art, his themes reach distinctly further than the accommodation of life's drawbacks.

Trepliov has written a play of which only a part is performed, a monologue, recited by Nina: a futuristic vision of the world when everything alive has disappeared. What remains is the "common soul of the world" into which the other "souls have all been merged" (35).

This is not unlike the passage at the close of *Sebastian Knight*: "[t]he hereafter may be the full ability of consciously living in any chosen soul, in any number of souls" (202).

Trepliov's metaphysical claim is presented without preamble and relies largely on enumerations and grotesque sounding concoctions as "Eternal Matter" and "the Kingdom of Cosmic Will" (36). This might explain why some of the spectators think that Trepliov has meant his play to be a joke. But Trepliov, who admires Tolstoy, might have been inspired by the ideas ventured by Pierre about a cosmic consciousness, thoughts that Prince Andrei attributes to Johann Gottfried Herder (*War and Peace* 415). Nabokov does not dismiss the contents of Nina's speech as nonsense although of course he cannot but censure its phrasing as it is "in a Maeterlinck style, mystically commonplace" and "obscurely trite" (*Lectures on Russian Literature* 284).

Trepliov's relationship with Nina closely resembles the love affair Mme. Lecerf depicts with so much fervor during V.'s second visit to her (friend's) Paris apartment. Nina Zarechny thinks that Trepliov "grows so irritable lately, and most of the time [has] been talking unintelligibly, in a sort of symbolic way" (51). When she fell in love with Trigorin, Nina "refused to see [Trepliov], and the servants wouldn't let [him] go up to her room at the hotel" (77). And although Trepliov "hated" her, it was "not in [his] power to stop loving [her]" (85). This is all very much the same (although Chekhov's "servants" have become "ruffians"

[*Sebastian Knight* 181]) as what happens to Sebastian while courting his Nina.

Trepliov, who cannot accept that Nina leaves him, commits suicide and that is the end of the play.

16. OTHELLO

Othello is married to Desdemona who is completely devoted to her husband. Othello let himself be persuaded by Iago that Desdemona is unfaithful to him and in a rage he kills her. It is not by words alone that Iago convinces Othello, he also arranges that a handkerchief, a symbol of the bond between Othello and Desdemona, is noticed by Othello's deluded eyes, as the crowning evidence of her guilt. This handkerchief, introduced in the third scene of the third act, reappears frequently until the last scene of the play.

The fulcrums of the story in *Othello* are repeated in *Sebastian Knight*. Like Desdemona, Clare is a caring consort, she too drops her handkerchief and her relationship has a catastrophic end caused by a (professed) sexual infatuation. Clare's sweet and gentle character is not affected by her ordeal; her commitment to Sebastian is as unwavering as that of Desdemona to Othello. Short of killing her, Sebastian's treatment of Clare is as heartless as Othello's of his wife. But, one may ask, when do the correspondences stop, as the real tragedy of Othello is based on the fact that the alleged sexual infatuation is non-existent?

17. PINKS AND DAFFODILS

The opinion, expressed by Roy Carswell, that Sebastian's new lover "smashed his life" (perhaps rather a guess than a judgment "as nobody seems to know anything about her") is anticipated by the reference to Keats's poem "La Belle Dame sans Merci" (118, 27). In this poem a knight is held "in thrall" by sorcerers. The color of his cheeks, compared with a rose, "fast withereth" until, one suspects, he looks as "death-pale" as her other captives.

V.'s conviction that Nina Rechnoy (trapped in his arachnoid trick) is Sebastian's fatal Circe should be weighted with her remark that "all flowers except pinks and daffodils weathered if I touched them" (164). This seems to annul V.'s unmasking.

That all flowers (now representing men rather than their cheeks) wither by her touch except "pinks and daffodils," excludes Sebastian as he is associated with these flowers. A daffodil is pale yellow narcissus, formerly called "affodill" and the root of this name is the Greek "asphodelos" (*Concise Oxford Dictionary* 284).

A daffodil thus combines a reference to the "Narcissus-like" portrait of Sebastian by Roy Carswell (with a withered leaf on his brow) as well as a reference to Sebastian's last novel *The Doubtful Asphodel*.

Pinks are carnations, the flowers V. observes in the boudoir of Madame von Graun's apartment during his second visit. "To pink" means to "pierce with sword etc.," another allusion to Sebastian via his namesake "the martyr with the arrows in his side" (123).

18. THE QUEST FOR CORVO

The Quest for Corvo: An Experiment in Biography, by A.J.A. Symons, was first published in 1934. The book is an account of the search its author made to learn more about the writer of *Hadrian the VII*, named Fr. Rolfe. Starting with some insignificant and unpromising clues Symons is able to reconstruct a rather intriguing life of Rolfe, alias Baron Corvo, based on testimonies from his correspondents and finally on letters and notes from Rolfe himself. Born in London 1860 he died in Venice in 1913 after a miserable life. Rolfe was a painter, a poet and a writer, a priest manqué and a soi-disant baron, and above all a most querulous man, belligerent especially to all his benefactors.

When *Sebastian Knight* appeared in 1941, two reviewers compared it with *The Quest for Corvo*: P.M. Jack for the *New York Times Book Review* and Walter Allen, writing for the *Spectator* (Page, *Nabokov* 67–70; Karlinsky, *Dear Bunny* 64). Paul Barolsky, in a 1998 article, even says that Nabokov's novel is "rooted in Symons's quest" (412). Baron Corvo is also mentioned in Paul Fussell's 1966 review of Nabokov's *Notes on Prosody* (76) to which Nabokov responds with saying that he does "not know who Baron Corvo is" (*SO* 213) although Wilson had sent him Jack's review in 1942 (Karlinsky, *Dear Bunny* 64).

The comparison makes sense, first because of the way the biographee's life is researched is in a way comparable, second because of the high degree of involvement of the biographer with his informants. Symons visits Rolfe's brother in his office and the account of it, mixed with reflections on his impressions and on his own emotions, resembles, short of its caricatural aspect, V.'s visit to Mr. Goodman.

There is also a great contrast, however. Symons gives the reader all the details he gathers, "impartially bringing out all aspects of the case," while V. quite soon confines his biography to a quest for the femme fatale (Symons 116).

19. STAG HUNT

Nina Rechnoy, née Toorovetz, acquired this name by marrying Monsieur Lecerf. "Le Cerf" is French for "the stag." Madame Lecerf's home is in Lescaux, which sounds similar to Lescaut, the surname of Manon, the mistress of a knight, the Chevalier des Grieux, the hero of Abbé Prévost's short novel *Manon Lescaut* (1731).

Lescaux also closely resembles the famous caves of Lascaux, with its many murals of aurochs and stags (*Encyclopaedia Britannica* 6: 792). The cave was discovered in 1940. *The Real Life of Sebastian Knight* was published on December 18, 1941 (Boyd *VNAY* 40). As Nabokov read the galleys in October 1941, he had ample opportunity to use the name of Lescaut for Mme. Lecerf's domicile (*VNAY* 39). In *Lolita*'s penultimate sentence Nabokov refers explicitly to the wonders of Lascaux.

The pursuit of a lover represented as a stag hunt is hinted at unambiguously when V., anticipating the meeting with the enchantress, congratulates himself with "having captured his prey" (168).

The eroticism that in mythology is associated with stag hunts is alluded to in *Lolita*, by calling Jean Farlow's dogs "Cavall and Melampus" (89). In his *Metamorphoses* Ovid tells how Actaeon interrupts a hunt to wander around and by chance sees Diana and her nymphs, all bathing. Diana turns the uninvited spectator into a stag, and Actaeon, now fearing his own dogs, tries to flee but is caught and devoured. Melampus is the first dog of his pack that is mentioned by Ovid (79).

In the medieval Welsh tale *The Mabinogion*, Cavall, King Arthur's dog, is the first who enables him to kill a unique, "pure white" hart, and its head is offered to the loveliest girl of the court (260–273; see Boyd *Stalking* 333).

In view of the associations between hunting and love making, one wonders to what extent V.'s eagerness to find the Russian enchantress was free of hedonistic motivations.

Motifs: Narrative

V's pursuit of the Russian lady brings him from London to Blauberg, Berlin, Paris, and finally Lescaux. Such a chase deserves to be called a quest. As has been discussed above a quest can denote the effort in acquiring perfection. In the end V. does not succumb to Nina's seductiveness (in the "green room" she sits down invitingly close to V. and in the garden even so close that their shoulders touch [165] but eventually V. recoils from her deceitfulness). Instead of ending in Nina's arms, V. finishes his biography by announcing that he has learnt a secret, the metaphysical idea of the migration of souls.

Such a transition from chasing an animal and finally winning a philosophical insight parallels the development in medieval French poetry with respect to one of its "traditional element[s]": "le cerf amoureux," or "the stag of love" (Morgan 321). According to Boyd "the deep love [Nabokov] acquired for the [French] medieval masterpieces" was probably the "greatest gain" of his "formal studies at Cambridge" [*VNRY 174*]). As Paul Morgan discusses, the poetry about stag-hunts became allegorical, and the contest between hunter and hunted game, turned into the pursuit of some "acquisition or burden of wisdom with which [the hunter] must learn to endure" (Marcelle Thiébaux, qtd. in Morgan [322]).

20. "THAT PIG OF A MORIN"

In Guy de Maupassant's story a rural draper, Morin, travels to Paris, sees a beautiful girl in the train and, inflamed by the prospect of Parisian pleasures, seizes and kisses her. She, Henriette, cries for help, Morin is arrested and faces prosecution. Two acquaintances, one of them the narrator, offer their help and, to find out whether they can appease the insulted party, visit the young lady who is sojourning with her uncle and aunt for her holidays. During their stay the narrator falls in love with the girl, and visits her room at night under the pretence that he has forgotten something to read, and then compares the ensuing love making with "the most divine of poems" (146).

Just like the narrator of the Maupassant's story, V. sets out to talk with a beautiful girl in order to clarify the nature of the encounter she had with the narrator's acquaintance. The reference to Maupassant's story is made precisely before the point where the parallel ceases: the narrator's being on the verge of making love with a most desirable lady. If the parallel can be traced backwards this would mean that the affair

Sebastian had with Nina might be compared to that of Morin with Henriette: an affair that is actually non-existent.

21. THE COLONEL

The Colonel by F.C. Burnand was a play first performed in 1881. It is about a family that lives peacefully in the country until its harmony is disturbed by an imposter, Lambert Strekye, who proposes, with the help of his cousin, Basil Giorgone, to refurbish the family's home according to the latest fashion of the Aesthetic Movement. A friend of the family, Colonel Woottweell W. Woodd, happens to come along and restores the peace.

Among Sebastian's books V. has selected as worthy of mention is one titled *About Buying a Horse*. This book contains "[h]umorous autobiographical sketches" by Burnand (Boyd, "Notes" 676).

Burnand's writings have now long been forgotten, but one comes across his name in biographies on Oscar Wilde, because he portrayed Wilde in *The Colonel* as Strekye, "a charlatan and a swindler" (Pearson 44; see also Holland). Wilde did not retort but remarks in *The Decay of Lying*, written in 1889, that "the aim of the liar is simply to charm, to delight, to give pleasure. He is the very basis of civilized society, and without him a dinner-party, even at the mansions of the great, is as dull as a lecture at the Royal Society, or a debate at the Incorporate Authors, or one of Mr. Burnand's farcical comedies" (Wilde 834).

In *The Prismatic Bezel* Burnand's *Colonel* is parodied using some of its details. The setting is also a "country house" and the number of characters, "twelve persons. . . . Plus a chance passer-by" matches the thirteen dramatis personae of *The Colonel* (*Sebastian Knight* 90–91). Sebastian's sleuth "drops his h's," but adds an 'h' as well: "'u]llo,' he says, 'ow about Hart?'" (92). This is borrowed from a dialogue in the play's first act, between Richard Forrester, the head of the family, and the colonel:

For. My father-in-law, the late Sir John . . . had no society aspirations
Col. And no society aspirates.
      Dropped his "h's" and
      saved his dollars

      . . .

For.	Ah! If Sir John had lived we should have heard Nothing about Art.
Col.	No ... he'd have called It *H*art.

(Burnand)

For his novel Sebastian retains the colonel from Burnand's play and in chapter 6 it will be argued that the play's title is a main reason for referring to Burnand.

The summary of *The Prismatic Bezel* as given by V. is delightfully funny, and one can only regret that there is no original version. The most ludicrous figure is doubtless the London detective who is to some extent duplicated by V. after he assumes the role of a detective engrossed in finding the unidentified femme fatale. V.'s quest brings him to a hotel and a country house, and likewise the scenery in *The Prismatic Bezel* switches from a "boarding-house" to a "country-house." Due to the detective "the lodgers are examined afresh" just as V. is not content with Mr. Silbermann's list of "all the hotel-gentleman's" but wishes to have all the hotel-guests investigated anew. Both are invited to come to the respective country houses. And just as the sleuth decides to concentrate on "Hart" ("ow about Hart?"), so V. focusses on Mme. Lecerf, "le cerf" is French for "the hart."

Even V.'s attempt to see Sebastian before he dies, as described in chapters 19 and 20, is epitomized in *The Prismatic Bezel*. Like V., the sleuth is summoned "to come at once." The London inspector has the same inclination and runs dangerous risks when using a car; V. to such an extent that he is expelled from his taxi by the cabman; and the detective even "runs over an old woman." And both, having reached their destination, are confronted with the wrong room (the sealed door is not a person's room but "that of a forgotten lumber-room's," and the room shown to V. is not Sebastian's).

22. TRAINS

Like cars, trains serve as a medium for fate to direct or divert the course of the lives of the characters in *Sebastian Knight*. Trains are even more frequently mentioned than cars, about thirty times. There is a deplorable decay in the quality of the trains during the run of the novel. The Great European Express Trains and the Pullman car make way for second and even third-class carriages where people instead of "reading" (22) are seen "eating" and "snor[ing]" (194, 175).

The first trip V. makes by train mirrors his last as they are both connected with Sebastian's life: if Sebastian had not arrived in time at the St. Petersburg railway station he would probably have been shot like Captain Belov. But V. did not arrive in time in St. Damier to find Sebastian still alive. And it was on a train that the nonpareil Mr. Silbermann wished to meet V. and offer him his help. And fate arranged that Sebastian just missed Clare on her way to the underground. Had Sebastian been there "a minute earlier" he would have seen Clare. And perhaps Sebastian might then, being lonely and ill (it was his last summer) have explained to Clare why he had stepped out of her life six years ago (182). Why, one may wonder, has fate (the novel's author) withheld from the reader this perspective? Perhaps to press on the reader that such an explanation might exist.

23. TRANSMIGRATION BY LANGUAGE

The English language is Sebastian Knight's coat of arms and expresses his strong emotional bond with his mother and her native country. Instead of using his own paternal name, he adopts his mother's surname. His mother probably never learnt to speak Russian properly; when visiting her son in 1908 she spoke to V.'s mother in "bad French" (8). English therefore must have been the language spoken daily in the household during Sebastian's father's first marriage. When Sebastian is twelve years old he reads *Chums*, and at the age sixteen he writes poetry in English. He has at the same time English lessons (by Mrs. Forbes), probably to maintain his fluency, since during his father's second marriage the use of English might have lost its attractiveness. His partiality to pass for an Englishman drives Sebastian to such a point that he denies that he was born in Russia. Contrary to his creator, whose "closest friends were Russian" no Russian acquaintance is mentioned by Sebastian's Cambridge friend (Boyd, *VNRY* 168). Although he had a Swiss governess and his French was apparently strong enough to read Proust's *Le Temps Retrouvé,* he prefers to "pronounce French as a real healthy Britisher would" (71).

That his English grammar and vocabulary needs correction is no reason for Sebastian to view his non-English extraction with greater tolerance.

Somehow his Russophobia does not prevent him from making a trip for a couple of days with "a man he had known age ago, in Russia" (86). And some years later he dines with V. in a Russian restaurant, probably Sebastian's choice as he proposes to have "'pelmenies'" (106). He writes letters in Russian, even uses a rare Russian word such as *vypolziny*, talks about his "emigré existence," and becomes a patient of the old family doctor Starov, who pronounces his given name in the Russian fashion, "Sevastian" (188). And, as Neil Cornwall has observed, he registers in the St. Damier hospital with his Russian surname and not the adopted name "Knight" (Cornwell 161).

V.'s use of English and Russian inversely mirrors that of his half-brother. As he has lived in France for eighteen years, his command of French must be fairly complete. But, of course, when visiting Paul Rechnoy, their conversation is carried out in Russian. However, V.'s talks with another compatriot, Nina Lecerf (née Toorevetz) are held in French (which must have been her choice as she learned from V.'s card that he is Russian). But it was V.'s choice when, although recognizing Silbermann's "thick guttural French," he prefers to talk with him in English. The last conversation reported in *Sebastian Knight* is V.'s discussion with an Englishman about *The Doubtful Asphodel*, and is certainly carried out in English: here, all traces of the Russian origin of the half-brothers have disappeared. That V.'s English is "miserable" is contradicted by the unusual richness of his vocabulary, the preciseness of his sentences, and the ease of his linguistic transitions in his biography.

V. seems to have attained what Sebastian as a writer aspires to, while Sebastian has returned to his childhood Russian as V. so eagerly wishes. In realizing their linguistic ideals, the half-brothers have changed places.

24. UNFINISHED PICTURES

Starting from his observation that "a deep theme of Vasari's biography of Leonardo [is] the painter's tendency to leave works unfinished or 'imperfect,'" Paul Barolsky discusses how literary art has generated many verbal paintings and portraits to learn the secrets of art and artists. He argues how such quests have often ultimately become obsessions, but unfortunately for them the "elusive" artists do not succumb to the scrutinizers as is indicated by the fact that the portraits remain unfinished (414). Barolsky mentions Leonardo, Flaubert and Sebastian Knight as examples of artists whose true identity remain mysterious. In *Sebastian Knight* it is not Sebastian's portrait alone that remains "incomplete" and "unfinished" (118, 123). The portraits of Natasha are conspicuously fragmentary, only a "mere outline" is presented and a bit later she disappears altogether "except for the arm and a thin brown hand" (136, 137). (The "achrometic" representation is discussed in section 4, 6.) "The presentation of absence is obviously not a gratuitous device"; writes Lara Delage-Toriel, "it brings into relief the importance of the visual portraits by creating a sense of frustrated scopic desire which parallels the narrator's own unfulfilled quest for Sebastian's last love" (146). Without answering the question why Sebastian felt himself always "hopelessly alone" (42), V.'s quest, doomed by his obsessive fixation on a Russian lady, is bound to remain unaccomplished.

25. VALENTINO

Sebastian's uncontrollable laughing when he sees a film with Clare trying to curb his mirth "prefigures," writes Stacy Schiff, "the same scene at Cornell" (188). She refers to a recollection of Alfred Appel Jr. who in 1954 saw Nabokov laughing loudly when seeing *Beat the Devil* (Appel, *Cinema* 311). The movie that exhilarated Sebastian is *The Sheik,* which caused a furor in the 1920s. It features Rudolph Valentino, the patent beau, in his most famous role. The film was made after E.M. Hull's novel *The Sheik* and Claud Cockburn summarizes its theme by quoting "rape, rape, rape all summer long" (139). Sebastian was not the only one who could not stand the movie as many viewers in the 1920s howled at some scenes and droves of men walked out of the cinema during its showings (Leider 165, 169).

26. VARVARA

Pahl Pahlich Rechnoy remarried, after having divorced his first wife Nina, Varvara Mitrofanna, who comes from Sebastopol and who "has taken up dressmaking" (142). Varvara's patronymic recalls the name of the youth, Mitrofán, in Denis Fonvizin's play *The Infant* (1782). This badly bred boy professes that he would like to get married, but finally concedes to join the army. The main intention of the comedy is to ridicule the terribly bad manners many characters of the play have.

Varvara is also the name of the second companion of Andrey Kovrin, the protagonist of Chekhov's story *The Black Monk*, which Sebastian uses to pull "Mr. Goodman's leg" (62).

Kovrin, a strained student, hallucinates that he sees a black monk who praises Kovrin's "astonishing scholarship" and much more. Elated, he marries Tanya, who has him treated for his illness, but when he regains his health he misses the "delusions of grandeur," starts hating Tanya and leaves her (84, 96). It is only in the last, ninth, section that one learns that Kovrin now lives with Varvara and that they have arrived in Sebastopol. They find a hotel and Varvara, being tired, goes to bed. Then she is "asleep behind the screen and her breathing [is] audible" (Chekhov, *Selected Stories* 102), just as "the sleeper's breath" behind "a screen" (*Sebastian Knight* 200–201) is heard by V.

Like V. who takes the sleeper to be Sebastian, Kovrin is mistaken as he, mortally ill, falls and cries for Tanya.

27. WILDER

Thornton Wilder's novel *The Bridge of San Luis Rey* is about a quest comparable to that of Sebastian Knight's novel *Success*: "to discover the exact way in which . . . lines of life were made to come into contact" (*Sebastian Knight* 94). Five people died when the bridge broke; "[w]hy did this happen to those five? If there were any plan in the universe at all, if there were any pattern in a human life, surely it could be discovered" (Wilder 9). The answer, a rather panacean one, might have disappointed Sebastian: "the bridge is love, the only survival, the only meaning" (Wilder 124). Perhaps more opportune to the mysteries of *The Real Life of Sebastian Knight* is the story (told in the third of the novel's five parts) of the brothers Manuel and Esteban who live together and are very close. Manuel falls in love with the beautiful actress Camila Perichole. As Esteban feels painfully excluded from his brother's exalted emotions and grows miserable, Manuel stops seeing her. And the question is suggested who was more in love with Camila, Manual, her putative admirer, or his reticent brother Esteban? The same question can be asked with respect to the half-brothers in *Sebastian Knight,* as it is not clear who was captured more by Nina's charms, Sebastian or V.

28. ZELLE

When V. visits Mademoiselle, the Swiss lady who had been his and Sebastian's governess in St. Petersburg, she recalls Sebastian's way of addressing her as "Zelle" (20). Maurice Couturier explains this by calling it an "[a]bréviation affectuese de 'Mademoiselle'" (*Oeuvres* 1546). After the interview V. is much dismayed having spend time on "this useless pilgrimage" (21).

In V.'s interview with Pahl Rechnoy, he compares his former wife with "an international spy. Mata Hari! That's her type Oh, absolutely" (143).

Mata Hari is the name the Dutch Margarete Getrude Zelle (1876–1917) used for her performances as a dancer in France. By coupling Nina Rechnoy with Mata Hari/"Zelle," it is implied that V.'s search for Nina might turn out to be another "useless pilgrimage."

Motifs: Identities

CHAPTER 4

CONTENTS

1. Baring 110
2. Brooke, Gray, Housman, and Kipling 111
3. Byron's "Dream" 114
4. Celadon 114
5. Chess 115
6. Colors 115
7. Cox 120
8. *Dead Souls* 120
9. Douglas 122
10. Enchanted Garden 123
11. *Jekyll and Hyde* 124
12. Joan of Arc 125
13. "L" and "V" 126
14. Mann 127
15. Moon 130
16. "Mrs. Bathurst" 131
17. Nesbit 131
18. Proust 132
19. Queer 134
20. Robinsonnade 135
21. *Rubáiyát* 136
22. Sexuality 138
23. Sherlock Holmes 140
24. Snakes 142

25. St Sebastian 145
26. *Success* 145
27. *The Tragedy of Sebastian Knight* 146
28. *Ulysses* 150
29. Uncle Ruka... 153
30. Velimir Khlebnikov 156
31. V.'s Dream 158
32. *Woman in White* 159

1. BARING

Nabokov was acquainted with Maurice Baring as well as with his works and connections. Coming from the Baring family of bankers, he was educated at Eton, Cambridge, and Oxford (he entered Trinity College in 1894 about a quarter of a century before Sebastian and Nabokov, and like Sebastian, frequented the Pitt Club [Baring *Puppet* 143, 153]). He was a highly prolific writer and, having become a staunch Russophile, many of his books are devoted to Russia, its people and its literature. In 1914 Baring accompanied H.G. Wells during his visit to Russia (Boyd, *VNRY* 178). When in St. Petersburg Wells was invited to dinner at the Nabokovs and this invitation was extended to Baring, whose social standing was similar to that of Nabokov's father (*Letters to Véra* 663). Two decades later Nabokov, in a letter to his friend Gleb Struve in which he inquired about the possibility for lecturing on literature in England, mentions Baring as someone who might help in furthering this idea (Efimov 228; see also Boyd, *VNRY* 431). In 1948 Nabokov commented to Edmund Wilson on Thornton Wilder's *The Ides of March*: "The thing is much too easy—and has been done so many times in England. Maurice Baring did it quite as well" (Karlinsky, *Dear Bunny* 226).

In his article on Nabokov and Prince D.S. Mirsky, Mikhail Efimov writes that "[a]ccording to Gennady Barabtarlo's recent discovery, the manuscript copy of the third chapter of Nabokov's first English novel, *The Real Life of Sebastian Knight*, contains 'a deleted paragraph which among Knight's "not very numerous friends-literati" mentions a well-known English philologist Maurice Baring'" (229).

Like Sebastian, Baring happened to throw inkpots and wrote an experimental detective novel, *Overlooked* (Baring, *Puppet* 183; Smyth

239). But one is tempted to explain the initial inclusion as well as the final exclusion of Baring in *Sebastian Knight* in the same way as in which V. tries to discover the secret of Sebastian's life, that is by means of his love affairs. In Baring's case it was rather the absence of any love affair that puzzled his acquaintances. In her biography of Baring, Emma Letley records the many speculations about this subject, and provides a key to its answer as well (216). When discussing Baring's friendship's she writes: "The women Maurice knew well at this time divide sharply into the Beauties (that succession of lovely women with whom Maurice populated his life . . .) and on the other hand the redoubtable Sapphists" (196). Although no greater distinction can be imagined than between the elegance of the "Beauties" whom Letley mentions and the formidability of the Sapphists, no amorous overtures were expected from Baring as all the beautiful ladies were married. In his autobiography, *The Puppet Show of Memory*, which spans the years until 1914 and was published in 1932 (Ethel Smyth's biography followed in 1938) no romances are mentioned. But perhaps one should not forget Baring's friendship with Auberon Herbert, "the most intensely admired of his friends" (Smyth 50). Herbert was killed in World War I, which caused Baring to write one of his best poems, the elegiac *In Memoriam, A.H.* Of course the likeness with Tennyson's great poem *In Memoriam A.H.H.* cannot be missed and does not end with the titles. And the line "And on your sandals the strong wings of youth" recalls the perplexing effect Baring felt when seeing "the Hermes of Praxiteles" (*In Memoriam* 259; *Puppet* 254).

2. BROOKE, GRAY, HOUSMAN, AND KIPLING

In order to illustrate "one of the barest emotions," the "pining after the land of [one's] birth," Sebastian uses scenic images from poems by Brooke, Gray, and Housman (24). And, in expressing "the love with the country which was [his] home" Sebastian had his "Kipling moods," his "Rupert Brooke moods" and his "Housman moods" (66).

The festive evocation of the English countryside in lines 25/ 1–3 is cunningly composed, as the poets cited have earned their fame for quite different reasons than for their ability to eulogize England's landscapes. Brooke and Housman gained their prestige due to World War I because premature death is one of the great themes of their poetry

(Keynes 9; Sampson 845). Brooke is one of the so-called War Poets and his prophetic "The Soldier" is probably his most anthologized poem. Nabokov admired Brooke for similar reasons: "[n]o other poet has so often, with such tormented and creative vigilance, looked into the dusk of the beyond" (qtd. in Boyd, *VNRY* 182; see also Johnson, "Brooke"). But Brooke's "The Old Vicarage, Granchester" is a truly nostalgic poem that he wrote in Berlin in 1912 about the place where he stayed in 1911 and where he enjoyed "one of his happiest summers" (Lehmann 46).

Housman's poetry also has many Arcadian evocations, all inspired by his homeland Shropshire, but these cannot mask his real theme, that of doomed lads. In the poem referred to by Sebastian, numbered XL in Housman's collection of poems, the bitterness of the poet's melancholy is all to clear, as the wind that is blown from "those blue remembered hills" carries "an air that kills" (Housman 70). The same can be said of Thomas Gray who was one of the first man of letters to discover the picturesque beauties of Wordsworth's Lake District but who had a splenetic disposition. His "Ode on a Distant Prospect of Eton College" from which Nabokov quotes, has a jubilant opening ("Ye distant spires, ye antique towers That Crown the watery glade,") but soon takes a morbid turn, disastrously so after the stanza beginning with

> Alas! Regardless of their doom
> The little victims play (Gray 255)

What links Gray and Housman is the source of their melancholy. Housman, writes John Sparrow, "could not confess to affections of which a poet could speak openly in ancient Greece. Like Gray, therefore, and for the same reason, Housman 'never spoke out'" (Sparrow 13). Doubtless, Sparrow must have had Matthew Arnold's essay on Thomas Gray in mind, in which the phrase "*He never spoke out*" is taken as a guiding motif (Arnold 267–281).

Arnold quotes Gray's close friend Charles de Bonstetten who "thinks that Gray's life was poisoned by an unsatisfied sensibility, was withered by his having never loved" (277). Both men, Housman and Gray, became professors at Cambridge, the university serving as a refuge. Both, writes Edmund Wilson, "belong to the monastic order of English university ascetics" just as "Walter Pater, Lewis Carroll, Edward Fitzgerald and Gerard Manley Hopkins" (83). The relevance of Edward

Motifs: Identities | 113

Fitzgerald for *Sebastian Knight* is discussed in section 21; the relevance of Walter Pater is discussed in chapter 6).

"Not to speak out" is the theme of Housman's poem beginning with the lines "Because I liked you better / Than suits a man to say" or the one opening with "Ask me no more, for fear I should reply" (Housman 191, 221). The "nameless" in "Additional Poems," XVIII with its first line "Oh who is that young sinner with the handcuffs on his wrists?" is about Oscar Wilde who, sentenced to hard labor, was forced to stand handcuffed on the platform of a London station "'for the world to look at'" (Pearson 281). The "nameless" refers to the "Love that dare not speak its name" of which Wilde was accused of and which he defended so bravely and eloquently during his trial (Pearson 268; the phrase "Love that dare not speak its name" comes from "Two Loves," a poem by Alfred Douglas, Oscar Wilde's lover [Wright 206]).

"Not to speak out," characterizes Sebastian's behavior when his relationship with Clare becomes unbearable. "He has stopped talking to me," says Clare, and Sheldon's appeal "out with it, man" is answered with silence (108).

Rupert Brooke lived from 1887 until 1915 when he died on April 23 (Nabokov's birthday) during a military expedition. He studied in Cambridge, at King's College, from 1905 until 1912 and his verse amounts to 120 short poems. Brooke had varied sexual experiences and in *Look at the Harlequins!* Nabokov remarks that "the naked-neck photo of Rupert Brooke" is found "a-*houri-sang*," a play on the French *ahurissant*, meaning 'staggering' or 'stupefying,' and 'houri,' meaning an alluring woman (28).

(The "photo" is most likely taken of Brooke's memorial plaque in the chapel of his old school in Rugby, which shows a bas-relief sculpture of the poet's head and neck, the latter rather pronounced. The bas-relief is photographically reproduced in Lehmann's monograph.)

Kipling is certainly mentioned because of his dictum that the human heart can love only its native land (Boyd, *VNRY 182)*, but possibly also because of his partiality for male characters. Nabokov was sensitive on this point as is clear from his comment on Gogol: "I am depressed and puzzled by his utter inability to describe young women" (*SO* 156.) Inevitably, Nabokov may have been struck by the "general shortage of women in Kipling's world" (Page 90). In his article "Kipling's World of Men" Norman Page discusses many critics who have observed that

"Kipling despised women" and how he preferred "the world of soldiers and sailors" (91, 85). (Incidentally, it was Joseph Conrad [see comment on line 40/ 9] who also preferred the company of "soldiers and sailors"; see Seymour, *Otteline Morrell* 254.)

3. BYRON'S "DREAM"

The reminiscences Natasha Rosanov has of the summer of 1916 and her rendezvous with Sebastian, as retold by V., have four scenes, separated by the following phrases: "The picture changes"; "As in Byron's dream, again the picture changes"; "A last change" (136/37). Byron's poem "The Dream" consists of nine stanzas, of which six have the same opening line, "A change came over the spirit of my dream." Written in 1816 the poem recalls Byron's love for Mary Chaworth and their meetings in 1803. Byron was fifteen years old and Mary seventeen but an even more serious obstacle was Mary's engagement to another (Marchand 26).

Sebastian and Natasha are the same age, but Natasha was also in love with someone else. In both cases the rowing together seems, for Byron and Sebastian, the most cherished memory. When Byron and Mary had to pass under a rock they had to lie down in the small boat, and this intimacy moved him greatly (Marchand 27). The outing of Sebastian and Natasha is painted in a paradisical way (the sun is shining, flowers abound, the air is filled with dragonflies and swifts), but no intimacy is mentioned. And the final comment suggests that Sebastian's broken heart could be mended rather easily: "next summer was mainly devoted to the futurist Pan" (138).

Byron had a similar consolation: "in the autumn . . . he turned to the reassuring affection of his Harrow friends" (Marchand [30–31] adds that "a strong attraction to boys persisted in Byron from his Harrow days throughout his life.")

4. CELADON

The cat of Sebastian's Cambridge friend has received some attention among critics because of the color of the cat's fur (see, for example, Fischman, and Rutledge[180]). Here the color of the cat's eyes, "celadon," is discussed (45). "[C]eladon" refers to Céladon, one of the main characters of the novel *L'Astrée* by Honoré d'Urfé, an imposing work written between 1607 and 1627. "The work's immense popularity . . . led to the naming of the colour shades as 'Céladon' and 'Astrée'" (Levi 872). More important than its hues (a grayish yellow green, beautifully reflecting the polychromatic, rayed eyes of cats) is the literary connotation of "celadon." Nabokov who studied French and had to write an "essay, on a topic in seventeenth-century French literature or history," most certainly was well acquainted with this celebrated romance (Boyd, *VNRY* 183). Although "peopled with hundreds of characters" the love story of Astrée and Celadon is the central part of it (Gregorio 783). Celadon loves Astrée and, disguised as a girl and assuming the name Alexis, gains intimacy with her. Celadon's beauty and complexion facilitates this travesty, which is not even discovered when they exchange kisses. Celadon who passes the greater part of the work as the girl Alexis, gets confused about his own identity: "Am I Alexis? . . . Am I Celadon? . . . So I am Alexis and Celadon mixed together" (qtd. in Gregorio [796]). As Astrée does not find out that Alexis is a boy, her love can be regarded as of a Sapphic nature. The confusion and deliberate imprecision where "signs of sexual identity are concerned" appear "to be the intended effect of the thematic plan of d'Urfé's novel" (Gregorio 782). This might explain why in this work "[i]n spite of explicit moral pronouncements against the practice of homosexuality, apologies and defenses are made for appearances of it" (Gregorio 798).

5. CHESS

Nina Rechnoy's maiden name is Toorovetz and the first part of this name is close to "tura," the Russian for "rook."

All the chessmen seem to be presented in *The Real Life of Sebastian Knight*: rook, knight, bishop, and queen, except the king who is not mentioned explicitly. This subject is addressed again in chapter 6.

6. COLORS

To study the colors Nabokov mentions in his novels, and the emblematic significance he attributed to them, using their synaesthetic, etymological, iconographical, literary, and mythological meanings and nuances, would require a book-length survey.

The subject is especially so elusive because colors, as in real life, cannot be perceived without a context. To some extent the meaning of the colors Nabokov refers to, depend on their setting. It would also require a study of the numerous flowers Nabokov mentions, as these are the principal original bearers of colors. A short survey of Nabokov's statements of what colors meant to him can be found in my "Introduction" (Vries and Johnson 20–22). Nabokov's expressions show his wide knowledge of and great involvement in chromatics.

6.1 Violet (I)

In his article "Oculate Paradise" Erik Martiny writes that it is argued "that violet is the prevalent colour of [*Sebastian Knight*] but there are arguably more objects tinted with blue" (100). Although the chapter devoted to *Sebastian Knight* makes no claim about a prevalent color, it is true that the color violet is its main topic (Vries and Johnson 39–43). Martiny gives fourteen examples to support his statement, whereas I have stopped after having listed thirteen samples. But numerical considerations should not be counted decisive in matters where so much depends on contexts. The color violet has a crucial role, because, as Barbara Wyllie writes, it is "central to notions of transition and transcendence" (101). In Nabokov's work numerous momentous transitions occur, from past to present, from day to night, from one country to another, from one lover to another, from one identity to the next, from one language to another, from life to death, and from death to life.

This is reflected in *Sebastian Knight*. In it, colors define "time," a "book," and a "romance." The dominant color—violet—symbolizes the transition Nabokov (and Sebastian) had to make from Russian to English, and prefigures the merging of Sebastian and V. as described in the novel's last section, while the flower violet is connected with the novel's discussion of the hereafter (Vries and Johnson 39–43). The color violet results from mixing red and blue, a combination of colors that recur often in *Sebastian Knight* (39). Another instance of a possible red and blue combination is discussed in section 4, 20.

The color violet's special meaning follows from its position in the rainbow, "the ultimate tint of the spectrum" (*Speak, Memory* 293) from where one can transmigrate to the next sphere. The "solar spectrum is not a closed circle but a spiral of tints from cadmium red and oranges through the strontium yellow and a pale paradisal green to cobalt blues and violets, at which point the sequence does not grade into red again but passes into another spiral, which starts with a lavender gray and goes on to Cinderella shades transcending human perception," writes Nabokov in *Pnin* (96).

The passing from an uppermost arc into another dimension is also illustrated in *Sebastian Knight*'s eighth chapter in the seminal picture of the swarm of pigeons that settle on the frieze of the Arc de Triomphe and "fluttered off again . . . as if bits of the carved entablure were turned into flaky life," an image condensed by Sebastian into the phrase "stone melting into wing." With this swarm of pigeons Nabokov commemorates the "flight of doves" that inspired Uncle Ruka's best composition (*Speak, Memory* 74). Before the pigeons perch on the Arc de Triomphe they have already been observed by Clare and commented on by Sebastian who complains about their smell. "What kind of smell?" asks Clare, to which Sebastian answers: "Iris and rubber." As Sebastian refers to their odious smell he must have in mind the so-called "stinking iris" or gladdon (*Iris foetidissima*), which has an odor "like burning rubber" (Breverton 191). This plant has violet flowers instead of the commoner yellow flowers that belong to the *Iris pseudacorus* (Nicholson, Ary, and Gregory 28, 162). Iris is also the name of the goddess of Greek mythology who personifies the rainbow. This rainbow links the flower with the semicircle of the Arc de Triomphe, while its color violet catalyses the metamorphosis of stone into wing. This association with the rainbow may explain the route Sebastian takes to accompany his half-brother to the underground station.

Sebastian and Clare see the pigeons on the Arc de Triomphe when they are "about to cross the Avenue Kleber" where they arrive coming from the Champs-Élysées. The main façade of the Arc de Triomphe is directed toward the Champs-Élysées. Why is the view of the petrified birds taking wing in *Sebastian Knight* seen from the Avenue Kléber?

The Arc de Triomphe is a rectangular construction, with two crossing archways. The southern, smaller, side of the Arc is faced toward the Avenue Kléber, from where one can see through its smaller archway. A rainbow also consists of two arches, a smaller and a bigger one. Instead of a single rainbow, one can often see a double rainbow, which has a fainter one (the so-called secondary rainbow) above the smaller, more colorful and easier visible (primary) rainbow. As D. Barton Johnson has explained, "the primary rainbow" represents "Nabokov's literary creation in his native Russian," and the "larger, fainter secondary rainbow" "his English language writing" (*Worlds in Regression* 22). *Sebastian Knight* is the first novel Nabokov wrote in English and this might be regarded as a farewell to his Russian literary career. The birds taking leave from the smaller arc aptly suggest the transition from Russian to English.

6.2 Violet (II)

The pertinacious presence of the color violet or its corresponding flower throughout the novel deserves attention as well because of its recurrence in other novels, where it has often been used to signal deviations from heterosexual orientations. In *The Gift* "the violet rust of pansies" is noticed "in every garden" on the eve of Yasha Chernyshevsky's suicide, the poor homophile boy, whose poems have so many "autumn scenes à la Esenin" (46, 38). In *Pale Fire* Nabokov "has gone to a great deal of trouble to associate Shade's 'ready to become a floweret' . . . with the homosexual Kinbote" as this floweret is meant to be a violet (Boyd, *Nabokov's* Pale Fire 122). In *Ada* three men are introduced, all with a "'pansy' character": "Captain Tapper, of Wild Violet Lodge"; Johnny Rafin, Esq., a "pun on 'Rafinesque,' after whom a violet is named," and Arwin Birdfoot (600, 304–306, 600).

In *Look at the Harlequins!* another kind of violet is mentioned, lavender: "Sebastian—whoever that was—might still be coming for the grape season or lavender gala" (5).

In *Sebastian Knight* this lavender color can also be detected in the phrase "a sunlit laundry: blue water and scarlet wrists" (98). Not only is the combination of "blue" and "scarlet" suggestive of violet or purple, the word "laundry" does the same. According to the second edition of *The Oxford English Dictionary* "laundry" is an "[a]ltered form of lavendry," and "launder" a "[c]ontraction of lavender" (VIII: 703 and 702).

In *Pale Fire* Kinbote writes that "the name [lavender] hails from the laundry, not the laund" (197). Although Kinbote playfully reverses the root (lavender) and the derivative (laundry), he emphasizes the etymological correctness by dismissing the plausible candidate "laund" as a possible root. (According to *Webster's Second* "laund" is an obsolete word meaning "a lawn," and in former times laundered linen was spread on a lawn to let it dry and bleach.)

Dieter Zimmer writes that the name lavender is selected because lavender as a color symbolizes homosexuality (Zimmer, *Fahles Feuer* 489). The many pairings of lavender with homosexuality in literary and historical documents has been traced back to "descriptions of the lesbian poet Sappho as violet haired," while another explanation might be that "lavender consists of the combination of red and blue, gender-specific colors used in Western society to distinguish between girls and boys at birth" (Zimmerman 747).

6.3 Heliotrope

The word heliotrope denotes the name of a plant with violet flowers, or the name of that color. Because Nabokov discusses this color's position in "European literature" this section will be finished with a small digression about this particular variant of violet. Marcel Proust mentions the "colour of heliotrope" in an exquisite sentence of exceptional length (almost the length of a whole page, see *Remembrance of Things Past* 1: 428–429) in which he reflects on "Gilberte," the name of a little girl, "playing battledore and shuttlecock" in a public garden along the Champs-Élysées. The sentence contains a multitude of elevated thoughts and emotions this name evokes, connected with the little girl and the narrator's own reminiscences. Proust concludes by saying that "finally" this name casts "a marvellous little band of light, the colour of heliotrope." (In his *Lectures on Literature* Nabokov expertedly paraphrases this inimitable sentence, highlighting its beauties by interspersing them verbatim in his elucidation [240–241].)

This band of light is, according to Nabokov, "the violet tint that runs through the whole book, the very color of time. The rose-purple mauve, a pinkish lilac, a violet flush, is linked in European literature with certain sophistications of the artistic temperament" (*Lectures on Literature* 241). At the end of his opus, when Proust recapitulates his childhood memories and tried to unravel the very sources of the happiness they brought about, he mentions some purple passages from French literature where "a sensation of the same species as the taste of the madeleine" figures (3: 959). One of these is the "loviest episode in [Chateaubriand's] *Mémoires d'Outre-tombe*": "A sweet and subtle scent of heliotrope was exhaled by a little patch of beans that where in flower" (3: 958–959). Because it is in this last part of his work that Proust learns how to recapture the past, the time lost, it may be that

Nabokov calls this recurrent color heliotrope the "color of time," the very subject of a speech Nina was not amused to listen to.

In *The Gift* Nabokov mentions "a Turgenevian odor of heliotrope" (150) and in *Pale Fire* he gives its source a Latinate aura: "*Heliotropium turgenevi*" (98). These fragrances refer to the heliotropes in Turgenev's novel *Smoke*, in which the hero, Grigory Litvinov, has to choose between two women, "the gentle, domestic, virtuous and compassionate Tania, and the elemental, cynical, strong-willed, sensual and dominant Irina" (Schapiro 202). Twice a bouquet of heliotropes is offered, once by Grigory to Irina just before he loses her, the second time (about a decade later) by Irina to Grigory in attempt to win him back (*Smoke* 46, 63). In *Sebastian Knight* a reference is made to the crucial stage in the story when Grigory is once more ensnared by the femme fatale (see comment on lines 7/ 15–16). In *The Seagull*, which Chekhov wrote about two decades after *Smoke* appeared, a "scent of heliotrope in the air" is mentioned in, what Nabokov calls, "a delightful speech" delivered by Trigorin, the succesful writer, who reflects on his métier and concludes by saying that he is a good writer "but Turgenev is better" (*The Seagull* 54; *Lectures on Russian Literature* 287; see also section 3, 15).

7. COX

"'You're a very poor cox,'" Sebastian tells Natasha Rosanov when she has steered the boat into the rushes. "Cox" is an abbreviated form of "coxswain," which comes from cockboat + swain, while a "swain" is a young male lover. Had Sebastian used words like "hand," "helper," "mate," or "rower" his mild reproof would have sounded less artificial and without attributing a masculine undertone. But the reproof itself is surprising as well. Would not any young lover be delighted when his sweetheart let the rowing boat they are sitting in disappear between rushes? One can be assured that Ganin responded quite differently when Mary let "the boat sail into the reeds" (*Mary* 58).

8. DEAD SOULS

When V. visits the Rechnoy family he looks "round the room" while Rechnoy and Uncle Black discuss their chess moves. He notes "the moustache of a famous general," and the family's triple bed and remembers "Chichikov's round of weird visits in Gogol's *Dead Souls*."

Zimmer (*Das wahre Leben* 294–295) and Couturier (*Oeuvres* 1556) suggest that the owner of the moustache is Alexander Kutepov, a general in the White Army, kidnapped in Paris in 1930 by the Soviets and destined to be murdered in Moscow, hence the "moscowed" (see also Boyd, *VNAY* 59).

Like V., Chichikov, when visiting Mikhail Sobakevitch, looks around and sees pictures of military men (all with "incredible mustachios"): Mavrocordato; Kolokotronis, Miaulis and Kanaris (*Dead Souls* 109). These are the names of the military leaders of the Greek nationalists who wished to free their country from Turkish domination. This war for independence lasted from 1821 until 1827. Miaulis and Kanaris were admirals; the two military men mentioned first were also political leaders (*Encyclopaedia Britannica* 10: 849–850). Gogol proposes an explanation for Sobakevitch's preference for these pictures: "[t]he owner being himself a hardy and hefty man apparently wished his room to be adorned with hardy and hefty people too" (quoted and translated by Nabokov [*Gogol* 97]).

Nabokov in his *Nikolay Gogol*, however, dissents: "was this the only reason? Is there not something singular in this leaning towards romantic Greece on Sobakevitch's part? Was there not a 'thin wispy little' poet concealed in that burly breast? For nothing in those days provoked a greater emotion in poetically inclined Russian than Byron's quest."

Elsewhere in his monograph Nabokov uses the word "romantic" to indicate sentimentality, such as Gogol's "romantic" invention of having fallen in love with a "goddess" (23, 17) or Gogol's "brief romantic friendship with Prince Vielgorsky" (159; its fervor lasted five months until the Prince's death).

It is, however, unlikely that the "romantic" feelings were aroused by the Greek struggle. As Nabokov writes in his *Commentary to Eugene Onegin* Russia supported the Greeks but with many reservations (3: 330–331). Pushkin was "sick of Greece" (Wolff 92). For this reason it must be assumed that it is "Byron's quest" that, according to Nabokov, must have moved Sobakevitch to have his room decorated with these soldiers. Byron knew only Mavrocordato well; it was he who welcomed Byron on his arrival at Missolonghi on January 4, 1824 (and where he died of marsh fever on April 19 of the same year). Byron's reputation was already established in 1812 when the first two Cantos of *Childe Harold* were published. The second part of Byron's biography by Peter Quennell, *Byron: The Years of Fame*, published in 1935, covers the years 1811–1816, thus omitting his Greek escapade altogether. It was the Byronic hero that impressed Russian men of letters, not Byron as a Greek hero. Byron's interest in the Greek cause cannot be properly regarded as "Byron's quest." Byron's quarry was rather his unquenchable thirst for "the ideal love, forever sought and forever unattainable" (Marchand 435). In Byron's case, according to Leslie Marchand (435), this ideal was approximated by his love for handsome boys. In Missolonghi it was the page boy Loukas who absorbed most of Byron's attention and who inspired Byron's last poem (as well as his last financial arrangement) (Marchand 435, 450–451, 459).

For these reasons it seems plausible that Nabokov's digression is meant as a hint to "Greek love" as a specimen of the "romantic Greece," that might have moved Sobakevitch. This might also explain why V. remembers *Dead Souls* not when he notes the portrait of the moustached general, but only when he has also made his impertinent observations on the sleeping accommodations of the Rechnoy family.

9. DOUGLAS

Although Nabokov lists Norman Douglas among his favorite authors (*SO* 43) it was not for his literary merits alone that Nabokov mentions him in Gaston's gallery in *Lolita* (181). Like Oscar Wilde, Norman Douglas was (in 1917) prosecuted and imprisoned in England for homosexual assaults (in Norman Douglas's case on minors; Alfred Douglas was twenty-one when he met Wilde). But unlike Wilde who thought it dishonorable to leave England before his final trial in court, Norman Douglas left the country as soon as he could (Holloway 232; Pearson 274). Wilde was sentenced to two years hard labor, which was essentially a death sentence, since "men of Wilde's class usually died within two years after completing a sentence of hard labour" (Wright 299).

In a letter to Véra (April 1939) Nabokov wrote that it "turns out that Norman Douglas is a malicious pederast" but this left no traces in the opinion he gave in the 1964 interview, referenced earlier.

10. ENCHANTED GARDEN

A well-tended garden can satisfy all the senses while its seclusion indulges more intimate pleasures. In his *Commentary* on *Eugene Onegin* Nabokov's mentions "the indolent delights of an enchanted garden" in which the "handsome . . . Armida lures and lulls knights" (2: 182).

Here Nabokov discusses *Gerusalemme liberata* by Torquato Tasso (1544–1595), a near contemporary of Edmund Spenser (1552–1599) who in Canto XII of the second Book of *The Faerie Queen* probably wrote the locus classicus of English literature concerning the lascivious excesses such a garden can offer: Spencer's "Gardin" is the "Bowre of blisse" visited by the knight Guyon who becomes engrossed by two "Damzelles," amorously engaged with each other while bathing in a fountain (Spenser 131, 135, 137).

Although the sensuous enjoyment of its flora and fauna seems much more inherent in a garden than the carnal pleasures one can have with its inhabitants, they are put on a par by Marcel Proust, in his description of the "two 'ways,'" Proust's name for two promenades in Combray: "Swann's way" and the "Guermantes way" (*Remembrance of Things Past* 1: 146–204). (Nabokov in his lecture on Proust devotes one fifth of its pages to this part although it is only about one percent of the total length of *Remembrance of Things Past*.)

The narrator in Proust's opus observes that he makes no distinction "between the earth and its creatures" and calls the local girls of the woods of Roussainville "their secret treasure, their deep-hidden beauty" (*Remembrance of Things Past* 1: 171). At the end of his walk (of Swann's way) and reaching Montjouvain, he does not find a local girl, but he espies two girls who are making love. Nabokov (who also mentions the Proustian confluence of nature and human love as it "is on the Swann way walk that the theme of the hawthorns and the theme of love . . . come together") calls this lesbian affair the start of "the long series of homosexual revelations . . ." in Proust's work (*Lectures on Literature* 232). Likewise in *Ada*, epitomized by Bobbie Ann Mason as *Nabokov's Garden*, the incestuous love affair of Van and Ada is measured by nature: "[t]heir immoderate exploitation of physical joy" wanes when summer, "a boundless flow of green glory," nears its end (*Ada* 139).

The enchanted garden as a metaphor for the concealment of outlawed loves reoccurs in Evelyn Waugh's *Brideshead Revisited*, a novel about a passionate friendship between two young men, Sebastian Flyte and Charles Ryder. Margarit Tadevosyan and Maxim D. Shrayer, in their article "Thou Are Not Thou: Evelyn Waugh and Vladimir Nabokov" argue that it "is quite likely, that Waugh's Sebastian Flyte owes his appearance to Nabokov's Sebastian Knight" (28). They call the relationship in Waugh's novel a "love affair," and indeed many details evidencing their homosexual affair have been investigated by David Leon Higdon. The friendship begins when Charles accepts Sebastian's invitation to have luncheon with him. "I was in search of love," writes Charles, apprehending that he had at last found the door to "an enclosed and enchanted garden" (*Brideshead Revisited* 32). And when their relationship has finished, he knows that the "enchanted garden" has disappeared as well (163).

11. JEKYLL AND HYDE

Although Robert Louis Stevenson's *Strange Case of Dr. Jekyll and Mr. Hyde* may differ in numerous respects from *The Real Life of Sebastian Knight*, the works share the mysterious drastic change their main characters show. Sebastian's behavior becomes so utterly unrecognizable that Clare calls him "mad, quite mad" (108). And the charming Dr. Jekyll, despite his possessing "every mark of ... kindness," harbours enough evil to fill another person, Hyde, with it (Stevenson 43). There is much debate about the nature of this evil. The explanation Stevenson offers is more puzzling than clarifying: "a certain impatient gaiety of disposition," "pleasures" and "irregularities" seems to be Jekyll's main faults (81). Nabokov cannot appreciate this vagueness, which he qualifies as "irritating" (*Lectures on Literature* 194). He suggests a more distinct explanation. Referring to the observation by Stephen Gwynn that the male characters in Stevenson's novel are bachelors and that women scarcely have any role in it, he proposes that "Jekyll's secret adventures were homosexual practices" (194). It is clear from the copious quotations that Nabokov has read Gwynn's considerations carefully, but disagreed with Gwynn's conclusion that Jekyll's fault is "his savage indifference to the infliction of pain" (131). It seems likely that Nabokov refers to Stevenson's novel in order to emphasize that a reader, when confronted with a secret, should not always be satisfied with the explanations put forward by the narrator.

12. JOAN OF ARC

"Dot chetu" is the phonetic rendering of the word "Domremy" when its handwritten letters are read as Cyrillic text. Domrémy was the birthplace of Joan of Arc (present-day Domrémy-La-Pucelle) and it was there, in the garden of her parental house, that she heard angelic voices. These urged her to liberate France from the English occupation, and have the French pretender to the throne, the Dauphin Charles, crowned as the rightful king. She went to the Dauphin's court and gained access to him. The Dauphin believed the girl (although seventeen years old and of peasant stock), equipped her as a knight and within a year she brought him victories and the French crown. Then she was captured by the enemy, turned over to the inquisition, and burned to death. As a warrior she was a splendid knight, beautifully accoutered, riding a black horse, bearing a banner, and accompanied by an ample retinue (Warner 165–173). Sebastian deftly compares the destination of his letters with Joan's fate: "they have heard voices . . . they must suffer the stake" (184). However, it is not the voices that demand their destruction, as Sebastian writes "but they must suffer the stake." If it were the voices that require their burning, then one would expect to read "[and] they must suffer the stake." What secret do these letters contain that they needed to be burned? As Sebastian compares their fate to that of Joan of Arc, the reasons for her fall might provide a key for revealing their secret.

Marina Warner writes that hearing voices was not the only reason why Joan of Arc was put on trial: "Joan went to the stake because she refused to yield to the authority of the Church, as represented by the Inquisition that tried her. That defiance focused on two counts: first, the truth of her voices; second, her male dress. Standing up to authority has cost many a life, but to lose one's life for one's dress, to express one's separateness, one's inalienable self through one's clothes, is unusual. Yet Joan's transvestism was taken very seriously indeed, by the assessors of Rouen, who condemned her for it, and also by herself. It ranked of equal significance for her with the truth of her voices" (146–147). Most likely it is this issue of "sexual ambiguity" that makes the comparison between Joan of Arc's fate and that of Sebastian's letters acute, as the female gender of the addressee of Sebastian's letter has never been ascertained satisfactorily (Warner 152).

13. "L" & "V"

Letters, or characters, have sounds and shapes, as well as—for those gifted with synaesthesia—colors. In *Invitation to a Beheading* Cincinnatus describes a character as "an upsilamba, becoming a bird or a catapult with wondrous consequences" (26). D. Barton Johnson has explained that this character "represents a blending of the ancient Greek 'upsilon' . . . and the 'lambda'" and the "shapes and the tropes are suggestive of Cincinnatus 's desire that his imprisoned words (as well as his person) take flight" ("The Alpha and Omega" 125). In *Sebastian Knight* V and L also have a significant role. "V." is the initial the narrator uses for his name. And the character in Knight's novel *Lost Property* which reads as an apology written by Sebastian to Clare is signed with an "L" (112). Both characters are singled out in one of the letters: "Life with you was lovely—and when I say lovely, I mean doves and lilies, and velvet, and that soft pink 'v' in the middle and the way your tongue curved up to the long, lingering 'l'" (110).

The origin of the letter "L" may be the Greek letter lambda, which has approximately the shape of an inverted "V" (just as the l-sound in the Cyrillic alphabet has the form of an inverted "v," especially in its handwritten variant) (*Encyclopaedia Britannica* 13: 533). (The letter "V" is closely related to the Greek letter upsilon as it was with the shape of a "V" that this letter passed into the Latin alphabet [*Encyclopaedia Britannica* 22: 656 and 921]).

If both letters are combined into one (much like the "upsilamba") the "V" and the inverted "V" form together (points touching) the letter "X." This letter is mentioned when V. travels to his dying brother and, worrying about the name of his destination, recalls the name of Dr. Starov who has warned him: "Doctor Starov. Alexander Alexandrovich Starov. The train chattered over the points, repeating those x's" (191).

Johnson has beautifully elucidated its triple echoes: "[t]he letter 'x' links the doctor, the sound of the train on the tracks, and the unknown name of the village, the 'x,' that the narrator seeks" (*Worlds in Regression* 30). "The letter (and sound) 'x,'" Johnson continues, "figures in another passage in which the biographer refuses to speculate about Sebastian's sex life." The decomposition of the letter "x" in a "V" and an inverted "V" may point to sexual inversion as homosexuality was called in the first half of the previous century, just as "the lambda is a lesbian and gay symbol with an only partly recovered history" (Zimmerman 747).

14. MANN

One of the more serious frictions Sebastian has with one of his publishers is about the latter's stricture of the way in which Sebastian expresses his disdain for a contemporary writer. This author is "influential and esteemed"; "an old story of his has just been selected for *Modern Masterpieces*," and his "sales in Germany are almost as tremendous" as in England, and who, according to Sebastian, owns his success to a "dark secret" (52/ 53).

Doubtless this writer is Nabokov's *bête noire*, Thomas Mann. His *Death in Venice* (1912) and *Magic Mountain* (1924) were soon after their publication translated into English. Nabokov called Mann "ridiculous" and a "quack" and *Death in Venice* "asinine" (Karlinsky, *Dear Bunny* 263 and 164; *SO* 57; see also *Selected Letters* 525–526).

The Oxford Companion to English Literature states that "*Death in Venice*, influenced particularly by the thought of Schopenhauer and Nietzsche, presents the artist and artistic creation in a highly ironic light" (614). Such a baffling comment is in line with the reverence usually observed for Mann and its actual wording is well tuned to the subject it praises. *Death in Venice* is more factually a catalogue of pederastic desires. The sybarite, a man of at least fifty years, is the famous Gustav Aschenbach, the object of his concupiscence Tadzio, a boy of about fourteen years. Aschenbach's prose is drenched in a bombastic aestheticism to give it respectability or to mask his real idolatry. Aschenbach is close to Aschenbecher, German for 'ashtray' and this might explain its repeated occurrence in *Sebastian Knight*.

As Emily Emery observes, the title of Sebastian Knight's story *The Funny Mountain* is a play on Mann's *Magic Mountain* (29). The hotel in Blauberg that is visited by Sebastian Knight is not a luxurious resort for regular quests. It is "a famous kurort" which offers special "treatment" for serious ailments (144, 104). The Beaumont hotel is situated on a mountain slope, past of "a cluster of hotels and sanatoriums" and both Sebastian and Nina expect to find there relief for their illnesses (119).

Plot and setting, a passionate but frustrated love affair in an upland kurort is elaborated at length in Mann's novel. The hotel, called

Berghof, is a Swiss sanatorium. The hero, Hans Castorp is "over head and ears in love" with Claudia Chauchat, a femme fatale, a "belle dame sans merci," whose maiden name, like Mme. Lecerf's "was not French but Russian" (*Magic Mountain* 229, 327, 136).

Like Mme. Lecerf's usage, Mme. Chauchat prefers to converse in French. Alluring as Mme. Chauchat may be, the origin of Castorp's love should be sought elsewhere. Castorp is infatuated with Mme. Chauchat because everything of her appearance "was precisely Pribislaw" (146). Much later, long after Mme. Chauchat has turned her attention to someone else, he still recalls their eyes, "'Tartar slits' and 'wolf's eyes' . . . the eyes of Pribislaw Hippe and Claudia Chauchat" (479). Pribislaw Hippe, "a grafting of German stock with Slavic" is the name of the boy Castorp was passionately in love with in his youth (120). The very summit of intimacy he had with Hippe occurs when Castorp borrows a pencil from him. It happens to be "a silver pencil-holder," and when its mechanism is shown by Hippe, "their two heads bent over it" (123). This motif, the amorous handling of a pencil, returns during the "carnival" party when "women dressed as men" and men wear women's clothes (322, 326). Again Castorp needs a pencil and this time it is Mme. Chauchat who lends him her "silver pencil" and when she shows him its mechanism "[t]heir heads [are] bent over it together" (332, 333).

Much later, in a dream, this silver pencil (which has not failed to raise Freudian attention among critics) becomes Hippe's: "I gave back to the ailing Claudia Chauchat Pribislaw Hippe's lead-pencil" (495).

That Mr. Silbermann handed "a delightful silver pencil" to V. is a token that the Castorp-Hippe story (mentioned so very incidentally in Mann's lengthy novel that it can be missed easily) should not be neglected when the traces *The Magic Mountain* has left in *Sebastian Knight* are considered. "Silber" is German for "silver," thus the name "Silbermann" combines the name of Mann with an important key to Mann's best-known novel. (The "masonic bond" Sebastian mentions in his castigation of second-class contemporary writers such as Mann, might refer to the "Masonic conferences" in *The Magic Mountain* [518]. One of the guests holding forth on this subject is Herr Settembrini, himself a "Freemason" [5–7], who borrows his name from Luigi Settembrini [1813–1876] who wrote "*I Neoplatonici* the tale of 'the platonic love' of two youths, and vaunts the superiority of male homosexuality" [Haggerty 786]).

The motif of the silver pencil has been used by Nabokov earlier in his novel *Despair*. Its hero, Hermann, comes across a tramp, Felix, whom he thinks is the very likeness of himself. He exchanges clothes with him and kills him in order to try to cash the insurance on his own life. During their first meeting Hermann wishes to note the wanderer's address and takes out his "notebook and silver pencil." But Felix prefers to write the address himself and while doing this Hermann observes that Felix "writes with his left hand." When Hermann leaves Felix, he suddenly feels "some long and disgusting orgy. The reason for this sickly-sweet afterglow was that he had, with a cool show of absentmindedness, pocketed my silver pencil" (13–14). The remarkable thing is that, although Hermann could still see Felix, he makes no attempt to ask for his pencil. During their next meeting it appears that Felix indeed "stole it." However, Hermann does not really mind the theft: "Well, anyway, let's let bygones—Have a cigarette" (76). And although Hermann makes fun of his French readers who may "discern mirages of sodomy in my partiality for a vagabond," he also remarks that a "procession of silver pencils marched down an endless tunnel of corruption" (159, 14).

At the end of this tunnel are probably the silver pencils stolen from Leonardo da Vinci. In his *Notebooks* he wrote down for the year 1458 that one Giacomo Andrea "comes to live with [him]" and twice stole a silver pencil, one "on the 7th day of September . . . a silver point of the value of 22 soldi" and the other "on the 2nd April . . . a silver point . . . of the value of 24 soldi" (*Notebooks* II: 438, 439).

The second stolen pencil sugggests that the first one had been replaced, not returned. Having young pupils in their shops was customary at that time, Leonardo started his own career in this way. But Giacomo Andrea, whatever his artistic skills might have been, had much to offer. According to Giorgio Vasari, Giacomo was "a pleasingly graceful and handsome boy . . . with beautiful thick, curly hair which greatly pleased Leonardo" (234). "This," writes Leonardo's recent biographer Charles Nicholl, "says a lot without actually saying" that theirs was "a homosexual relationship" (272). Most likely Nabokov, who lectured on Leonardo and whom he regarded as a supreme artist (see my chapter on Leonardo in *Nabokov and the Art of Painting*), had some knowledge of this part of the painter's life. And Nabokov might have seen Freud's *Leonardo da Vinci. A Psychosexual Study of an Infantile Reminiscence*, where the silver pencil episode is discussed in its chapter 3. (A silverpoint, or silver stylus, and a silver pen are both used exclusively for scribing and drawing. After the discovery of graphite in 1554 [*Encyclopaedia Britannica* 17: 460–462] the lead pencil began to replace the silver point. In *Transparent Things* "Shakespeare's birth year" is mentioned as the one "when pencil lead was discovered," which is the year 1564 [7].)

15. MOON

The moon is frequently seen in the universe of Nabokov's oeuvre, very often associated with homosexuals. Nabokov with this connection follows a tradition well established in Russia's Silver Age as has been discussed in Olga Skonechnaia's article on "People of the Moonlight." In Shakespeare's *As You Like It* Rosalind, travestied as Master Ganymede (what is in a name?) is called an "effeminate" and "a moonish youth" (3.2.436). Possibly this association goes back to the speech of Aristophanes who in Plato's *Symposium* says that "originally the male sprang from the sun . . . while the sex which was both male and female came from the moon" (59–60).

In *The Gift* Yasha writes in her diary "I am fiercely in love with . . . Rudolf . . . - and this is just as fruitless as falling in love with the moon" (43). After Yasha has committed suicide Nabokov switches the attention to "the cast-off banana skin," which image combines "fruitless" and "moon" with a banana, which has the shape and color of a crescent moon (48). In *Glory* Archibald Moon, who is addicted "to uranism," yearns for a slice of "lemon," also a falcate yellow piece of fruit (97, 69). The "Brazil nut," "stolen" by the "white-robed armchair" in Sebastian's bedroom, is another lunate fruit (35). In *Pnin* the blond Englishman, Jack Cockerell, "evidently one of the people of the lunar light" is described as "moon-faced" (Naiman 101; *Pnin* 187). *Pale Fire*'s Kinbote, Nabokov's homosexual par excellence, is persistently associated with the moon. In *Sebastian Knight* Mr. H. looks at a photograph of him as a boy, "a moonfaced urchin," and the butler to the old colonel in *The Prismatic Bezel* is also "moonfaced" (38, 91).

In *Mary* Kolin one of the two ballet dancers (a "Harmless couple" . . . "happy as a pair of ring doves") is powdering his nose (64). Archibald Moon's nose is also powdered, and one may wonder for what reason the "talc-powder tin" in Sebastian's bathroom has been emptied (35).

And it is noteworthy that V., while discussing his own ideas about the role sex has in a relationship, quotes from Sebastian's *The Back of the Moon*.

16. "MRS. BATHURST"

In Rudyard Kiplin's story "Mrs. Bathurst" (1904), a number of men sit together, gossiping, to kill time. The main character who is introduced into the tale, is a man whose "name begins with a V.," from Vickery (78). Vickery, a married man, meets in Auckland a Mrs. Bathurst, reputed to make a man who "gets struck" with her "crazy" unless he "saves himself" (83). It is also known that Vickery turns up in Cape Town where he, day after day, goes to see the same movie because its shows Mrs. Bathurst very briefly among the many passengers leaving a ship. Finally, Vickery is found dead in a teak forest near the Zambesi, together with another dead man "looking up at him." Both are "burned to charcoal" but Vickery is recognized because of a tattoo saying "M. V.," as easily readable as writing which "shows up white on a burned letter" (91).

The coincidences with *Sebastian Knight* are striking: the use of the initial "V"; the femme fatale, the repeated seeing of a movie that shows the woman concerned for only a few seconds, and the identifying burnt letter. The main mystery of Kipling's story is of course why a man so deeply enraptured by a woman ends his life in the close company of a man.

17. NESBIT

In February 1937 Nabokov went to England in search of an academic job. He used his stay also for a day's visit to Cambridge, which left many reminiscences in *Speak, Memory* (271–273). And, as Brian Boyd remarks, it inspired Nabokov to compose V.'s trip to Cambridge to interview Sebastian's friend. What is "a raw February day" in *Speak Memory* is the "bleak day in February" in *Sebastian Knight*. Part of that day Nabokov spent talking with his old friend Nesbit, who was absent-minded due to his concern for his "cousin or maiden sister who kept house for him." Sebastian's friend, who was quite easily distracted by his cat, has a sister who takes care of part of his belongings. Like Nesbit, Sebastian's friend had literary interests and an academic career. Whether the correspondences stop with respect to the fact that "Nesbit and his friends . . . frowned upon . . . things . . . such as . . . girls," is another question (267).

18. PROUST

Marcel Proust is, together with William Shakespeare, the author most frequently alluded to in *Sebastian Knight*. When asked, in 1930, whether he liked Proust, Nabokov replied "[n]ot just like; I simply adore him. I have read all twelve volumes through twice" (qtd. in Boyd, *VNRY* 354).

Le Temps Retrouvé, the last part of *À la recherche du temps perdu*, his magnum opus, known by English readers as *Remembrance of Things Past*, is among Sebastian's books. In it Proust explains that the past cannot truly be revived by "the artificial impression of it which we form for ourselves when we attempt by an act of will to imagine it." Instead we have to rely on details and "things which logically had no connection with it and which later have been separated from it by our intellect which could make nothing of them for its own rational purposes" (3: 902). Sebastian could have learned from it that *Lost Property*, "his most autobiographical work" cannot hold his "purest emotions" because of the added Britishness, alien to Sebastian's Russian childhood (6, 24). And Sebastian uses the adjective "Proustian" for a digression, seemingly because of its length (but which might possibly indicate a Proustian side of Sebastian) (52).

In Goodman's opinion, Sebastian "copied" Proust, and is he inclined to the same "listless 'interesting' pose" as Proust (114).

The habit Sebastian had in Cambridge of writing in bed, he shares with Proust. The same goes for their fondness of taxis; it was with a taxi driver, Alfred Agostinelli, that Proust was deeply in love. In the last part of his life Sebastian is seen "wearing a scarf round his neck even in the warmest dining-room" (181). Proust was equally easily affected by cold; in the spring of 1922 (he died half a year later) Proust was invited to a black-tie dinner (James Joyce was among the other guests) and "kept his fur coat on throughout the evening" (De Botton 120). Sebastian's reverence for the memory of his mother recalls Proust's deep admiration for his mother (see Painter 585).

In *Lectures on Literature*, written in 1940 before *Sebastian Knight* was published, Nabokov writes that Proust hides his "keen appreciation of male beauty" "under the masks of recognizable paintings . . . and young females" (vii, 228). Proust began writing his opus in 1906 and at that time masculine beauty was praised rather unrestrainedly in Oscar Wilde's *The Portrait of Dorian Gray* (1890), André Gide's *The Immoralist* (1902), Michael Kuzmin's *Wings* (1906), and later in Thomas Mann's *Death in Venice* (1912). Proust preferred to comply publicly with the prevailing correct norms of his time, even to such an extent that in the part titled *Cities of the Plain* (its original title was *Sodome et Gomorrhe* [1921–1922]) he presented a most painful diatribe against homosexuals, full of hatred. It starts with the narrator's spying on the overtures M. de Charles (who has been given, according to Nabokov, "the greatest portrait in literature of a homosexual" [*Lectures on Literature* 234]) makes to the former tailor Jupien (*Remembrance of Things Past* 2: 623–637). This spying reminds the narrator "of the scene at Montjouvain" which has been mentioned in section 4, 10 on "The Enchanted Garden" (*Remembrance of Things Past* 2: 630). The "purpose" of this scene, Nabokov writes, is "to start the long series of homosexual revelations and revaluations of characters that occupy so many pages in the later volumes and produces such changes in the aspects of various characters" (*Lectures on Literature* 232).

In his "Proustian parenthesis" Sebastian admonishes his publisher for dubbing him "a budding author," which seems "misapplied" by Sebastian who claims to be a writer who springs "into blossom in one bound" (52). "Budding" and "blossom" recall titles from parts of Proust's opus. Its second part is titled *A l'ombre de jeunes filles en fleurs*, which Nabokov translates as *In the Shade of Blooming Young Girls*. Proust's first translator, C.K. Scott Moncrieff, selected the title *Within a Budding Grove* and translated "*jeunes filles en fleurs*" as "blossoming girls" (*Lectures on Literature* 207; *Remembrance of Things Past* 1: 1040). If a writer is "budding" and "blossoming" he is compared with flowers. The question, though, is to what flowers is the writer being compared? The answer to this question is given at the end of the lyrical passages in which Proust's narrator describes his enrapture with the hawthorns along the "Swann's way," which "could but and blossom in pink flowers alone" (qtd. in Nabokov [233]). (Nabokov uses Scott Moncrieff's translation, published in 1922. Moncrieff's translation has been revised because the French edition from which he worked was imperfect; the revision by Terence Kilmartin has: "which, wherever it budded, wherever it was about to blossom, could do so in pink alone" [*Remembrance of Things Past* 1: 153].) Like violet, whose color results from mixing red with blue, lavender, and pink are lighter shades of bluish red.

19. QUEER

"Queer" denotes a variety of meanings such as "strange," "odd," and "eccentric." It is also a synonym for "homosexual." The *Oxford English Dictionary* recorded this latter meaning for the first time in 1932. Sherron E. Knopp mentions that Vita Sackville-West used this word in this sense two years earlier in her novel *The Edwardians*. Its hero is a young aristocrat, Sebastian. He meets "a sailor and an adventurer," Leonard Anquetil, "twenty-odd years" his senior (55–56). Sebastian, who has inspired Anquetil with "romantic notions," tells him that he is "a queer sort of fellow" to which Anquetil answers: "Do I seem queer to you? I assure you, you seem equally queer to me" (56, 57). Anquetil invites Sebastian to join him on his next trip, but Sebastian declines. Six years later, Sebastian happens to see Anquetil again and is "flooded by an inexplicable happiness" (221). The novel ends with Sebastian's acceptance of Anquetil's extended invitation, "Come with me" (222). Sackville-West was married to Harold Nicholson, diplomat, biographer, and author of the popular collection of fictitious biographical sketches of acquaintances, *Some People*. Of this book Nabokov wrote "I greatly admired *Some People* and I may have added that in my thirties (when writing *Sebastian Knight*) I was careful to steer clear of its hypnotic style" (*Selected Letters* 442). As *The Edwardians* was a bestseller as well, it will have been noticed by Nabokov, the more so as the successful authors were presented in the newspapers together as a couple (Glendinning 231).

Sackville-West uses the word "queer" in isolation: there is nothing to indicate what Sebastian or Anquetil might have had in mind when calling each other "queer." The same goes for *Sebastian Knight*; no hint is given as to what prompts Sheldon to find that Sebastian looks "queer" (107). This is the only instance in which Nabokov, who in *Sebastian Knight* very frequently uses the word "queer," does not substantiate its intended meaning with ample and specific illustrations. For example, Sebastian's "queer mistakes" in his usage of English are

Motifs: Identities

followed by no less than six specimens (46). It can also be observed that in *Sebastian Knight* "queer" is always used to qualify things or incidents, with two exceptions when it typifies characters, Sebastian and William, a character from *Success*. William is the heroine's "first queer effeminate fiancé, who afterwards jilted her"; who is on familiar terms with an old conjuror, who has troubles with his heart for which he consults a doctor, Coates, and who entertains mental pictures of "forbidden bliss" (96–98). The similarities with the author of the novel seem conspicuous and are listed in section 4, 26. (Sebastian, who "liked to display [his hands] with feminine coquetry," is reported to "experience a queer twinge . . . in his left arm" [114, 87]. In *The Eye*, the protagonist Smurov, who has also "mincing gestures," "belongs" according to an acquaintance, to "the sexual lefties" [88].)

20. ROBINSONNADA

The suffix "-ade," (if it is supposed that "Robinsonnada" is a mispronunciation of Robinsonade) turns a word into an act or product. But because "Robinson" is not a verb or noun, the suffix is perhaps added to suggest a collection of Robinsons, just as in words like "salade" and "parade" a number of its components is implied. Robinson, just like Robin, is a name derived from Robert. In *Sebastian Knight* only one Robin is mentioned, in *Cock Robin Hits Back*, the title Sebastian proposed for the novel that was published as *The Prismatic Bezel* (see comment on line 70/ 11). Clare was by no means in favor of Sebastian's first choice "[a] title," she says, "must convey the colour of the book, not its subject" (70).

In this way Clare associates Cock Robin with a color. The robin is well known for its red breast. The robin is also alluded to in the color "egg-shell blue" of the notepaper used by Sebastian's correspondent, as its best known variant is the color "Robin's Egg Blue" (see comment on line 36/ 7). In this way the robin adds another combination of red and blue (see section 3, 6, where the motif of colors is reviewed in more detail).

"Cock Robin" is a nursery thyme and with the "red-capped German gnome" and the "brownie" one seems to have entered a childhood's fairyland. The "red-capped" directs its residents to Grimm's fairy tale of "Little Red Riding Hood." This tale is referred to in *The Enchanter*: "the lone wolf was getting ready to don Granny's nightcap" (67). Gnomes were, in popular traditions called dwarfs or goblins, malicious spirits that branched into well-disposed hobgoblins (Briggs 193–194).

The best known "Hobgoblin" is Puck, also called "Robin Goodfellow," the fairy from Shakespeare's *Midsummer-Night's Dream* (2.1.40, 2.1.34). Oberon, King of the Fairies, desires to have a young knight whom the Queen

> [A]s her attendant hath
> A lovely boy, stol'n from an Indian King;
> She never had so sweet a changeling;
> And jealous Oberon would have the child
> Knight of his train, to trace the forest wild.
> (2.1.21–25)

As the Queen Titania refuses to part with the boy, Oberon asks Puck to cast a spell on Titania by squeezing a magic juice on her eyelids while she sleeps. This juice, a love potion, can be obtained from

> [A] little western flower,
> Before milk-white, now purple with love's wound,
> And maidens call it, love-in-idleness.
> (2.1.166–168)

This flower is the "Viola tricolor" from which the pansy has been cultivated (Kerr 23). Once under the charm Titania consents to give Oberon "her changeling" (4.1.65). When V. during his visit to Mme. Lecerf in her country house ponders the idea to make love to her (instead of returning to Paris), he calls this thought "a changeling" (169).

21. RUBÁIYÁT

Omar Khayyám's quatrains collected in the *Rubáiyát* as translated by Edward Fitzgerald were immensely popular in the first half of the twentieth century. The many editions (about 2,000 separate editions and reprints have been published since 1859, the year of the first edition, see Martin and Mason [4]) are often lavishly illustrated by well known artists. The fourth quatrain, as illustrated by Edmund J. Sullivan, a British artist who lived from 1869 to 1933, shows a lady among blossoming trees. The illustration for the same quatrain by Gordon Ross, an

American artist (1873–1946), is very similar, although this lady is actually touching some boughs. The similarity suggests that this representation is a typical icon for this quatrain, of which the text, in Fitzgerald's translation, is:

> Now the New Year reviving old Desires,
> The thoughtful Soul to Solitude retires,
> Where the White Hand of Moses on the Bough
> Puts out, and Jesus from the Ground suspires.

In a note the "White Hand of Moses" is elucidated: "In the *Koran* Moses draws forth his hand and it becomes magically white, and thus the bough whitens with blossoms perhaps" (Khayyám [Pocket Book] 8; the other consulted edition is published by Avon).

The highly erotic way in which the Rubáiyát has usually been illustrated (girls often in dishabille) deserves attention as the text of the quatrains is never explicit on this point. Sometimes, as in XX a beloved is addressed ("Ah my Belovéd, fill the Cup that clears") or suggested as in XI ("A Flask of Whine, a Book of Verse—and Thou") but these are rare exceptions.

"Where FitzGerald," writes Doris Alexander, "worked most intimately from his own interacting memories and treated the original Omar most freely and even cavalierly, was in the quatrains about sexual pleasure. Not only did he cut the proportion of such quatrains drastically, but he differed even more drastically in his conception of the subject from his originals. In a Mohammedan culture, were women are looked upon as domestic breeding animals and kept in careful seclusion to produce authentic sons, they are not thought of as companions. In the original Persian quatrains love is mentioned ironically, for they recommend transitory sexual delight. So the boy wine-bearer, the 'Saki' ready to fulfill all desires, is the traditional companion in pleasure among the epigrams of the Persian *Rubáiyát*" (69–70). Curiously, William Martin and Sandra Mason mention the reference in Khayyám's verses "to the idea of 'a happy opportunity with a moon faced one'" (28).

On the webpage titled "Keys to *The Gift*" (keystogift.com), edited by Yuri Leving, the note on page 71 concerning the Persian miniaturist Riza Abbasi gives interesting details about the amorous role of the "Saki." Nabokov refers to the *Rubáiyát* in his *Lectures on Don Quixote* where he quotes Fitzgerald's quatrain XLIX (168) and in *Lolita*, quoting from VI (262, see also 381). Nabokov liked FitzGerald's translation "tremendously," an admiration that ended "suddenly" when in the 1960s Nabokov learned about the nature of FitzGerald's paraphrases (Zimmer, Nabokv-L, 2 November 2003; *Strong Opinions* 246).

As most editions of Fitzgerald's translations are illustrated, one can distinguish three versions of the *Rubáiyát*:

- the original Persian version with the "Saki" as lover
- the purified sexless Fitzgerald translation
- the erotic heterosexual version as depicted by the illustrating artists

And the English reader might as well (instead of to the *Koran*) refer to the *Bible* to clarify the comparison with Moses in quatrain IV: And [Moses] put his hand into his bosom: and when he took it out, behold, his hand was leprous as snow" (51). This reference and the illustrated *Rubáiyát* might explain why Mme. Lecerf compares herself to a "Persian princess" who "blighted the Palace Gardens" just as the flowers "withered" as she touched them" (164).

22. SEXUALITY

According to V. the tragic turns Sebastian life takes during his last ten years (the break-up with Clare, the estrangements from his friends, his loneliness, and the aggravation of his health problems) are all due to Sebastian's infatuation with Nina Rechnoy. This enthrallment must have been exclusively sexual, "[f]or what could her conversation have been, if indeed she *had* managed to get acquainted with that quiet, unsociable, absent-minded Englishman at the Beaumont Hotel?" (147). Notwithstanding this sensible comment V. thinks that "granting 'sex' a special situation when tackling a human problem, or worse still, letting the 'sexual idea,' if such a thing exists, pervade and 'explain' all the rest, is a grave error of reasoning" (103). Such an unrestrictive formulation seems a rather flagrant dictum for an author writing a biography of a person who, according to this biographer, let his life, when the occasion was there, be governed by sexual impulses.

By quoting from Sebastian's writings V. suggests that Sebastian shares his opinions that sex does not matter.

Motifs: Identities 139

As Lara Delage-Toriel has demonstrated, these quotations contradict rather than support V.'s statement:

> Under the pretext that "the word 'sex' with its hissing vulgarity and 'ks, ks' catcall at the end" (*Sebastian Knight* 103) is so inane as to be senseless, V. brushes the subject away, grouping a series of cryptic quotations 'randomly' picked from Sebastian's works:
> 'The breaking of a wave cannot explain the whole sea, from its moon to its serpent; but a pool in the cup of a rock and the diamond-rippled road to Cathay are both water.' (*The Back of the Moon.*)
> 'Physical love is but another way of saying the same thing and not a special sexophone note, which once heard is echoed in every other region of the soul' (*Lost Property*, page 82).
> 'All things belong to the same order of things, for such is the oneness of human perception, the oneness of individuality, the oneness of matter, whatever matter may be. The only real number is one, the rest are mere repetition' (ibid, page 83)" (*Sebastian Knight* 103).
> Broken down to their essential meaning, these quotations do, however, emerge in radical contradiction with their sophistic purpose and their apparently haphazard juxtaposition helps gradually to enforce the idea that sex is part and parcel of an amorous relationship ("a pool in the cup of a rock and the diamond-rippled road to Cathay" are all made of the same element), that sex therefore cannot be distinguished as a seperate entity within the configuration of this relationship ("physical love" is "not a special sexophone note," it resonates throughout), since this relationship is indivisible ("The only real number is one, the rest are mere repetition"). From a crude analogy to a monistic profession of faith, these quotations distil the idea that sex is a fundamental constituant of a relationship, and should therefore not be shrugged off as irrelevant. The whole episode in fact is steeped in irony at V.'s expense, since his preteritive allegation—"naturally, I cannot touch upon the intimate side of their relationship" (103)—is followed by a lengthy and rather contorted treatment of the very subject that had been dismissed, with the final admission that "being dissatisfied with things in general, [Sebastian] might have been dissatisfied with the colour of his romance too" (104). (Delage-Toriel, "Ultraviolet Darlings" 37–38)

Even more curious is that *Sebastian Knight* seems to have no homosexual characters. *Mary* has its couple of ballet dancers, *The Eye* its protagonist Smurov, *Glory*, as has been discussed, Archibald Moon, and poor Yasha Chernyshevski's fate is felt throughout *The Gift*. The protagonist of *Despair* has distinct homosexual inclinations and so has Pierre, the executioner in *Invitation to a Beheading*. These novels were written before *Sebastian Knight*. About a year after having finished this novel, Nabokov wrote the story "Solus Rex" with its protagonist Prince Adolf, an ostentatious homosexual and exhibitionist who makes Kinbote seem a prudish ascetic.

23. SHERLOCK HOLMES

V., in search of Lydia Bohemsky, uses "an old Sherlock Holmes stratagem" (151). Bohemsky is of course the same person as "the fat Bohemian woman" mentioned by Sebastian in *The Doubtful Asphodel* (173).

In Arthur Conan Doyle's story, "A Scandal in Bohemia," this historic Kingdom (under the Habsburg rule until 1918, when it became part of Czechoslovakia) is supposed to still have a king of its own. The adjective Bohemian has another meaning as it is applied to people having an unconventional lifestyle. Holmes, a drug-addicted bachelor who loathes "every form of society" is said to have a "Bohemian soul" (Doyle, *The Complete Sherlock Holmes* 3–4).

The plot of "A Scandal in Bohemia" is grounded on the threat of blackmail, as Irene Adler, the former lover of the King of Bohemia, has a photograph showing both the king and herself. The king, now wishing to marry with the second daughter of the King of Scandinavia, is convinced that Irene Adler will send the photograph to the bride's family and that the marriage will be canceled. Irene Adler is a "contralto" and a "prima donna," like Helene von Graun, who has "a splendid contralto" and is a "lovely tall primadonna" (Doyle, *Complete* 11; *Sebastian Knight* 130, 173).

When Mr. Silbermann tells V. that he is with the police, not a uniformed policeman but a "[p]lain-clothes," he suggests to V. the idea of "consult[ing] a private detective" (125–126).

Eventually it is Mr. Silbermann himself who takes up this role. What is farcical in Mr. Silbermann's acting is that he can produce within a few days a complete list of all the guests who stayed at the Beaumont Hotel in June 1929, with numerous details (which even the hotel manager could not have provided) including addresses, appearances, positions in society and even the first names of the female guests. Still more ridiculous is that he can produce a list of the addresses of "all the hotel-gentleman's" instantaneously (128). This is not a parody of the plot-saving technique of a *deus ex machina*, but rather a parody, albeit a burlesque one, "of the Sherlock Holmes vogue" (92). In the Doyle story Holmes receives a note and within a few seconds deduces that the "paper was made in Bohemia" and that "the man who wrote the note is a German" (7). While reasoning, Holmes mentions "factories and paper mills," words repeated incoherently by Mr. Silbermann: "factory. Paper" (Doyle, *Complete* 7; *Sebastian Knight* 124). And when Holmes wishes to know a bit more about Irene Adler he simply sees what his archive says on this matter, because Holmes "has adopted a system of docketing all paragraphs concerning men and things" (Doyle, *Complete* 11).

The Author of Trixie by William Caine (published in 1924, about forty years after the publication of the first Sherlock Holmes story), is a frivolous tale consisting of nugatory dialogues. In the course of the narrative a private detective is employed to find out whether a Mr. Roache has committed any misdemeanors during his life. Without any delay at all, the dectective has a long list with all Mr. Roache's peccadillos enumerated. This is explained by the sleuth: "since I started this little business of mine . . . I have accumulated data, of one sort or another, relative to not less than sixty-five thousand ladies and gentlemen of position and means" (151–152). Mr. Silbermann seems to fit in a tradition of detectives who have a gift of producing the most unexpected information on whatever subject at the very moment that it is required.

Like the King of Bohemia, Sherlock Holmes falls in love with Irene Adler. It is the only woman Holmes is attracted to, as he has an "aversion to women" (Doyle, *Complete* 478). Irene was an exception "with a face a man might die for" (17). But perhaps it was not her loveliness (which has it limits anyhow as "she has a soul of steel") but her mind, which appealed to Holmes, as it was "the mind of the most resolute of men" (12, 13). A "male costume" suits her as well and she "often take[s] advantage of the freedom which it gives" (27). One may compare Holmes's admiration of Irene's mind with V's appreciation of Clare's imagination, which "was of a particularly strong, almost masculine, quality" (*Sebastian Knight* 81).

Susan Elizabeth Sweeney, in her article "Purloined Letters: Poe, Doyle, Nabokov," has studied in great detail how much Doyle's story owes to Edgar Allan Poe's "The Purloined Letter." In this story the threat of blackmail is based on a letter stolen from the Queen of France, evidence of an illicit love affair which she wishes to hide from the King. The letter is stolen by Minister D. who, in order to prevent its being recaptured, has turned the letter inside out and has given it a new address. Poe emphasizes "the radicalness of these differences" between the original and the new address: the first was written "markedly bold and decided," the other "diminutive and feminine" (150). That Clare's handwriting is described as a "bold feminine scrawl" (*Sebastian Knight* 36), mirrors the handwriting in Poe's letter. But now the masculine "bold" (which characterizes the Queen's lover's script) is merged with the "feminine" aspect.

The Russian letter in which V. sees the words, "thy manner always," is in a way purloined as well, because V. attributes it to a woman without knowing who the sender was. It is this letter which "perplexe[s]" V. and prompts his quest (36). But unlike Poe's story in which the purloined letter is retrieved, the true sender of the Russian letter is never identified. (Nina Rechnoy can of course be crossed out, because someone who "never read, anyway" her admirer's letters is the least likely person to write (a bundle of) letters to the same [159].)

Lydia Bohemsky seems to be a bohemian *pur-sang*. In a few months she has three different addresses, the most recent in Paris, near "the Santé prison," that is in the 14th Arrondissement and on the avant-garde Left Bank (151). She has "waved bright orange hair, purplish jowls and some dark fluff over her painted lip" (151). "It is . . . intriguing," writes Sweeney, "given Irene Adler's transsexual disguise . . . , that Lydia Bohemsky is described as visibly masculine beneath her feminine surface, to the extent that she seems a transvestite" ("Purloined Letters" 235). The proximity of the prison may be mentioned as a reminder how liable to punishment homosexual practices were.

As a nonconformist Lydia Bohemsky seems to be the ideal person to interrogate about the social communications between the guests in the Beaumont Hotel, an opportunity that does not even cross V.'s mind to profit from.

24. SNAKES

The casting of skins, as snakes and caterpillars do, is often associated with the renewal of life and immortality. Sebastian who writes that he is "fed up with . . . the patterns of [his] shed snake-skins," is speaking of worries of a different kind (183). The simile is remarkable as the pattern

Motifs: Identities 143

of a snake's skin returns when the snake has sloughed off its older one. Perhaps Sebastian suggests that his person has undergone more drastic changes, incompatible with the pattern of his exterior appearance.

The comparison with a snake, having movements that can be described as "a series of waves" (*Encyclopaedia Britannica* 20: 850) recalls the "succession of waves," which Sebastian employs in *The Doubtful Asphodel* to "express" a "hidden meaning" (174), or the "wavy lines," which in *Success* precedes the successful meeting of two persons bound to share their lives (95). It is also worth mentioning that Sebastian in *The Back of the Moon* (quoted by V. when discussing the role of sexuality) links a "wave" with the "moon" and a "serpent" (103). As Sebastian, after having referred to his "shed snake-skins," writes that he finds "a poetic solace in the obvious and the ordinary which for some reason or other [he] had overlooked in the course of [his] life," it seems unlikely this change in his life is related to Nina Rechnoy as it is difficult to see how she can be classified as a "solace" by Sebastian (183).

The passage "[t]he breaking of a wave cannot explain the whole sea, from its moon to its serpent" is supposed to elucidate the role of sexuality in relationships. The waves with its own moon and its own serpent, jointly presented in one sentence to express a certain psychological meaning, seem to belong to a particular seascape. It recalls one of the engravings by Gustave Doré, made to illustrate Samuel Coleridge's famous poem *The Rhyme of the Ancient Mariner*. In the engraving number 20, called "The water-snakes," a sea is depicted with huge snakes coiling in the light of the moon. It illustrates a scene from Part IV of the poem, in which the doomed mariner, after "[t]he moving Moon went up to the sky," watches "water-snakes" whose "rich attire" he admires as well as the way "they coiled and swam."

Then, suddenly, "A spring of love gushed from [his] heart," and this appears to be the turning point in the mariner's life (Coleridge 197–198). His curse is lifted from him and the time of peril comes to an end. (In *Look at the Harlequins!* Nabokov refers to Coleridge's "little golden sea snakes" and to Coleridge's mariner, "a naked old man with a rag around his foremast, gliding supine into full moon whose shaky reflections rippled among the water lilies" [166, 243].)

Curiously, it is a snake (or rather snakeskins) to which Sebastian refers in his last letter, to mark a turning point in "the course of [his] life." He writes that he is "fed up [*osskomina*] with a number of tortuous things and especially with the patterns of my shed snake-skins [*vypolziny*]." In section 3.2 the correspondences between Sebastian's and Pushkin's dates of their death are mentioned. The word *vypolziny* forms another link between Sebastian and Pushkin, because they both use this rare word a few days before their death. (The reference to Joan of Arc in Sebastian's letter may also echo Pushkin's "The Last of the Relatives of Joan of Arc," written also shortly before his death [see Binyon 601]. "The Last of the Relatives of Joan of Arc" is the title of a little sketch in which Voltaire is berated for having written *La Pucelle*, a scandalous mock-epic on the French heroine replete with sexual innuendoes [see Stewart].)

Late in January 1837 Pushkin met Vladimir Dal, a doctor and a lexicographer (Nabokov, who acquired his four-volume Russian dictionary in Cambridge, transliterates his name as "Dahl" [*Speak, Memory* 265]). "It was at this meeting with Dal," writes Serena Vitale, "that Pushkin first heard the word *vypolzina* (from *vypolzat*, 'to creep or cawl out') designating the skin sloughed off by snakes every year. 'We call ourselves writers,' he exclaimed, 'yet we are ignorant of half of the words of the Russian language!' When he saw Dal again the next day, he was wearing a black frock coat fresh from the tailor. 'Do you like my new skin?' he asked with a laugh. 'This one's going to last me quite a while. I won't shed it soon.' In fact he was to wear it for just a few days" because it had to be removed from his body after his deadly duel with d'Anthès (Vitale 247).

Nabokov had already used this rare word in *The Gift* (originally written in Russian) in the phrase "*banannaia vypolzina*" (qtd. in Shvabrin, *Nabokov as a Translator* 380 note 3).

In the English version this is translated as "the cast-off banana skin," which is seen in Yasha's room at the very moment of Yasha's suicide near a lake. Yasha was "in love with the soul" of another boy, an attachment he felt "as fruitless as falling in love with moon" (*The Gift* 48, 43). In *Pale Fire* it is Kinbote, who, like Pushkin, compares a garment with a skin by calling a "gorgeous silk dressing gown" a "veritable dragonskin of oriental chromas" (159). One may also recall Uncle Ruka's ophidian ring (*Speak, Memory* 69).

The shedding of one's skin or the stripping of one's garment means a degree of exposure, while the combination with the three homophile characters (Yasha, Kinbote, Uncle Ruka) suggests that Sebastian's use of the word *vypolziny* can be understood as his coming out.

25. ST. SEBASTIAN

When in 1926 Nabokov's brother Sergey converted to Catholicism it "conjure[d] in Vladimir's mind the depictions of the suffering Saint Sebastian," writes Stacy Schiff (99). "Repeated in a thousand forms in Italian painting and sculpture, he is the ultimate symbol of Renaissance art" (Paglia 148). Will Ogrinc, who has collected some 850 pictorial images of St. Sebastian, has described the development in the representations of the saint. In the thirteenth century he appears as a mediaeval knight, until the beginning of the fifteenth century when he is shown as a martyr: a young man, nude apart from a loincloth, tied to a tree or a pillar, pierced with arrows. The Italian Renaissance has given him an Apollonian beauty often with feminine traits; a well curved body, long well groomed hair, and girlish looks. It is this androgynous image that has become a homoerotic icon. Tadevosyan and Shrayer discuss many examples of literary expressions of the "'homosexual cult' of St. Sebastian" (30–35). Sebastian is also the name adopted by Oscar Wilde after his release from prison: Sebastian Melmoth. The second name is borrowed from Charles Maturin's Faust-like novel *Melmoth the Wanderer*, but Wilde changed its protagonist's first name, John, into Sebastian. This name might have been selected because Wilde, while in prison, had to wear his convict costume, "an ill-fitting suit printed with arrows all over it" (Wright 240).

The historical change in the pictorial representations of St. Sebastian is mirrored in the turn Sebastian Knight's life takes, from autonomous knight to vulnerable sufferer.

It is interesting to note that V., when making a similar comparison, specifies the color as the main omission in his biography at that stage: "[a]n unfinished picture—uncoloured limbs of the martyr with the arrows in his side" (123).

In *Speak, Memory* Nabokov mentions "a bullfight in San Sebastian," probably to indicate that a bull pierced with lances suffers no less than the martyr pierced with arrows (151).

26. SUCCESS

Sebastian Knight's novel *Success* is, according to V.'s summary, an imaginative tour de force in tracing the manœuvers fate employs to bring together two people's lives, those of Anne and of Percival. Anne, a conjuror's assistant, has a queer effeminate fiancé, William, who jilts her as he has done with "May, Judy, Juliette, Augusta" (98). William, whose talk to Anne is unintelligible, is much more at ease with the conjuror. As V. observes, the lengthy passage he quotes about William is "strangely connected with Sebastian's inner life at the time" (96). Indeed some incidents in the novel resemble those of Sebastian's life:

- Sebastian jilts Clare, just as William jilts Anne.
- William broke earlier with May, Judy, Juliette, and Augusta; Sebastian left Clare "in September" (109).
- Anne "hate[s]" William's "silly" "talking" Nina found the "way [Sebastian] spoke," his "obscure speech," "appalling" (96, 158).
- William has heart troubles, Sebastian has serious complaints about his heart (97)
- William's doctor is named "Coates," Sebastian's "Oates" (97, 104).
- William is the "queer effeminate fiancé," Sebastian displays his hands with "feminine coquetry" and looks "queer" (96, 114, 107).
- "I'm more bald than grey," is a remark by the conjuror, which recalls a line from Southey's "The Old Man's Comforts": "The few locks which are left you are grey"; and links it with the "elenctic" manager of the Blauberg hotel where Sebastian stayed, as discussed in section 3, 7.

Not related to William, but the ultimate goal of the quest in *Success* is the successful meeting, which, although it "seems accidental," happens when the lovers-to-be "use the same car" (94). This resembles Sebastian's meeting a man after which "they had gone in the man's car" (86).

27. THE TRAGEDY OF SEBASTIAN KNIGHT

Although V. jeers frequently at Mr. Goodman and his work, the reader should not dismiss Goodman's biography as readily as V. does. The main reason for this is that the quotations which V. gives from *The Tragedy of Sebastian Knight* provide the only information (apart from Sebastian's last letter) about Sebastian's life that does not depend on V.'s

Motifs: Identities — 147

manner of reporting. Of course, the selection of the samples is entirely V.'s and one can trust that he took the trouble to find the passages most open to ridicule. When V. met Goodman he does not know that Sebastian's former secretary has been writing Sebastian's biography. But for some reason V.'s animosity toward Goodman is already there. V.'s reason for visiting Goodman is not to learn something about Sebastian's life (it was too early for that as V. "intended to follow his [Sebastian's] life stage to stage") but "merely to obtain a few suggestions as to what people I ought to see who might know something of Sebastian's post-Cambridge period" (51–52). Before V. begins describing his visit he quotes a long and rather indignant letter written by Sebastian before *The Prismatic Bezel* was published. By inserting this letter in his report just when V. is about to enter Goodman's office, he contrives to suggest that the letter was addressed to Goodman. (It was not; the letter was written no later than 1925, while Sebastian engaged Goodman in 1930.) Entering Goodman's room, V. sees that a "black mask covered his face." This seems to justify V.'s distrust toward the Janus-faced secretary. However, the reader is informed at the end of the interview that Goodman "returned the black mask which [V.] pocketed." Obviously, the use of this mask has been premeditated by V. as a measure to ensure that Goodman would act according to the role V. had assigned for him.

Goodman was employed by Sebastian in 1930, after publication of his first three novels. Because his second novel, *Success*, was "brightly heralded and warmly acclaimed" (100), Sebastian was at that time a well-established author. It seems unlikely that the opinions expressed by Goodman about Sebastian as a writer differed widely from those of other critics or from the obituaries that appeared in the papers after Sebastian's death, as his biography "enjoyed a very good press" (59).

V. quotes several passages from Goodman's biography, all but one castigated severely. In chapter 3 V. discusses Goodman's assessment of Sebastian's attitude toward his Russian past, by quoting a passage from *The Doubtful Asphodel*. V. tries to counteract its suggestion of Russophobia by a quotation from *Lost Property* but this backfires as V. seems not to realize that the Russian countryside has no "spire[s]," but only domes and cupolas (25).

In chapter 7 V. examines with unbridled derision Goodman's attempts to position Sebastian as a writer thoroughly troubled by the disastrous Great War. V. ridicules the, what he calls, "chronometric concepts" Goodman uses, such as "Postwar Unrest" and "Postwar Generation," as the sources of Sebastian's major concerns (60). Although Goodman seems to be indeed outside the mark, one cannot blame him too much.

The Great War had an enormous impact on writers and poets and left hardly anyone unaffected (James Joyce might be the notorious exception). Marcel Proust includes this war in his *Remembrance of Things Past* in a substantial section, titled "M. de Charlus during the War" (3: 743–885). Nabokov entered Cambridge University soon after the conclusion of the Great War. There he had endless political discussions with another student who "had fought in the trenches," whom Nabokov, in *Speak, Memory*, calls Nesbit, acknowledges the strong influence of "the Georgian poets, Rupert Brooke, De la Mare, etc. by whom I was much fascinated at the time" (Boyd, *VNRY* 168; Karlinsky, *Dear Bunny* 87).

(The works of the Georgian poets appeared in numbered anthologies titled *Georgian Poetry*, which included poetry of all major "war poets" like Edmund Blunden, Robert Graves, Wilfred Owen, and Siegfried Sassoon. It was their prosody as well as their interest in the supernatural, which appealed to Nabokov. D. Barton Johnson writes that "Nabokov arrived in England at a time when British interest in spiritualism was exceptionally high—thanks to the thousands of families grieving for the First World War dead" ["Vladimir Nabokov and Walter de la Mare's 'Otherworld'" 84].)

In chapter 12 V. quotes from Goodman's biography some pictures of Sebastian's traits and habits. Goodman tells that he was usually received by Sebastian "lying in bed," that Sebastian "copied" Proust, that he "liked to pour half a bottle of French perfume into his morning bath." He also mentions that Sebastian "made a great show of Byronic languor," and dwells on Sebastian's aversion to "contemporary questions."

Although V.'s retaliations are always marked by a high measure of rudeness (he calls Goodman a "meddlesome old rogue" and his work and opinions "slapdash," "utterly preposterous," and "rubbish" [51, 13, 64, 67]), he now refrains from such affronts or even from any refutation at all. His only comment concerns "Mr. Goodman's glibness," a word qualifying Goodman's style rather than the contents of his prose (116).

This is remarkable as Sebastian's exuberant use of perfume, his display of his "sensitive hands . . . with feminine coquetry" and especially the comparisons with Proust and Byron, might be taken as indications of a homophile disposition (114). Why did V. let this pass, while it must have sounded inadmissible to his orthodox ears? Or does V. refer to this passage when he writes, "at a certain point of my search I was blindly enraged by a trashy concoction" (63)?

In *The Eye* a comparable puzzle is presented. Its hero, Smurov, professes to be deeply in love with a girl called Vanya. Somehow he reads a letter in which he is dubbed a homophile. This because of his "entire appearance, his frailness, his decadence, his mincing gestures, his fondness for Eau de Cologne" and his "passionate glances" at a male acquaintance (*The Eye* 88). In the same letter he is accused of being "a thief" and a kleptomaniac (89). What happens next is that Smurov feverishly but vainly tries to convince another acquaintance that he is no thief at all, but makes no attempt to contradict the statement about his sexual "perversion."

In his description of Sebastian appearance, V. is selective and repetitious. The reader is informed about a tiny birthmark once, twice about the physiognomy of his ears, thrice about the ("glossy") darkness of his hair, while his pale complexion is mentioned four times (69). It is from Roy Carswell that one learns that Sebastian was a "gaunt man" (114). Goodman also writes that Sebastian is "very thin" (114).

Goodman writes that Sebastian usually received him lying in his bed, and that Sebastian, copying Marcel Proust, favored "a certain listless 'interesting' pose," and that he even was "the perfect 'poseur'" (114). Writing in bed is a habit already noticed by Sebastian's Cambridge friend. The writer most famously connected with his bed is Marcel Proust. During the last decade of his life, Proust, due to ill health, spent most of his time in bed where he worked on *Remembrance of Things Past*. And Proust often received visitors in his bedroom. But it is not this reclusive way of life that Goodman points out as a habit which Sebastian shares with Proust, but their alleged "interesting pose."

Being a "perfect 'poseur'" is an indulgence that can be practiced only when there is an audience. But Sebastian was averse to receptions and dinners, and this is confirmed by what Goodman calls his "uncongeniality" (115). Not in the least uncongenial was Marcel Proust. He was a socialite with beautiful manners who delighted in soirées and receptions and used to talk with his many friends and acquaintances far too intensively to be able to act as a poseur simultaneously.

The references to Marcel Proust come much more to the point when one thinks of his friend, Comte Robert de Montesquiou, who is the main prototype for Proust's character Baron de Charlus, the principal protagonist of *Remembrance of Things Past* (Davenport-Hines 135; Painter 117). Montesquiou was an aristocrat and a *littérateur* whose main creation was his own public persona. In the portraits by James Whistler (*Portrait of Count Robert de Montesquiou*. 1891–92. The Frick Collection, New York) and by Giovanni Boldini (*Comte Robert de Montesquiou*. 1897. Musée d'Orsay, Paris) he is by all means what William Sansom calls him, "the *poseur* absolute" (49; see also the photographic portrait of Montesquiou reproduced on the same page, where he is holding two large stalks with white roses). These portraits all exhibit Montesquiou's "impenetrable façade of his vanity," but of course cannot disclose his "beautiful gestures" or the fragrance of his "lilac perfume" (Painter 125, 120).

V. writes that Sebastian "emphatically did not want to see [people]" (100), and his aloofness is mentioned so often that one must take this for granted. And the fact that Sebastian in his short life wrote four novels and three stories does not suggest that he gave much priority to impress the beau monde. Because he had to give his attention to the translations and new editions of his works as well, one should rather think of a man wedded to his desk than of a dandy.

This contrasts with Goodman's portrait of Sebastian, which shows him as an "extraordinary vain person" with a taste for posing with "Byronic languor" and who delights in the uxorial habits of using "French perfume" and whose gestures are noted for their "feminine coquetry." But is this portrait less plausible than that sketched by V. who wishes his readers to believe that Sebastian chases a woman for more than six years despite the fact that soon after their first meetings she repulsed him most fiercely?

28. ULYSSES

In Sebastian Knight's *The Prismatic Bezel* one of the twelve persons staying in the country house is "G. Abeson, art dealer" who is found murdered. The number of the company accrues as a chance passer-by, old Nosebag, happens to be in the lobby. But when old Nosebag removes his beard, it is G. Abeson who reappears.

Motifs: Identities

"Nosebag" is a word used by James Joyce in *Ulysses* when Mr. Bloom muses on the cabman's horses feeding on oats in the bags hanging on their heads: "Nosebag time." Next he passes the "cabman's shelter" (78). It is to this place that Bloom returns with Stephen Dedalus in the middle of the night. They hope that "they might hit upon some drinkables in the shape of a milk" (533). Instead of milk they are offered "coffee" by the keeper of the cabman's shelter (543). John Burt Foster Jr. has observed the correspondence with Sebastian's drinking "hot milk in the middle of the night at coffee stalls with taxi drivers" (*Sebastian Knight* 182; see also Foster 167). It is not explained why Sebastian prefers to enjoy his nocturnal hot milk in the company of taxi drivers, but the clear references to *Ulysses* indicate that Bloom's similar visit might help to answer this question.

The most conspicuous other guest in the Dublin shelter is a "red-bearded sailor" who has not seen his wife "for seven years" (Joyce 543–544). His name is "W.B. Murphy" but he might as well be "A. Boudin." On his chest he has several tattoos; representing an anchor, "the figure 16," and "a young man's side face" who appears to be "a Greek" named "Antonio" (551–552). On this "Antonio personage" Joyce comments that he has "no relation to the dramatic personage of identical name who sprang from the pen of our national poet" (556). This helpful hint should be honored by looking at the five Antonio's in Shakespeare's plays. One is the sea captain in *Twelfth Night*.

Curiously this play has received some considerable attention from critics of *Sebastian Knight*, independent from the reference to Joyce (see Frank 166–168). The first to discuss Shakespeare's play is Page Stegner because of its "mistaken identities," those of Sebastian and his twin sister Viola whose initial is the same as V.'s (70). In Samuel Schumann's *Nabokov's Shakespeare*, the same play is discussed (but most attention in Schumann's chapter on *Sebastian Knight* is devoted to *The Tempest*, because it also points to "self-reflective art," "a frequent feature of Nabokov's work" [42]).

In *Twelfth Night* a young lady, Viola, arrives, after a shipwreck, in Illyria. In order to enter in the service of the Duke of Illyria, she decides to appear "in man's attire" (1.4. stage direction) and to call herself "Cesario." The Duke woos Olivia (a wealthy lady of Illyria) and asks Cesario to act as a go-between. Olivia falls in love with Cesario while the Duke grows fond of his squire as well. Then Sebastian, Viola's twin brother, rescued from drowning by Antonio, arrives in Illyria. Because the twins look very much the same, the confusion is complete: "One face, one voice, one habit, and two persons!" (5.1.226). Even Antonio cannot tell his friend from his sister: "two creatures. Which is Sebastian?" (5.1.234).

The question which one is Sebastian can be transmitted to *Sebastian Knight*: Is Sebastian depicted in V.'s biography the real Sebastian, or a Sebastian shaped according to V.'s opinions as becomes his half-brother?

But the confusion in *Twelfth Night* is simply caused by Viola's transvestism of which the spectator is well aware. And the reference in *Ulysses* pertains not to Sebastian but to Antonio. The relationship between these two carachters in *Twelfth Night* is noteworthy as it has been called "the strongest and most direct expression of homoerotic feeling in Shakespeare's plays" (Adelman, qtd. in Bruce R. Smith [67]).

A more substantial role than Antonio has in *Twelfth Night*, has his namesake, the merchant of Venice in Shakespeare's eponymous play. As Don Gifford has indicated there is an allusion in *Ulysses* to *The Merchant of Venice* when Mr. Bloom mentions "the harmless necessary animal of the feline persuasion" (557), as in Shylock's monologue the caprices of man are considered, one of them being the delight in "a harmless necessary cat" (4.1.55).

In this play Antonio's friend, Bassanio, needs money to marry the wealthy Portia. Antonio is so kind as to borrow the amount needed from Shylock, pledges his ships and agrees that when he does not repay his debt in time, Shylock is entitled to "an equal pound/ Of [Antonio's] fair flesh" (1.3.150–151). Such an outrageous commitment bares the dept of the affectionate bond between the two men, Antonio and Bassanio, whose "name is a diminutive of Sebastian" (Lindheim 690). Another allusion to a cat appears in Bassanio's song that ends with "Ding, dong, bell" [3.2.71], a nursery rhyme about a cat. Another version of this verse contains the lines "what a jolly boy was that / To get some milk for pussy cat," a possible precursor of Sebastian's Cambridge friend who also offered his cat some milk [Baring-Gould and Baring-Gould 54–56].)

Peter Quennell and Hamish Johnson who published their book on Shakespeare's characters in 1973, long before the gender-based Shakespearean studies have made so much progress, and who are aware that they "must always beware . . . of adopting a twentieth century approach toward a sixteenth-century work of literature, and editing Shakespeare with a degree of 'psychological' expertise that no Elizabethan playwright would either have appreciated or understood," write that it "has frequently been suggested that [Antonio] is a repressed, *unconscious* homosexual" (14, 29). "Certainly," they continue, Antonio's "love for Bassanio is all-absorbing" (30; see also Pequigney). And so is Bassanio's love for Antonio:

> Antonio, I am married to a wife
> Which is as dear to me as life itself;
> But life itself, my wife, and all the world,
> Are not with me esteem'd above thy life:
> I would lose all, ay, sacrifice them all,
> Here to this devil, to deliver you. (4.1.283–288)

Whether Joyce had the Venetian Antonio in mind or the *Twelfth Night* Antonio, he doubtless refers to this name to point out Murphy's sexual orientation. But even without this reference, Murphy's sexual inclination has already been clearly marked: he is a sailor, he avoids his wife, he has a double identity, he has the face of a young man tattooed on his chest as well the number 16, which number in "European slang and numerology . . . means homosexuality" (Gifford 544).

29. UNCLE RUKA

It has often been observed that some facts of Sebastian's life correspond with events and episodes in the life of Vladimir Nabokov. This is also acknowledged by the author in a letter he wrote to Edmund Wilson (who had tried to interrogate an old Cambridge roommate of Nabokov). "Your running into yet another dead fish [out] of my past" writes Nabokov, "is very amusing as you seem to be trying to reconstruct me much in the same way as I did in regard to Sebastian" (Karlinsky, *Dear Bunny* 208). Sebastian and his author share their year of birth, they both fled from Bolshevik Russia, both studied in Cambridge, and both became novelists. Even specific details tally, as has been noted in the annotations. Reminiscences of their adolescence romances are adorned by the presence of a Camberwell Beauty, and their daily routines overlap to some degree. More than a few habits and opinions they have as writers coincide. And they both visit their old Swiss governess in Lausanne. Such frames, which coordinate the outline of the life of the protagonist with his own, is not unique for *Sebastian Knight* among Nabokov's novels. Martin, the hero of *Glory*, is, for example, also born into an Anglophile St. Petersburg family and also finds his way to Trinity College.

What is more remarkable is that Sebastian has been given some traits that are pertinently related to his Uncle Ruka, whose portrait is presented in chapter 3 of *Speak, Memory*. Like Sebastian Uncle Ruka spoke English with more ease than Russian. He had a "heart ailment" as incurable as Sebastian's. When the seizures came he could obtain relief by lying supine on the floor, "spread-eagled," in exactly the same way as one day Leslie finds Sebastian on the floor of his study. Uncle Ruka was extremely good at poker and in the original Russian version of his autobiography Nabokov relates how his uncle got mixed up in a fraudulent game of poker, just as happens to Sebastian (Boyd, *VNRY* 73; *Sebastian Knight* 182).

Uncle Ruka "almost lost his life in an airplane crash" and when young Nabokov asked how the pilot took it, his uncle replied, "*Il sanglotait assis sur un rocher*" (He sobbed seated on a rock) (*Speak, Memory* 70). In *Lost Property* Sebastian also talks about a plane crash and its survivor found "sitting on a stone. He sat huddled up—the picture of misery and pain" (110).

"In the autumn of 1916," writes Brian Boyd, Uncle Ruka "died, alone, at a hospital in St. Maude, near Paris . . . and twenty years later at the climax of his first English novel Nabokov paid a curious atonement by having Sebastian Knight die, also alone and also of angina, in a hospital in St. Damier, near Paris" (*VNRY* 121). This might explain why V. when trying to recall the name of the place of the hospital, persists in thinking that it "began with an 'M'" (190–193).

Like Sebastian (and his mother), Uncle Ruka was possessed by a restlessness that caused him to peregrinate during most of his adult life. It was only in the summer that he stayed briefly at his Russian manor house. He had houses in France and Italy, and traveled to America as well as to his "beloved Egypt." If Sebastian had also traveled to the Arab world, then it becomes explicable why he had an "Anglo-Persian dictionary" among his books, and an "Oriental amethyst" as a memento.

Nabokov attributes his uncle's wanderlust, his "search for a travelling shadow" to his "colorful neurosis," his homosexuality. The color of this neurosis might be guessed by gathering the hues of some of his uncle's belongings, his "[p]ink" coat, the "pink" globe of coral cupped in a gold coronet which knobbed his cane (*Speak, Memory* 243), the "Bibliothèque Rose"—a collection of stories for children that contained Uncle Ruka's favorites, and the "scarlet" of the sleeves of Uncle Ruka's handsome coachman with his Assyrian profile.

The precious cane with the pink globe, a "collector's item" Nabokov inherited from his uncle, played a fateful role during Nabokov's voyage into exile, just as fateful as the cane found by V. in Lescaux and which was instrumental in discovering Mme. Lecerf's real identity.

It was on a day that Uncle Ruka was "on the terrace of his Pau castle" with its view on the "empurpled mountains" in the distance, that he saw "a flight of doves striating the tender sky" and he, visited by "a Proustian excoriation of the senses," composed his best work, "a romance," its music as well as its words. Likewise Sebastian was struck by doves "wheeling across the sky," a view he rewrote for inclusion in his third book (*Sebastian Knight* 72).

Nabokov recalls with the "utmost repulsion" "the sarcastic comments that Monsieur Noyer, my Swiss tutor used to make" on this composition. Noyer's real name is Nussbaum (Boyd, *VNRY* 105) and in *The Doubtful Asphodel* a "Professor Nussbaum, a Swiss scientist" shoots himself dead (173).

Nabokov quotes two lines from Uncle Ruka's romance:

Un vol de tourtelles strie le ciel tender
Les chrysanthèmes se parent pour la Toussaint
(A flight of doves striates the tender sky
The chrysanthemums deck themselves out for All Saints' Day
[Translated by Brian Boyd, "Notes" 699])

The origin of All Saints' Day is a Celtic festival named Samhain (*Encyclopaedia Britannica* 11: 15) and this recalls the name of Colonel Samain who also stayed at the Beaumont hotel.

Like Sebastian Uncle Ruka is linked to Proust. "Ruka's belle époque affluence, his poor health, and his homosexuality all recall Proust," writes John Burt Foster, Jr. "and in his Russian version of his autobiography, Nabokov even states that his uncle looked like him" (204). (In his letter from July 15, 1943 to Edmund Wilson, Nabokov associates a Cambridge friend, Bobby de Calry, a "passive pansy" with Proust: "He is something of an indifferent imitation of Proust." Nabokov made a sharp distinction between homosexuals who, like for example Diaghilev, Gide and Wilde, did not hide their proclivity in public, whom he invariably calls "pederasts," and closeted homosexuals, whose inclination he only indicates in a much more subtle, indirect way.)

In the chapter of *Speak, Memory* where Nabokov portrays his Uncle Ruka, there are several signals to Proust and his chef d'oeuvre. The chapter's last section opens with a sentence about "recalling a patch of the past." "Patch," or "*pan*" in French, is a word crucial for Proust's excursions into his childhood (Foster 119).

In the first part of *Remembrance of Things Past,* titled "Ouverture," Proust tells the well-known story of how he (that is, the narrator) as a young boy waits in his bedroom for his mother's goodnight kiss. As his parents have visitors, this kiss is withheld from him. This upsets him to such a degree that, when his mother finally sees the boy upstairs, she decides to read to him to calm him. The book she chooses is *François le Champi,* by George Sand (*Remembrance of Things Past* 1: 39–44). Decades, as well as thousands of pages, later the narrator enters the library of the Prince of Guermantes where he comes across the very same book, and "tears came to [his] eyes" (3: 918). The happiness he feels then, as the narrator discovers after much introspection, he learns to regard as "something whose value is eternal" (3: 1093).

In the last section of chapter 3 of his autobiography Nabokov tells how his Uncle Ruka, "in 1908 or 1909" found in the house of his nephew's parents in a French children's book "a passage he had loved in his childhood," a recollection resulting in "agony and delight." The book Uncle Ruka so readily recognized belonged to the series that Comtesse de Ségur wrote for small children, the first being *Les Malheurs de Sophie.* Nabokov also tells how many years later, he too, in "a chance nursery" rediscovered that same series, and also experiences that same agony and delight, which, as with Proust, leads him to conclude that "[e]verything is as it should be, nothing will ever change." (In *Ada* he would conflate the titles of Proust and De Ségur, *Swann's Way* and *Les Malheurs de Sophie,* into one: *Les Malheurs de Swann* [*Ada* 55].)

30. VELIMIR KHLEBNIKOV

Futurism, an important movement among the poets of pre-Revolutionary Russia, was a reaction to the works of the Symbolists and Acmeists intent on "destroy[ing] all the poetic canons of the past" (Mirsky 496). The founder of Russian futurism is Velimir Khlebnikov and it is this poet (together with Vladimir Mayakovsky) whom Brian Boyd mentions as the origin of some of the traits of the futurist Alexis Pan ("Notes" 676). In some of his writings Khlebnikov calls himself "the Head of the Universe" or "President of the Planet Earth" (Douglas 333, 362). Nabokov ridiculed this in a lecture (Boyd, *VNRY* 92) which might explain why he chose the name of Pan, the god of the universe (Bulfinch 206) as a cover-up for his staging of Khlebnikov in *Sebastian Knight*.

Khlebnikov published poems and articles in close cooperation with Alexei Kruchonykh. "To both men," writes Charlotte Douglas, "*zaum*, beyonsense, was an extension of poetic language that rejected the mediation of common sense and deemphasized denotative meaning" (20). It is this kind of vocalization that Nabokov had in mind when he calls Pan "the inventor of the 'submental grunt'" (see also Boyd, "Notes" 676; *VNRY* 95).

Sebastian joins Alexis Pan when he and his wife travel to the "East," to embark on "a Marcopolian journey." The first expedition narrated in Marco Polo's *Travels* is "to the Middle East," which is mainly a voyage to Persia (Polo 58–74). Khlebnikov too spent about half a year in Persia. Pan traveled "from one provincial town to another" giving performances consisting of recitals and dances "dressed in a morning coat, perfectly correct but for its being embroidered with huge lotus flowers." The "net profit" of these performances "was supposed to get him, his wife and Sebastian to the next town." This is almost a replica of the way Khlebnikov strayed through Persia "dressed in robes, and living on handouts" ("from their listeners") while he "explored coastal and inland villages" (Douglas 28–29).

Pan's dances are a "mixture of Javanese wrist-play and his own rhythmic inventions." A photograph of the performance of the choreographed *L'Après-midi d'un Faune* by Diaghilev's *Ballets Russes* in Paris in 1912 may serve as a possible illustration of such a gestural show, as the players resemble Balinese dancers (the photograph is reproduced in Camilla Gray [42]). The custom to display hand gestures while dancing is widespread in Asia, and some of the choreographies Diaghilev produced were inspired by Siamese dancing (Grigoriev 72).

Khlebnikov went to high school in Simbirsk, the place where Pan's ends. Pan died "in 1922 or 1923," Khlebnikov in 1922.

During the performances Pan had a "constellation (the Greater Dog) painted on his brow." Futurists used to paint "pictures on their faces" (Mirsky 496). The important futurist David Burliuk (who read lectures, one entitled "Pushkin and Khlebnikov," in St Petersburg and Moscow, and whose art was denounced together with Nabokov's in an anti-Semitic article during the Nazi-hegemony) walked regularly in Moscow's main streets with flowers, algebraic or artistic signs painted on his cheeks (Camilla Gray 115; Douglas 21; Shrayer, "Jewish Questions" 76–77). The *Wikipedia* article on David Burliuk opens with a photograph showing him with a dog painted on his cheek.

The interesting thing is that amid so many correspondences between Alexei Pan and Velimir Khlebnikov, there is no original for Larissa, Pan's wife. Charlotte Douglas's outline of his life does not even suggest that there has ever been an attachment to another female than to his sister Vera in his life. He lived often alone or shared a home with another man. The time in Persia Khlebnikov spent together with his friend Mechislav Dobrokovsky (Douglas 28). If one would like to complete the parallels between Pan's and Khlebnikov's lives, one has to suggest that Sebastian, and not Larissa, was Pan's main companion.

31. V.'S DREAM

If V.'s dream is synopsized as far as it concerns the relationship between the two half-brothers, it may become less mysterious. V. is waiting in a room with his mother for Sebastian's return from "some long journey" (perhaps one associated with his travels with Alexis Pan). He appears to be "ashamed of something," although his face "looked fairly cheerful." V. is horrified when he notices that Sebastian wears "a black glove on his left hand," a "sham thing" he never uses. Undoing this glove "a number of tiny hands" appear, "mauve-pink" colored. On seeing this V. wishes to leave the room, and, while going away, he hears Sebastian's voice "calling" and "promising to tell him something ... important" and finally making "one last loud insistent appeal" before the dream ends.

Contrary to what V. fears the black glove is not an artificial replacement for his left hand, but is full of liveliness, which shocks V. even more. It looks as if Sebastian is on the verge of offering V. an explanation that would end the quagmire caused by the uncovering. The embarrassment produced by the liveliness of Sebastian's left hand, so very different from what V. thinks a left hand should be, could have been lifted if only V. had heard Sebastian's revelation.

Another left hand might be detected in Roy Carswell's painting, if he had followed his idea to complete it. As Andrew Caulton has observed, the painter's name "anagrammatically hints at Lewis Carroll ('Roy Carswell' = 'Lewys Carrol') who wrote of Alice's adventures through the looking-glass and underground just as Carswell's picture shows Sebastian's face 'mirrored' in water" (186). In his notes in *The Annotated Alice* Martin Gardner writes that the "looking-glass theme seems to have been a late addition" to *Through the Looking-Glass* as it was originally "based on chess tales that Carroll told the Liddell girls" (180). Gardner relates how a distant cousin of Carroll "tells about her role in suggesting the mirror motif":

> "Now," he said, giving me an orange, just tell me which hand you have got that in." "The right," I said. "Now," he said, "go and stand before that glass, and tell me which hand the little girl you see there has got it in." After some perplexed contemplation I said, "The left hand." (180)

In discussing his portrait with V. the painter says that he could have completed his painting by hinting at Sebastian's lover "the shadow of a hand, perhaps." Because Carswell's portrait is painted as "mirrored," this hand would have introduced the very kind of inversion as demonstrated by Carroll (117). For more connotations of left hands, see section 4.27.

Other details of V.'s dream deserve attention as well. The painting on the wall, depicting a steamer, while the waves move like caterpillars, shows many similarities with the picture sketched by Sebastian in *The Back of the Moon*, as is discussed in the annotations. What also happens in V.'s dream is an endless going and coming of V.'s mother, busying herself with a "bike," "spurs and stirrups," "a silver cup," and a "thimble." Of these items, it is the last one that is of interest as it associates with Uncle Black, who, after winning the game of chess, put all the chessmen in a box, but not the thimble that replaced a white pawn.

32. WOMAN IN WHITE

In Sebastian Knight's novel *Success* the heroine Anne and William are reported to have seen a film titled *The Woman in White*, clearly a reference to the 1860 novel by Wilkie Collins with the same title (96).

The novel's heroine, Laura Fairlie, an heiress, marries an impoverished gentleman, Sir Percival Glyde, who turns out to be a villain. The marriage contract stipulates that Laura's inheritance, should she die before her husband, will be handed to him.

Laura has two half-sisters, Marian Halcombe, her close and devoted companion, and a stranger, Anne Catherick. The latter (she has the same father as Laura; see Collins 502) possesses evidence that Glyde is an imposter, and she is for this reason kept confined in an asylum. Anne manages to escape, falls ill, and dies. As Laura and Anne look very much the same, Glyde, in order to cash in the inheritance, contrives to make the world believe that it is Laura who has died. Initially, until Glyde is unmasked, this evil scheme succeeds: "it was plain that [Laura] had taken the dead woman's place" (388).

A surviving sibling impersonating a dead one is a theme familiar to the readers of *The Real Life of Sebastian Knight*.

Motifs: Death and Beyond

CHAPTER 5

CONTENTS

1. Donne 161
2. Executioners 165
3. *The Doubtful Asphodel* 166
4. V.'s Quest 167
5. Voices and Visions 169

1. DONNE

In the section with the annotations ten comments are made on passages referring or alluding to the poetry of John Donne. Many of these passages belong to chapter 18 in which V. discusses Knight's *Doubtful Asphodel*, which he calls "unquestionably his [Sebastian's] masterpiece" (172). The central theme of this novel is the revelation that is awaiting human beings when they die. This metaphysical postulation (contradictory as this combination of words may be) is discoursed upon in many of Nabokov's novels. In *The Gift* one reads "our future comprehension of [the other world's] surroundings . . . are due to be revealed to us with the disintegration of the soul from the eye sockets of the flesh" (310). The story "Ultima Thule" is entirely devoted to a man who, inconceivably, has "survived the bomb of truth," which can only explode at the moment of one's death (496). What then may happen is indicated in some detail in *The Doubtful Asphodel*, when "the world yield[s] its sense to the soul" (177). From V.'s discussion of and his quotations from this novel, it is clear that some of the novel's metaphysical beliefs, and the imagery employed, has much in common of those of Donne's "The Ecstacy." There is also a striking difference. The ecstasy in Donne's poem is the result of exalted communion with a beloved one, while the dying man in *The Doubtful Asphodel* who is followed so minutely, may be any man. This is surprising, as in most of Nabokov's novel, and most clearly in *Speak, Memory*, the contemplation of the hereafter is indissolubly tied to the love one feels for those nearest.

There seems to be no need to engage in the difficult task of discussing Donne's poem, because Nabokov's selective and focussed use of or references to subtexts seldom implies a commitment to all the ideas a subtext might convey. John Donne was one of Véra Nabokov's favorite poets (Schiff 99). In his commentary on Pushkin's *Eugene Onegin* Nabokov writes that Donne "has been somewhat overrated in recent years by lovers of religious verse" (3: 501). One may prefer to read this as a suggestion that lovers of religious verse could better turn their attention to more devout poets than Donne. Nabokov wrote this no later than 1963. Had he been able to read John Carey's 1981 *John Donne: Life, Mind and Art* one fancies that Nabokov might have chosen a less ambiguous note, leaving no room for a somewhat derogative reading of his comment.

According to Sebastian's novel, a dying man can already sense the imminent revelation, even when the soul is not yet liberated from its body: "We feel that we are on the brink of some absolute truth" (176). The actual disclosure of the revelation has been called an ecstasy: "a well-charted experience in devotional writings, occurring 'when as the servants of God were taken up in spirit, separate as it were from the body, and out of the body, that they might see some heavenly mystery revealed unto them.' It is the means of an immediate apprehension of truths which are normally inaccessible to us because of our necessary dependence upon sense and discursive reading" (Smith, "Notes" 367–368; the quotation is from J. Weemes *A Treatise of the Four Degenerate Sons* [1636]).

Although Donne's "Ecstacy" is distinctly about lovers and love, it is primarily a poem about the phenomenon of "ecstacy." To Coleridge it was "the quintessential 'metaphysical poem'" (Gardner 279). In it, writes Helen Gardner, Donne "is attempting to imagine and make intellectually conceivable the Neo-Platonic conception of ecstasy as the union of the soul with the object of its desire, attained by the abandonment of the body" (285).

- In Donne the relationship between soul and body is at the heart of the poem. But ecstasy belongs exclusively to the domain of souls and not of bodies ("whilst our souls negotiate there, / We like sepulchral statues lay" [ll. 17–18]). *The Doubtful Asphodel* has a similar conception as it is to "the soul" that the "world yield[s] its sense" (177).
- The souls of Donne's lovers, having experienced their exaltation, return to their bodies as their medium to express themselves: "Love's mysteries in souls do grow, / But yet the body is his book" (ll. 71–72). In his summary of *The Doubtful Asphodel* V. uses the same imagery and writes that the "man is the book" and that "you feel [the dying man] thinking throughout the book" (172–173).
- The immediacy of the revelation is compared in *Sebastian Knight* to the unravelling of a knot which suddenly gives way, because "the hardest knot is but a meandering string" (176). "[T]he dying man" is "that knot" (176), until the soul leaves the body and the knot is undone.

In Donne's poem, the "soul" repairing to its "body" becomes "[t]hat subtle knot, which makes us man" (ll. 59–64). The image of a man's body and soul as a knit can, as mentioned by A.J. Smith ("The Metaphysic of Love" 373), can be found in Chaucer's *Boethius*: as long as the soul is in the body, it will not "knowe the thinne subtil knittinges of things" (Chaucer 197). In Donne's poem as in *The Doubtful Asphodel* "fingers" are employed for doing or undoing the knitting (l. 63; 176). The violet, cropping up so frequently in *Sebastian Knight*, is in Donne's poem used as a metaphor to illustrate the enrichment gained by the lover's souls becoming "one"; oxymoronically the union is compared to a single violet that by transplanting becomes a double one (ll. 36–40).

When discussing *The Doubtful Asphodel*, V. mentions the notes Sebastian has "scribbled in the margins of a borrowed book" such as "Attraction of death," and "'the swamp of rank materialism and the golden paradises of those whom Dean Park calls the optimystics'" (175). These remarks all seem to refer to John Donne who wrestles with many religious questions, among them the materialist view that souls cannot exist outside the body (see Carey 162–164). However, Donne's views were orthodox enough to become Dean of St. Paul's (possibly the name "Dean Park" had to do with the fact that the deanery had a "sizable garden" [Parker 90]). (In his comments on Miss Irondell's translation of Donne's "Holy Sonnet X composed in his widowery" Kinbote refers to "the Dean of St. Paul's denouncement of Death." It has, however, been argued that Donne wrote most of his divine meditations "before his ordination" [*Pale Fire* 241; Smith, "Notes" 624].)

"Optimystics" might be a contraction of "optimistic" and "mystics." Donne might be regarded as an optimistic mystic (although William Blake was a greater mystic he was by no means an optimistic one) because of his firm esoteric aspiration that his future post-mortem life will be like "a *Lily* in Paradise" (Carey 225). No English poet was so attracted by his own death as Donne who was "happy" to die, and, having fallen ill in 1631, said that he "were miserable if I might not dye" (qtd. in Walton 81).

In "Pale Fire" Shade contemplates the arrangements in the hereafter when the sequences in one's life are annihilated by the "timelessness" of an afterlife (l. 568). Shade then reflects on a widower who remarried and so becomes a bigamist in eternity. Donne was quite outspoken that he wished to be resurrected including all the stages he experienced in his earthly life (Carey 225). He was even concerned about the recovery of his hairs and fingernails trimmed during his life ("Of the Progress of the Soul. The Second Anniversary" l. 278 and l. 337). In Sebastian Knight's *Success* this theological hair (and nails) splitting is derided.

While awaiting Sebastian's return to the German seaside hotel, Clare spends a rainy day reading Donne. It is a remarkable choice as Donne's poetry is no "pastime" poetry (Parker 113). Clare and Sebastian separated after Sebastian's return from Blauberg . Their estrangement however dates already from their return from Germany.

When Donne left London in 1611 for a long visit to the continent, he wrote a farewell for his wife, "A Valediction: Forbidding Mourning" proclaiming that their love is so spiritual that it cannot be harmed by remoteness. Such an emphasis on the spiritual side of love might be in line with the anaclitic nature of Clare's relationship with Sebastian. Julian Connolly also suggests a reconciliation between Sebastian and Clare "in the realm that lies beyond death" because the breach in their relationship "is irreparable in the here and now" ("From Biography to Autobiography" 43).

2. EXECUTIONERS

Being a character in *The Real Life of Sebastian Knight* often means premature death. The members of V.'s family die far too young and this goes for Clare as well. Captain Belov is shot by Russian revolutionaries. In Sebastian's apartment V. notices a photograph of a "Chinese stripped to the waist, in the act of being vigorously beheaded," a rather prosaic *momento mori* (39). Pahl Pahlich Rechnoy refers to an executioner as well, Anatole, "the executioner. The man with the guillotine here" (144). Violent death is implied in the comparison of Mr. Goodman's face to "a cow's udder," and when V. depicts the image of "Sebastian, struggling in a naughty world of Juggernauts" (58, 63).

The "cow's udder" comes from Nikolay Gumilev's poem "The Tram that Lost its Way," one of Gumilev's "best and most difficult poems" (Rusinko 383). Some of its images are excruciating: "The executioner, in a red shirt and with the face like an udder, chopped off my head, it lay together with the others here in the slippery box, right at the bottom" (translated from the Russian original by Dimitri Obolenski [302]. In *Look at the Harlequins!* the first half of this passage is rendered in French [246]).

Critics agree that the box with severed heads strongly suggests that Gumilev had the French Revolution in mind. Gumilev's tram is obviously a death machine and Yevgeny Slivkin points out that Gumilev, when he lived in Paris, might have seen a (photograph) of a public execution as at that time the guillotine was not put on a scaffold "but . . . was set up on a supporting rail" (144).

The name "Anatole" brings to mind Anatole France, the French novelist. France was obsessed by the massive use of the guillotine during the French Revolution and wrote a novel about this subject, titled *Les dieux ont soif* (*The Gods Are Thirsty*). This title is borrowed from the last issue of the journal *Vieux Cordelier* edited by Camille Desmoulins, the soi-disant originator of the French Revolution, which "ends with these words of Montezuma's, *Les dieux ont soif*, The Gods are athirst" (Carlyle 673). Thomas Carlyle compares the victims of the guillotine with "Juggernaut idols." A Juggernaut is a huge Indian chariot representing a Hindu god which, once on the move, crushes the devotees or zealots who happen to be in its way. It is unstoppable just as Gumilev's train.

Is V. suggesting with this allusion to Gumilev's poem that Goodman, who must have rushed to complete the final draft of his biography of Sebastian within less than two months after the novelist's death, and who did not stop the printing process to correct the omission about V.'s existence, has killed Sebastian's literary persona? Or is V., out of *jalousie de métier*, suggesting that Goodman's book is a deadly threat to his own biography (a serious threat, so it seems, as V.'s omissions are at least as blatant as Goodman's).

The name Anatole may also refer to the French executor Anatole Deibler. He officiated from 1899 to 1933 and executed almost 400 people. Due to this number, his long career, and his affable nature, he is probably France's best-known executor. He died, quite suddenly, while traveling to Rennes where he was expected to execute Maurice Pilorge, a young man who killed his male lover with a razor (see perso.numeri-cable.fr./~tessonmic/PILORGE.pdf).

His death and its circumstances might have been reported in the French papers. It might be that Pahl Pahlich mentions Anatole Deibler as the reason for not yielding to his impulse to kill his wife Nina who abuses him in so many ways; a *crime passionnel*, as Pilorge's case shows, does not protect the transgressor from the guillotine.

Perhaps the executions mentioned counterpoint the theme of dying in *The Real Life of Sebastian Knight*. Sebastian's novel *The Doubtful Asphodel* professes or prophesies the vision that the human soul, once liberated from the body, becomes omniscient and immortal. This is not a fearful perspective, but one cannot be sure that it will materialize. The motif of execution is therefore a forceful way to express this uncertainty. The fear of death (a dominating theme in *Invitation to a Beheading*) has a double edge: the fear of dying and the fear that the thaumaturgic transition to the other world will not happen.

3. THE DOUBTFUL ASPHODEL

This is the title of Sebastian Knight's last novel about a man who is dying. The closer he approaches his death, the stronger the premonition becomes that a revelation is awaiting him and that the mystery of his own life and that of the universe will be disclosed. The author, who is monitoring the dying man closely, expects to witness the revelation and to partake somehow in the disclosure. But when the moment finally arrives "the author seems to pause for a minute, as if he were pondering whether it were wise to let the truth out" (178). That "minute of doubt was fatal: the man is dead ... and we do not know." What then follows in V.'s retelling is puzzling: "The asphodel on the other shore is as doubtful as ever." If the asphodel on the other shore is the dead man, why then should he doubt, having regained universal knowledge (or, if not, having acquired the certainty that the revelation does not occur)?

An asphodel is a flower that belongs to the lily family. The name of a daffodil is a corruption of "asphodel" through its variant name of "affodil" (*Concise Oxford Dictionary* 64). The daffodil, or *Narcissus pseudonarcissus*, refers to the myth of Narcissus, who "heartlessly rejected lovers" and fell in love with the reflection of his own face in a pool, and "tried to kiss the beautiful boy who confronted him" (Graves 1: 287). Likewise Roy Carswell painted Sebastian's eyes and face "in such a manner that they are mirrored Narcissus-like in clear water" (117). This suggests that the asphodel on the other shore, separated by reflecting water, can be still one's mirror image. Does Sebastian Knight suggests that life after death might be a sort of continuation of earthly life?

The asphodel is also in another sense a significant flower in Greek mythology: when people die their ghosts are ferried across the river Styx by Charon, and they arrive on the Asphodel Fields, from whence they can proceed to hellish Tartarus or the heavenly orchards of Elysium (Graves 1: 120–121). Robert Graves writes that the Homeric adjective *asphodelos* "probably means 'in the valley of that which is not reduced to ashes' ... namely the hero's ghost after his body has been burned" (1: 123). This suggests that V.'s description of the "asphodel on the other shore" represents the soul of the man who has just died.

It is understandable that the author, having missed the precious moment of the revelation's manifestation, is condemned to doubt its existence. But why should this doom, this existential doubt, befall our souls as "the asphodel on the other shore is as doubtful as ever"? Is this doubt also part of a life that begins when earthly life stops?

4. V.'S QUEST

V.'s vigil at the bedside of the dying man (whom he thinks is Sebastian) forms a setting similar to that of the main episode in *The Doubtful Asphodel*. The close proximity is emphasized in both cases: the author of *The Doubtful Asphodel* is aware of all the movements of the dying man as when he "seems to move an arm or turn his head" (174). The "minute of doubt" that was "fatal" coincides with the slackening of the author's proximity; "He seems to lift his head and to leave the dying man" (178). In the St. Damier hospital the nearness of V. to the dying man is obvious as the latter's breathing is clearly audible since its minor irregularities are reported many times. Like the author of *The Doubtful Asphodel*, V.'s thoughts wander toward "some momentous truth [Sebastian] would impart to me" and his expectations seem well grounded as he is "learning something every instant" (200–201).

It seems as if it is not because of doubts that V.'s expectations might be threatened, but because the dying man is not Sebastian; the warmth of love V. radiated to the man whose breathing he could hear so well, went to a mere stranger.

This situation, however, is very similar as the one described by John Shade in "Pale Fire." He too had expectations based on the recurrence of a supernatural phenomenon. In Shade's case it is not the broaching of an absolute truth, but a kind of evidence for the existence of the hereafter. Alas, the recurrence appears to be based on a misprint, a mistaken spelling, just as the doorman of the St. Damier hospital misspells the name of Knight. But instead of ruining Shade's expectations, the misprint provides the very clue to the affirmation Shade has been searching for his whole life, as I have argued in "'Mountain, not Fountain': *Pale Fire*'s Saving Grace."

In the same manner the fact that Mr. Kegan and not Sebastian occupied the bed next to V. redeems his quest, instead of destroying it. It is thanks to this that V. has "learned one secret too" which changed his life "as completely as it would have been changed had Sebastian spoken to me before dying." What V. has learned is that "any soul may be yours if you find and follows its undulations" (202).

If this notion is inspired by V.'s reading of *The Doubtful Asphodel* than this transmigration of souls can be understood: if death means the instant and complete solutions of all the mysteries of the universe, then the differences between spirits cease to exist. One becomes an amorphous ghost without some inalienable individual intelligence. This means, to quote Leona Toker, that "the individual identity moves . . . toward a dissolution in something infinitely greater than itself" (*Mystery of Literary Structures* 7). But is an afterlife, where no "who is who" can be imagined, preferable above plain nothingness? "The need for maintaining a hold on one's identity and not letting it dissolve in the magma of the collective flow is among Nabokov's pervasive concerns," writes Toker ("Mixers" 94).

"The problem of the balance between the universal and the unique," as Toker calls it, is clearly noticeable in *Pale Fire* (*Mystery* 15). John Shade will "turn down eternity" if he can not retain in the afterlife everything which has been dear to him in his earthly life, while Kinbote is not in the least impressed by "the experience gathered in the course of corporeal confinement" and rejoices that he will ultimately deliquesce in a "Universal Mind" ("Pale Fire" l. 525; *Pale Fire* 227).

Shade's greatest wish is that he and his wife will be reunited with their deceased daughter Hazel. Mutatis mutandis, V. has the same wish with regard to Sebastian. There is however one great difference. Shade has loved his daughter all his life most intensely. V. has seen Sebastian hardly ever after his mother's death: two short meetings in Paris which ended abruptly. Invitations by Sebastian to come to London were turned down. "Why had I kept away from him so stubbornly," V. asks himself (193). And by writing Sebastian's biography V. wishes to learn of Sebastian what he has missed when he was alive.

V. must have realized that his many efforts (notably those to find Nina) did little to bring him closer to Sebastian. Sitting at the bedside of the man whose breathing he heeded so anxiously, he felt a deep attachment to the dying man. Having been told that it was not Sebastian but a Mr. Kegan whose presence filled him with so much compassion, he might have realized that "any soul may be yours." And, still more important, if it is so well imaginable that one can understand the soul of a mere stranger, then it is most likely that Sebastian's soul will be far more approachable.

And this knowledge might be what V. has won with his quest: although he fails to find the real person Sebastian has been, his belated love for his half-brother invigorates his belief that he ultimately will be on affectionate and intimate terms with Sebastian.

5. VOICES AND VISIONS

Nabokov has often expressed his belief that his existence is somehow not confined to his earthly life. His autobiography opens with a pronouncement of this "belief," and it can be regarded as a substantiation of his conviction (*Speak, Memory* 20). He has discovered numerous patterns in his life, "thematic lines," pliable but pertinent, which require a supranatural explanation. Nabokov attributes the design of these lines to "unknown players of games" who have "planned" his life ("Chapter Sixteen" 241). Likewise, John Shade discovers how his life might be the result of "a game of worlds" sported by players in "their involute / Abode" (*Pale Fire* 63). These fatidic factors, called "ghosts" in *Pnin*, continuously "attend to the destinies of the quick" (136). "[B]eings akin" to the living and former "friends" are parties most likely to partake in these recreations (*Invitation to a Beheading* 223; *The Gift* 314).

Nabokov's readers are likewise invited to detect such resistant patterns in the lives of the characters in his novels, and deduce from these the identity of the invisible designer. To trace such influences requires a great ability to see what is by no means obvious and to recognize the delicate details that belong to some telling pattern. Major discoveries in this realm have been made by Brian Boyd, especially with respect to *The Defense*, *The Gift*, and *Pale Fire* (see his VNRY 333; VNRY 467–478; and *Nabokov's* Pale Fire).

Apart from these interferences "ghosts" can manifest themselves in many other ways, such as vocally. In *Speak, Memory* Nabokov mentions his receptive quality for hearing anonymous voices, a quality he compares with the, admittedly more impressive, auditory endowments of Socrates and Joan of Arc (33). In *The Gift* an important pattern is evoked by the voice of the father of Fyodor, the novel's protagonist. This voice seems significant for Fyodor's formative years, for launching his literary career, for his meeting his beloved Zina, and for his apprehension of an otherworld. (In *Invitation to a Beheading* the protagonist recognizes his next to kin through their "voices" [223].)

In *Sebastian Knight* V. frequently mentions Sebastian's spectral presence: it is reported when V. visits Sebastian's Cambridge friend and also when V. gets enamoured by Mme. Lecerf. And twice V. suggests that his half-brother is monitoring and assisting him in writing Sebastian's biography. But ghosts cannot be summoned to perform, nor are their actions so easily made out; "that is not McFate's way" (*Lolita* 211). It is better not to take these ghosts too seriously, and to see them rather as V.'s wishful figments.

Quite different is the unsolicited voice heard by V., "the sudden voice in the mist" saying "Who is speaking of Sebastian Knight?" (49). V. experiences this message as a warning, a challenge of the biographer's claim: "don't be too certain of learning the past from the lips of the present" (50). This "sudden voice in the mist" recalls a similar event in *The Gift* when a "pulsating mist . . . suddenly began to speak with a human voice" (156). This voice inspires a spontaneous flow of poetic lines, which, despite their prosaic appearance, constitute poems. As Anna Maria Salehar has shown, in all these poems Fyodor's father figures. Most likely, this voice in the mist comes from Fyodor's deceased father, whose vocal presence is hinted at so frequently.

The warning voice in the mist heard by V. comes from the ghost of Sebastian who must have been concerned about V.'s decision to base his biography on intuition rather than on facts. Hearing voices is a phenomenon that interested Sebastian as he writes in his last letter about certain papers that "have heard voices" (184). These voices were, according to V.'s rendering of Sebastian's letter, heard in "Dot chetu," two words that result after transliterating "Domremy" (Joan of Arc's birthplace) when this name is mistakenly read as a word in handwritten Cyrillic.

It is curious, as Dieter Zimmer has observed, that "Chetu" is also the name of the place where, in *The Gift*, Fyodor's father has been seen for the last time (*The Gift* 134). It is a small Tibetan village that consists of several "'miserable log houses'" (Zimmer and Hartmann 69). (In his "Chinese Rhubarb and Caterpillars" Zimmer discusses the lepidopteral and botanical links between the death of Fyodor's father and the village named Chetu.)

The word "chetu" in *Sebastian Knight* represents the second half of the name of the place where Joan of Arc was born. But it is its most telling part, as Domrémy is not the only name of a place in France beginning with "Dom." ("Domrémy is the medieval form of "Saint Remy" ["dom" is short for the Latin "dominus"], Remy or Remigius [c. 438–533] was bishop of Reims.) As is discussed in section 4, 12 Joan of Arc heard voices that she obeyed. During his Asian journey Fyodor's father heard "the whisper of spirits calling you aside." Having mentioned "the last reliable evidence concerning [his] father" that he has been seen in Chetu, Fyodor writes that his father's voice, declaiming Pushkin's "The Prophet," might "still [vibrate] . . . to this day in some resonantly receptive Asian gully" (*The Gift* 124, 134, and 148). ("The Prophet" is the title of Pushkin's poem about a man, dying in forlorn circumstances, hearing celestial voices that he is ordered to carry out.)

That Nabokov, when writing *The Gift*, had already the correspondence between "Chetu" and Joan of Arc's "Remy" in mind, is plausible as the Tibetan place is named by the fictitious French missionary Barraud in the "*Exploration catholic.*"

Fyodor's father discusses with Barraud a "nomenclatorial point" about the name "iris." As Fyodor's father "greeted [Barraud] in French," and because it is likely that they mentioned the rainbow, personified in Greek mythology by the godess Iris, it may be assumed that they talked about the *arc-en-ciel*, the French word for rainbow, which can be read as "Arc in Heaven." Joan of Arc was in 1909, half a millenium after her death in 1431, beatified, and made a saint in 1920.

In the universe of Nabokov's novels ghosts can influence and to some extent direct the lives of the quick, but the living cannot command the spirits of the deceased, as V. tries to do. Ghosts act by exerting "the most indirect pressure" when "steering a favorite in the best direction" and they can only hope that their charges will respond adequately (*Transparent Things* 92). Responding to voices was essential in Joan of Arc's life, and is essential for Fyodor and is the final message in Pushkin's poem.

Unfortunately, V. is only willing to give the warning from the voice in the mist the merest recognition, and did not respond to Sebastian's alerting him to the voices that his papers have heard, although they could tell such dramatic messages that a comparison with Joan of Arc's voices seems justified. This is discussed in the next chapter.

Conclusion

CHAPTER 6

I

The conclusion of the previous chapter suggests that V. has been successful in finding a way that secures an affectionate bond with Sebastian's soul. At the outset of the writing of his biography it was V.'s aim to learn more about Sebastian's earthly life. This subject will be pursued now. The many subtexts investigated in chapters 3 and 4 strongly signal how to proceed. Seven of the motifs discussed in chapter 3 suggest, by analogy, that it should be doubted that there has ever been an affair between Sebastian and Nina (Motifs 1, 3, 9, 10, 16, 17, and 20). And from six motifs it may be derived that V. as a biographer has permitted himself some serious mistakes (Motifs 2, 7, 11, 14, 18, 21). Indeed, the love affair in *The Seagull* parallels that in *Sebastian Knight* (a young man, held in thrall by Nina Rechnoy/Zarechny, is ruined), but apart from the namesake there is no reference to Chekhov's play.

Turning to chapter 4 it appears that most of the motifs (twenty-one out of thirty-two) point to homosexuality and the remaining subtexts detail questions of sexual ambiguity. (Only one motif, 32, is related to a change of identity of a non-sexual nature.)

It seems advisable to temporarily dismiss V. as a guide and to see whether Sebastian might have homosexual affinities. If so, it might explain why Sebastian's attention is drawn by the naked man in Roquebrune, why Sebastian follows Alexis Pan as far as Simbirsk, and why Sebastian interrupts his reciting of his verse for Natasha when he sees a "nude bather." And perhaps the consequence that "[n]ever more may he ask of the boy who sits daily at the next school desk" about his sister, is the true reason why Sebastian regrets that Natasha is no longer his sweetheart (137).

Sebastian and Clare's relationship starts, ominously, by Clare entering "the wrong door" (79). Doubtless she is a "delightful companion" for Sebastian. She cheerfully types the text that Sebastian "dictate[s]" to her. This must have taxed her patience, as Sebastian used to "struggle with words" and also because typed sheets "had to be done over again" (81). Clare is "solely responsible for the managing of his literary affairs" (113). "Clare posted letters for him, and checked laundry returns, and saw that he was well supplied with shaving blades, tobacco, and salted almonds" (84). The pragmatic part of their alliance seems to be quite substantial. Dale Peterson calls Clare Sebastian's "amanuensis" (28). Although Sebastian appreciates her company (they visit restaurants and theaters) his eagerness to be with her is not unlimited. They meet in the spring of 1924 and when Clare spends the autumn in Paris Sebastian does not join her (although he visits her "more than once"). They also do not live together, Sebastian has his apartment, she her "lodgings" (109). They don't even dine together. When in 1925 Sebastian goes to Germany Clare follows "a week or two later" (85). And when Sebastian goes to the Alsace to a luxurious kurort, Clare is not allowed to join him.

Of course V. cannot avoid touching on the subject of "the intimate side of their relationship" but only to discard it categorically as a possible explanation (while at the same time accepting sexual attraction as the only explanation for Sebastian's ensorcellment by Nina) (103).

If it were true that Sebastian leaves Clare because of Nina's seductive powers, the problems would have arisen after Sebastian's stay in the Beaumont Hotel. It is however not after the summer of 1929 but already after the summer of 1926, when Sebastian went to the German seaside resort that the estrangement begins. Sebastian's dreadful fits of temper are "a new thing to Clare" (100). And "his relations with her appear more brittle than they perhaps were." And it was then, well before Sebastian's stay in Blauberg, that Clare "was left behind" by Sebastian (102).

What happened in Germany is that Sebastian "had come across a man he had known ages ago, in Russia, and they had gone in the man's car" to a place somewhere on the coast (86).

The man Sebastian met is most probably "Uncle Black" as V. calls him, or the "chess player Schwarz" as he is named by Sebastian.

"Schwarz" is German for "black" and links Uncle Black with the country where he met Sebastian. The only German word (apart from this proper name) in *Sebastian Knight*, "Schachbrett" is another connection between Uncle Black and Germany. And there is still another link.

When V. visits Pahl Rechnoy, Uncle Black takes his nephew out for a walk. When V. leaves Uncle Black and his nephew happen to return as they are "slowly coming up to the stairs" (146). It is then that V. hears Uncle Black saying: "Once upon a time there was a . . . ." Obviously, Uncle Black is so fond of fairy tales that, although their walk is finished, he starts telling one. It might be that this fondness is recalled by Nina when she, referring to Uncle Black, begins with saying "Once upon a time . . ." (169). In the same way Sebastian might have been stimulated to notice, after he has left Uncle Black, a fairy tale "brownie" (87).

The fairy tale that Uncle Black is telling his nephew is most likely of his own making as it is about "a racing motorist," a driver of a racing car. During his visit V. observes that Uncle Black excels in drawing racing cars. His nephew is very proud that Uncle Black is a taxi driver. And the only two things the reader learns about the man Sebastian meets in Germany is that he is a Russian and owns a car. Few exiled Russians were comfortable enough to afford a car, which probably means that such a possession matches Uncle Black's interest in cars.

That the alienation between Sebastian and Clare begins in 1926 and not three years later, is difficult to align with V.'s story about Nina. Even more serious is V.'s handling of the letter V. receives in January 1936 from Sebastian. This letter is written in Russian and the letter has, as has been discussed at some length in chapter (see comment on 183/ 18–184/ 21), two male addressees, and V., who has only seen the Russian version, must have known that the invitation he "if you can come, come," was originally directed by Sebastian to a man (183).

Who is this man? The gentle Uncle Black is such an affable and gifted man that one can imagine that a relationship with Sebastian that began after their meeting in 1926, might have lasted until 1936. Although his initial quality seems to be that of a chess player, he is, according to his cousin's laudation, a man of various talents. As a cousin he might have the same ancestors, among them the "famous general" whose portrait adorns Pahl Rechnoy's room. The other portrait, that of the Imperial Family, suggests White Russian sympathies. Uncle Black is also a taxi driver. This may not seem to be much of a distinction but in Paris at that time it was certainly a mark of class among Russian émigrés. "Many Russian cab drivers had been officers in the Imperial Army," writes Valerian Obolensky (III: 8). "Taxi drivers were the aristocrats of the *émigré* work force," says Robert H. Johnston, and their job "was one particularly attractive to military veterans" as it conferred a measure of independence (77, 76). Nabokov was well acquainted with their type; in Berlin he "interviewed numerous Russian taxi drivers," and called them "fine White Russians all of them" (Boyd, *VNRY* 246).

The best-known former White Russian officer who drives a cab is probably *Lolita*'s Mr. Taxovitch. Mr. Taxovitch, who liberated Valechka from her doomed relationship with Humbert Humbert, was a colonel in the Imperial army. In view of the colonels mentioned or alluded to in *Sebastian Knight*—Burnand's *Colonel*, *The Prismatic Bezel*'s colonel, his precursor, Agatha Christie's colonel, and Colonel Samain—one might suspect that Uncle Black has been a colonel as well. Colonel Samain was among the guests of the Beaumont Hotel, and might even be Uncle Black's real name. (His namesake Albert Samain, 1858–1900, wrote "gay poetry" [Schulz 277]. In his *Landmarks in Russian Literature*, Maurice Baring notes that Afanásy Fet "has something in common with the French poet Albert Samain" [*Landmarks*, 205].)

As the names of "Knight" and "Clare" are "homonyms for night and light (clair)" as Jessie Lokrantz has observed (70) it can be noticed that this antagonism is completely dispelled when "night" is associated with "black."

II

The real tragedy in *Sebastian Knight* is Sebastian's forsaking of Clare without offering her any explanation at all. By doing so he might have sentenced her to a lifelong doubt as to whether she must blame herself to some extent for the wrecking of their close friendship, which lasted five years, almost all her adult life. This, at least, is what V. is telling his readers.

How could Sebastian do this? It is the last thing one might expect from him. Let us remind ourselves what Sebastian's reaction was to his father's quixotic duel. Palchin was challenged by Sebastian's father because he was spreading the story that he was the lover for whom Sebastian's mother left her husband. This happened in 1912, eight years after the departure of Sebastian's mother, and three years after her death. The challenge was made by Sebastian's father to defend the posthumous honour of his former wife against a man whom she had preferred over him. Furthermore, he risks that his second wife might become a widow, a by all means serious risk as has been discussed in chapter 2, and particularly so because Palchin, unlike his adversary, aimed his shot at Sebastian's father. Despite this gratuitous, and ultimately ruinous behaviour, Sebastian was euphoric "when he learnt the reason for his father's fatal duel" (16).

How can someone admire such an extreme form of reverence for a woman, and maltreat another, much more devoted woman, to an equally extreme degree?

This question is the more compelling because several instances are presented showing Sebastian while he gives careful attention to people to whom he has no obligation whatsoever. He feels it a moral duty to take careful notice of "a taxi driver's hare-lip," to observe the cotton wool in the ears of a cloakroom attendant; the "very slight limp" of a chocolate girl, the advertisement offered by a beggar, and the predicaments of an "ugly woman" or an "old street violinist" (106–107; 174). Why should such a man refuse to see Clare's misery of which he is the sole perpetrator?

If what is suggested in the "love letter" from *Lost Property* ("I think you have guessed how things stand: the damned formula of 'another woman,'") is true, then his balking at telling Clare the truth could not have been insurmountable.

Nonetheless, the letter is a most interesting one. In chapter 2, six parts of its text have been commented on and most of these annotations point to the self-contradictory nature of its contents. This is reminiscent of André Gide's mise-en-scène technique and his novel *The Notebooks of André Walter*.

In this semi-autobiographical novel the protagonist wishes to love the heroine in a purely spiritual way, uncontaminated by carnal desires (an idea called "absurd" in the letter from *Lost Property*). Eventually, Walter decides to leave his Emmanuèle. In order to inflict no pain on his beloved, and to make the separation bearable for her, he resolves to make a "secret sacrifice," and "to accept [an] unjust accusation" and "so lose her esteem" (Gide *The Notebooks* 66–67).

Why does Walter wish to leave her? The novel opens with the answer to this question as Walter's mother on her death-bed asks her son "to leave Emmanuèle" because he cannot make her happy (20).

Walter consents to his mother's sincere wish. But is this the real reason for his compliance? His yearning for purity appears to have another cause: "I shall abstain from caressing her . . . for fear that she may later desire all the more that which I could never give her" (65) because her "body disturbs . . . and carnal possession frightens" him (54). Although he does not attribute this fear and his gamophobia to his homosexuality, the erotic desires aroused by "pale adolescents" demystify his tribulations (*The Notebooks* 86. The annotation by Walter Baskin on the same page refers to Gide's homosexuality as well.) Finally, Walter succumbs to the cul-de-sac of his perturbations and goes mad.

If one considers the possibility that Sebastian's new lover is a man and not a woman, then the way Sebastian disengages himself from Clare is much more understandable especially in light of the example of André Walter. Sebastian too accepts an "unjust accusation," consents "to lose her esteem" and finally he is rated as someone gone mad.

In Sebastian's case the unjust accusation is the alleged affair he has with "a woman he had met at Blauberg" (109). Although Clare is convinced that Sebastian "has gone mad. Quite mad" (108), the facts do not bear this out. His main employment, his literary work, is continued and progressing well. He begins writing *Lost Property* at the time of his separation from Clare, in the autumn of 1929, and proceeds with it in the beginning of 1930. V. calls it "his easiest book" (113) and, although it deals with "souls lost," it atmosphere is cloudless. It is characterized by V. as "the clinking sounds of unsaddled horses browsing in the dark; the glow of a camp-fire; stars overhead" (109/110). This pastoral and peaceful picture of an all-male company gleefully gathered around a fire, bantering, drinking and singing, is very incompatible with the grimness and gloom that, according to V.'s account, has taken possession of Sebastian. And *Lost Property* becomes a bestseller, just as Sebastian's novel *Success*, which brought him fame. There is really nothing suggestive of a tormented soul, let alone madness.

It is unlikely that Sebastian "had some final explanation with Clare" as he had "stopped talking" to her (109, 108). Of course, Sebastian was not disposed to lie straight to Clare's face, nor could he tell her the truth. If Sebastian had told Clare that he had fallen in love with a man, it is very likely that Clare would have tried to accommodate herself to the new circumstances. She would probably have continued with the many secretarial and managerial tasks she performed for Sebastian.

Nor would there have been much reason to disrupt their visits to theaters and restaurants. But having lost their shared consent that they were lovers, this would inevitably prove to be an arrangement bound to decompose. Sebastian was determined to sever all ties with Clare, thus enabling her to find a future Sebastian could not give her. For this reason Sebastian simply never spoke out and refused to answer Sheldon's urgent request "out with it, man" (108).

Feigning madness and remaining silent characterizes also Hamlet's way of ending his relationship with Ophelia. Hamlet's life's destination changed so drastically with the appearance of his father's ghost that he had to break with Ophelia. It "seemed to him necessary to convince Ophelia . . . that he was insane, and to destroy her hopes of any issue of their love," writes A.C. Bradley. To this end he "bid her a silent farewell" (Bradley 153). For similar reasons Sebastian's last meetings with Clare are marked with madness and reticence. Their relationship had to be ended too. Like Hamlet, Sebastian "must be cruel, only to be kind" (*Hamlet* 3, 4, 178).

Sebastian learned the "language of silence" from early age: he had to be "tongue-tied" because he could not express his love for his mother whose memory was met with hostility (48; 16). Confronted with his love for a man, he could not speak "out" to Clare. But the title for this book, *Silent Love*, is chosen for a second reason as well. It is taken from Shakespeare's *Sonnets* because its subject is, like *Sebastian Knight*'s, an enigmatic double love affair of a man with a woman and another man. (The actual citation, from "Sonnet 23" has, however, a different context, as Shakespeare's concern is one of expressibility, and not as Sebastian's, one of morality.)

But Sebastian did not wish to die without exoneration. In his last letter, ultimately addressed to V., he tries to settle this. Ruminating about this letter V. refers to *Hamlet*, by paraphrasing its line 1.5.79:

> With all my imperfections on my head

and alluding to the speaker of this line as "a revengeful ghost" (34). This refers to the ghost of Hamlet's father who complains that he is murdered

> [I]n the blossom of my sin,
> Unhouseled, disappointed, unameled,
> No reckoning made, but sent to my account
> With all my imperfections on my head.

This is not the way Sebastian wishes to die. In order to explain his seemingly heartless and ignoble behavior toward Clare, he has kept his letters and asks V. to find them. This would have been sufficient to reveal Sebastian's secret, because he writes to V. "I signed their death warrant, and by it you will know them" (184).

Now, what might this clause "and by it you will know them" mean? It can not mean "by it you will know that these letters exist" as somewhat earlier in the letter V. has already read Sebastian's request to "burn" them, and it is not possible to burn papers without seeing them. "[Y]ou will know them" must mean something else than "you will see them." Clearly, V. is supposed to learn more about these letters than their mere existence. Of course, one does not expect that V. would pore over the letters' contents, but he could have found out, by simply noticing the sender's name and address on the cover or from the letterhead, who had written them.

In this way V. could have traced Sebastian's correspondent, and could have written a truly real life of his half-brother in order to explain that Sebastian's behavior toward Clare was not void of mercy, but full of it.

By withholding the "striking disclosure" that the letter was addressed to a man (188), V. shows that he is so much embarrassed by it that he decided not to reveal this fact. When he, some months later, meets Nina Rechnoy, his bafflement must only have increased disastrously. Much as he admires her physical appearance, he also disapproves of Nina as a possible companion for Sebastian. He thinks that Sebastian would by all means "have avoided her," that she is "flighty," and intellectually the worst match imaginable as "books mean nothing to a woman of her kind" (147, 161, 172). It might have been that, on second thoughts, V. might have relented toward the male correspondent, especially after seeing that nothing could be worse than this female candidate. And perhaps V. has been able to find the male acquaintance and to apprehend Sebastian's reasons why he "never spoke out."

And if this is what V. has disclosed in a letter to Mr. Bishop, it can be understood that Clare's widower was this time more willing to acknowledge his communication in a receptive mood.

III

The writer referred to most frequently in *Sebastian Knight* is William Shakespeare. In the previous chapter references and allusions have been discussed concerning *Hamlet, King Lear, Macbeth, Othello, The Tempest, Twelfth Night, The Merchant of Venice,* and *A Midsummer-Night's Dream*. For his first novel in English Nabokov seems to have substituted Alexander Pushkin for Shakespeare as his muse. In Sebastian's novel *Success* the two characters Anne and William ("Anne's first queer effeminate fiancé, who afterwards jilted her") may recall William Shakespeare and his wife Anne Hathaway who had a marriage not marked by inseparability. Sebastian's William calls himself "Willy" who is "willy nilly a willow," which may be an allusion to "will he, nill he," the expression the clown in *Hamlet* uses, while reflecting on Ophelia's death when he digs her grave (5.1.16). The willow might refer to treacherous willow with its "envious sliver," precipitating Ophelia's death (4.7.174). And the "boil at the back of [Sebastian's] neck" that V, observes is remindful of the "blister" on "the fair forehead of innocent love" (105; *Hamlet* 3.4.43–44).

That insecure, disrespectful, or unrequited love affairs may hasten premature death is a motif in *Hamlet* equally visible in *Sebastian Knight*: by Roy Carswell's remark that the unknown femme fatale "smashed [Sebastian's] life" and by V.'s association of the pit dug out in Mme. Lecerf's garden with "murder" (118, 167). But rather than *Hamlet*, V.'s visit to Mme. Lecerf's country house mimics Shakespeare's *Sonnets*.

One hundred and fifty four sonnets by Shakespeare have been published. Of these, the first 126 are devoted to a beautiful fair youth, and another 26 are addressed to a dark lady. The difference in tenor is also striking. The sonnets to the fair youth are full of admiration, warmth and love, those for the dark lady frankly express that she is faithless and delusive yet irresistibly attractive. The sonnets for the fair youth are often marked by homosexual desires. (The term "homosexuality" did not exist in Shakespeare's time; it was called buggery and sodomy, and those engaged in such practices could be penalized by death, see Bruce R. Smith 11–14.) After the first edition of the sonnets, the homoerotic content of the first 126 of them caused such embarrassment that the next edition "cheerfully changed some of the pronouns from 'he' to 'she' and 'him' to 'her'" (Bate 39).

Shakespeare's two addressees, that is, the few things known of them, are nicely represented in the Lescaux country house. The dark lady is of course Mme. Lecerf with her "black hair" (148) and the beautiful fair youth is "the rather handsome man in plus-fours with a solemn face and . . . fair . . . hair" (165). The color of the hair of the man Shakespeare praises so passionately in his sonnets is repeatedly mentioned and so it is with the Lescaux beau: "the blond gentleman," "the blond gentleman," and "[t]he silent blond person" (165, 170).

In 1817 it has been suggested that Shakespeare's fair youth is Henry Wriothesley, third Earl of Southampton (pronounced, at least in the nineteenth century, as "Rosely" [Bate 47]). He is still regarded as the most likely person as he was when Nabokov wrote *Sebastian Knight* (Bate 49; Harrison 19). The portrait of Wriothesley, made about 1600, shows a young man with a stern look, wearing breeches. These breeches explain the "plus-fours" of the Lescaux beau (165). Plus-fours look like breeches but somewhat longer and baggier. (Wriothesley's portrait is reproduced in Bate [fig. 2] in an engraving after an original painting in the National Portrait Gallery.)

The number of sonnets devoted to the fair youth is 126, which equals two times the number 63. This figure is known as "the grand climacteric" (Boyd, *Lyrics* 104). A climacteric marks the end of a period of seven years and the ninth climacteric is called the "grand" one and was, in Shakepeare's time, regarded as decisive in human life (Harrison 123). In *Sebastian Knight* the figures 1, 3, 6, and 9 have special significance: Sebastian lives in London at 36 Oak Park Gardens, the telephone number of Dr. Starov is 61-93 and Sebastian died in 1936 (34, 194), most likely on 9-1-1936 (see 3, 2 Calender).

If one follows some of these figures it appears that sonnet 39 has the opening line "Oh how thy worth with manners may I sing," which line contains the words "thy" and "manner" V. reads in the burning letter (36). This might suggest that not only the addressee of Sebastian's last letter is a man, but the sender of the letters using blue stationery as well.

Sonnet 136, another combination of the relevant numbers, is addressed to the dark lady. The poet says that because the lady already has so many lovers, she should not mind (or even notice) that the poet would like to increase this number with one: "Among a number one is reckon'd none." This is strongly refuted in the "love letter" in *Lost Property* "There is only one real number: One" (111).

Shakespeare's black lady plays a virginal while Mme. Lecerf has a piano in her room in Madame Graun's apartment in Paris. Mme. Lecerf's bosom is called "hard," that of Shakespeare's mistress is of "steel" (166; Sonnet 133), and her "ramshackle" house recalls the "fading mansion" attributed to the dark lady in Sonnet 146 (162).

The blond young man in Lescaux is seen "examining the works of his watch." When V. jolts his elbow "he let drop a tiny screw," which shows that the blond gentleman is actually repairing his watch. Sebastian "never" has a wristwatch himself (104) and has to use that of others to learn the time. Thus, Sebastian can be said to be *In Search of Lost Time*, and that the fair man has *Time Regained*, as the title of the last part of Proust's novel, *Le Temps Rétrouvé*, might be translated.

It is no small feat that V. at the end of his long quest has found, willy nilly, a male lover instead of a female one. But this "silent blond person" too never spoke out.

IV

A small digression as an aside to the hypothesis that *Sebastian Knight* has basically an aporetic structure seems opportune because an infatuation with a femme fatale on the one hand and homosexuality on the other, are not so mutually exclusive as might be expected.

Although the phenomenon of the femme fatale (an attractive woman who is, actively or passively, destructive of her lovers) is as old as the world—see Homer's Helen of Troy and Circe and the *Bible*'s Delilah and Judith—the fascination with this sexual persona had its heyday during the fin de siècle (Gay 207; Kaye 56; Lucie-Smith 43; Meltzer 813). It is especially the biblical Salomé who often featured as its prototype. She was the daughter of Herodias and when her stepfather, King Herod, promised her whatever she might ask if she would dance before him, she, prompted by her mother, requested the head of St. John on a platter.

Walter Pater, whose aestheticism influenced Oscar Wilde, sees in his *The Renaissance* in the drawings of maiden heads by Leonardo da Vinci "[d]aughters of Herodias," an association no less perplexing as the much quoted comparison Pater makes of the *Mona Lisa* with a "vampire" (Pater 116, 123; see also Nicholl 368. Wilde calls Pater's view of the *Mona Lisa* "criticism of the highest kind" [873]).

Gustave Moreau, whose paintings have left many traces in the writings of French authors and poets during the turn of the century, painted several Salomés, and also many representations of Helen of Troy. He painted images of Narcissus and St Sebastian as well, both relevant to *Sebastian Knight*: it is in Roy Carswell's painting that Sebastian is portrayed as Narcissus.

The best-known paintings by Moreau of Salomé, *The Apparition* (1876), a watercolor, and an oil, *Salomé dancing before Herod* (1874–1876), are in J.-K. Huysmans's novel *Against Nature* bought by the protagonist Jean Floressas des Esseintes, and half a chapter is devoted to reflections on these pictures. Although *The Gospels* do not hint at a lasciviousness of Salomé's dance as rendered by Moreau, and attribute the cruelty committed to Herodias rather than to her daughter, it is Salomé who in Des Esseintes's eyes is the "true harlot, obedient to her passionate and cruel female temperament" (Huysmans 68).

Moreau's watercolor also adorns a wall in the narrator's room in Marcel Proust's *Jean Santeuil* (Caws 41; see also Reed 84–87). Proust's most famous femme fatale is Odette de Crécy. One of the real-life models for Odette was Léonie Closmesnil, "a celebrated cocotte," for whom young Proust felt a "platonic passion" (Painter 54). In his *Swann in Love* Proust connects "an iridescent mixture of unknown and demoniacal qualities" of "kept women" with "some fantasy of Gustave Moreau, with poison-dripping flowers interwoven with precious jewels" (a description which well applies to Moreau's *Apparition*) *(Remembrance of Things Past* 1: 292). *Swann in Love* tells of the wretched affair Swann has with this femme fatale, Odette de Crécy. Because of her unfaithfulness and Swann's inability to bear this, their relationship gradually turns into mutual hatred. Eventually Swann, feeling himself in a "circle of hell," deeply regrets his love for a woman "who didn't appeal to [him], who wasn't even [his] type!" (*Remembrance of Things Past* 1: 399 and 1: 415).

But even more famous than Moreau's *Salomé* became Oscar Wilde's eponymous play (Kaye 57; Praz 337). Here Salomé's erotomania culminates in kissing the decapitated head of St. John (Wilde 201), an act so demonic that it obliterates all the charms that she might have shown before this monstrosity.

Helen of Troy, although lacking Salomé's atrocity, figures also frequently as a femme fatale, especially in the poetry of Albert Samain (Praz 330–331, 406–407, 427). In chapter 4 of Mario Praz's *Romantic Agony*, titled "La Belle Dame sans Merci," this persona is discussed in great detail. He also mentions the emergence of the Russian femme fatale, due to the publication of E.M. de Vogüé's *Le roman Russe*.

Conclusion

Jean Lorrain, who, next to Count Robert de Montesquiou, provided the main components for Proust's character Baron de Charlus, wrote a novel *Très Russe*, whose heroine Mme. Livitinov "takes delight in tormenting her lover" (Praz 371).

The critics and artists associated with *The World of Art*, the Russian journal edited by Sergey Diaghilev, were "predominantly gay," but it was in its pages that Franz Stuck, the painter of many extremely lustful femmes fatales, is "mentioned perhaps more often than any other artist" (Karlinsky, "Russian Literature" 615; Granoien 401). Stuck's best-known painting, *The Sin* (1893), shows a nude vamp with an inviting look having a snake for a shawl, but he painted also a most voluptuous *Salome* (1906).

All these artists, Leonardo, Pater, Wilde, Moreau, Huysmans, Proust, Samain, Diaghilev, and Lorrain, have shown an interest in homoerotic aspects in their works, suggesting an inclination not at all incompatible with their ways of life, and their opinions and communications made in this respect (as far as can be inferred on the basis of the literature mentioned). Why such oriented artists feel obsessed by the persona of a femme fatale is a question difficult to answer. Misogyny, fear of female domination, anxiety about feminine sexuality and the pressure to abandon homoerotic relationships have been suggested as explanations (see also Gay 208 and Lucie-Smith 186). However, the fact remains that the less heterosexual one is, the more immune one becomes to the (possibly perfidious) seductiveness of women. Camilla Paglia (14/15) argues that "[m]ale homosexuality may be the most valorous attempt to evade the femme fatale and to defeat nature," but this also cannot explain the compulsive attention given by homosexuals to these malignant mistresses (why fear what can be evaded?).

The obsession might be understandable if one realizes that homosexually oriented men at that period of time might have felt compelled, by the demands of their social environment, public condemnation and the criminalization of homosexuality, to consider matrimony as a possible choice, for which the (simulation of) receptiveness for female beauty seems a prerequisite.

The artists mentioned gave expression to their obsession by means of their artistic work, Sebastian Knight, however, pursued his idol in real life. Despite her denial that she is a femme fatale, she is a genuine siren (160). She possesses a "delightful old-world suavity" and a jaunty conversation that agrees well with the "boudoir" in which she receives V. (148, 151). She has a winning predilection for cosy tête-à-têtes and her merriment as a quidnunc is fetching. But behind this façade hides a misanthrope: "[t]he men she liked proved dismal disappointments, all women with a very few exceptions were nothing but cats" (159), a Circe who thinks that "it is always entertaining to see that kind of refined, distant, brainy fellow suddenly go on all fours and wag his tail" (157). She brought her first husband to such despair that he longed to kill her, and dismisses her second husband from his own house in order to receive a young man whom she intends to make her new lover.

Is it likely that Sebastian was ruinously obsessed by this mistress, without being enraptured by her? When Sebastian visits her "he never stayed long with her" and he insults her for being "cheap and vain" or "vain and cheap" (157, 158). Instead of making love to her, the reader learns that Sebastian's main fixation is to inform her about his peculiar opinions, by holding forth on the trashiness of modern books, the foolishness of young people, religion, the form of an ashtray, or the color of time. This is certainly not the common course followed when a man meets a femme fatale: ravishment—courtship—love making—victimization—escape or ruin. Sebastian seems to have omitted the first stages, or rather to have replaced these by harangues bound to deter his addressee.

Somehow Sebastian's compulsion to see Nina again and again in order to renew their mutual aversion is as inexplicable as the obsession the artists discussed here have shown in portraying their femmes fatales.

V

Sebastian signed his juvenilia with a little black chess knight in ink. In his letter dated October 21, 1941 to Edmund Wilson, Nabokov draws attention to the chess game that indeed epitomizes the whole story. When V. meets Pahl Rechnoy, he has a black knight in his hand. The next thing is that the black knight loses his head. Losing his head is what happens when Nina Rechnoy has Sebastian in her thrall. But he does not tarry with her long, as is clear from Uncle Black's remark "I could take your rook if I wished." Nina Rechnoy's maiden name is "Toorovetz" and the first part is close to "tura," the Russian for "rook." Just as Uncle Black restores the chessman's head, he mends Sebastian's broken heart. Clare's marriage with Mr. Bishop is commemorated when Pahl Rechnoy takes "the queen with his bishop." The next and final move is a victorious one as Uncle Black wins.

The move of a chess knight can be compared to the L-shaped sides of a Pythagorean triangle, and a move along these sides is longer than along its slanted side. The longer move shows what the straight move hides. This detour characterizes Sebastian's advances: it is via Natasha Rosanov's brother that Sebastian gets in touch with her, and it is through Uncle Black that Sebastian meets Uncle Black's cousin's wife.

In this reconstruction chessmen have different roles. When the chessmen are arranged before a game starts, their position, for Black, is, from right to left: rook, knight, bishop, queen, king. The rook represents Nina, the knight Uncle Black, the bishop Mr. Bishop, the queen Clare, and the king the novel's hero, Sebastian. The letters forming the "egg-like alliteration" in the name of Olga Olegovna Orlova," O-O-O, is the chess notation for castling at the queen's side. Castling is the joining of the rook with the king and is allowed when all pieces in between them have been removed. As Mr. Bishop has taken the queen, the black knight still hinders the castling. The king remains nearer to the knight than to the rook.

VI

"There are so many parallels between the details of what happens in *Sebastian Knight* and what Nabokov has to say about his early life in *Speak, Memory* that it is impossible for a reader to ignore them," writes Michael Begnal in his careful study of the novel (3). In chapter 1 and in the annotations several correspondences have been mentioned, most of them between Sebastian's and Nabokov's lives. As *Sebastian Knight* is about two brothers, some parallels with Sergey's life might be expected to surface as well.

Sergey was about a year younger than Vladimir. After finishing their studies in Cambridge, Nabokov went to Berlin and Sergey "moved to Paris" (*Speak, Memory* 258). When Nabokov gave a lecture in Paris in 1932 he "began to see more of Sergey. Sergey's homosexuality had always made Vladimir awkward, and the brothers' first meeting in Paris had not been a success. Nevertheless Sergey indicated he wanted to speak seriously to Vladimir and confront their differences, and a week later they lunched near the Luxembourg Gardens with Sergey's partner" (Boyd, *VNRY* 396).

This partner is Hermann Thieme as Lev Grossman has discovered. Hermann's family owned a castle in Austria where he and Sergey sojourned regularly. The relationship was a happy one: "I'm just suffocating with happiness," Sergey wrote to his mother (Grossman). The social circle they moved in was different from Vladimir's purely literary connections: among Sergey's acquaintances was the painter Pavel Tchelitchew, the poet Jean Cocteau and the director of the *Ballets Russes*, Sergey Diaghilev. After Vladimir and his family settled in Paris in 1937 he was often visited by Sergey and they were "on quite amiable terms" (*Speak, Memory* 258). "When their mother died in Prague in 1939, and Vladimir was unable to get away from Paris, Sergei described the funeral for him in a letter. Writing on the spare, elegant stationery of Schloss Weissenstein, Sergei closed the letter affectionately: 'I want you to know that I am with you with all my heart'" (Grossman).

The Nabokovs left for America in 1940, Sergey continued to live in Europe. He was arrested by the Gestapo in 1941 and imprisoned for four months on charges of homosexuality, arrested again in 1943, sent to the concentration camp Neuengamme, where he perished in January 1945. Survivors testified of his heroic conduct: "he was extraordinary. He gave away lots of packages he was getting, of clothes and food, to people who were really suffering" (Grossman). ("The Neuengamme book of the dead and the hospital records," writes Andrea Pitzer, "seem to be at odds on whether Sergei died January 9 or 10; but the camp archivist Reimer Möller determined January 10th as the correct date" [414].)

That Nabokov begins his portrait of Sergey in *Speak, Memory* with a reference to *Sebastian Knight*, strongly suggests that he had his relationship with Sergey in mind when he wrote about the two half-brothers. "In *The Real Life of Sebastian Knight*, Nabokov's fictional account of a man's attempt to write the life of his mysterious half-brother, one finds uncanny references to Sergei everywhere, from the title character's name, which alliterates with Sergei's, to his foppishness and his failures at sports, to a series of uneasy meetings between the brother in Paris that closely parallel those of the real-life Nabokov brothers," writes Grossman. Next to the outer correspondence "the central mystery of Sebastian and Sergey" may be more deeply disguised (Begnal).

Conclusion

Nabokov was well aware of the difficult life Sergey had because of his homosexuality. In 1926, while living in Berlin, he received a letter from his mother that included another one that Sergey had written to her. He wrote about it to Véra, who at that time was convalescing in a sanatorium in the Black Forest. "I can't stop myself copying [Sergey's letter] out," Nabokov writes to his wife. What follows is one of the most painful documents connected with Nabokov's life.

"You know," writes Sergey to his mother, "my whole life for the last ten years has been a terrible one, not only a sinful life, but even a crime against myself" (*Letters to Véra* 77). Sergey also tells his mother that he has become a Catholic because this faith allows him "to take communion *every day* to kill the sin in me." The sin he refers to is his homosexuality.

Nabokov in his letter to Véra commiserates with his brother. "It is true," he writes, "Catholocism is a feminine, arrow-arched faith—the sweetness of painted glass, the suffering tenderness of young Sebastians" (*Letters to Véra* 78).

What makes this letter from Sergey so harrowing is the cause of his misery. Nabokov's family was struck by heavy blows—his father was assassinated, his mother as a widow lived in (sometimes extreme) poverty, and Sergey died in a German concentration camp. These merciless ordeals were part of the family's fateful history. Sergey's sufferings were different because, if they could not have been avoided entirely, they at least should not have been so tormenting. Sergey was born into a family that belonged to the highest strata of St. Petersburg society. In these circles homosexuality was regarded with no small degree of sophistication. "The decade of the 1890s saw a mass emergence of lesbians and gay men on the Russian cultural scene," writes Simon Karlinsky. "There were several quite visible grand dukes (brothers, uncles, or nephews of the last three tsars)." The uncle of Nicholas II "appeared with his current lover at official functions and at the theatre and opera" (Karlinsky, "Russian Literature" 615). "For many gays, lesbians and bisexuals today," writes Brian James Baer (183), "the decades immediately preceding the Revolution are looked on as something of a golden age, and not without reason."

This permissive atmosphere could not preclude individual cases of agony, as appears from the grand duke "Konstantin Romanov's anguished diary accounts of his personal battle against his 'secret vice' or Petr Ilyich Tchaikovsky's tortured letter to his brother in which he declares his intention to wed, unable to bear the idea that he could be a source of shame to those who love him" (Baer 186). The celebrated poet Mikhail Kuzmin, who wrote the pioneering gay novel *Wings* (1906), suffered, because of his homosexuality, from a "prolonged emotional crisis" and attempted suicide by poison (Barnstead 4).

Sergey seems to have hardly profited from the leniency existing in the upper class and artistic circles of St. Petersburg. This might be related with his father's (and to some extent to his elder brother's) attitude toward homosexuality. V. D. Nabokov was a most honest man, highly principled, courageous, well cultured and distinctly progressive in his political persuasions and artistic tastes. He was one of the main leaders of the Constitutional Democrats (the party which dominated Russia's parliament after the 1906 elections), edited the party's newspaper and wrote extensively on literature, music and the fine arts (see Shapiro, *The Tender Friendship,* and my "V. D. Nabokov, Literature and the Fine Arts," forthcoming). Unfortunately his reformative opinions did not reach far enough to prevail over his private view on homosexuality. As a liberal jurist he was influential in advocating the decriminalization of homosexual practices between adults. But this was the juridical side of the matter. "In the eyes of the healthy and the normal segment of the population," V. D. Nabokov writes, "sodomy will always and everywhere appear what it really is: an act inspiring profound disgust, perhaps pathological, perhaps merely a vice" (qtd. in Dragunoiu 176). His plea for decriminalization is also presented in a contribution to a German journal, in which V.D. Nabokov omitted his moral indictment of homosexuality just quoted. "Though the disclaimer's deletion was most likely a consequence of V. D. Nabokov's scrupulously politic and polite nature," writes Dana Dragunoiu, "it makes it also possible to imagine that his moral disapproval of homosexuality was less well-defined than the Russian text suggests" (177). In the same benevolent vein one could argue that by showing a personal aversion, V. D. Nabokov could sharpen his plea for legal abstention as to better persuade his adversaries. But the fact is that the actual wording of V. D. Nabokov's verdict is explicit and appears to be unnecessarily repetitious. In one sentence the reader is told that homosexual practices are unhealthy, abnormal, disgusting, vicious, and should be

Conclusion

regarded as sodomy. Certainly, given the legal context, the same could have been said by using more abstract phrases and without the anachronistic and unrelenting "always and everywhere." V.D. Nabokov's brother Konstantin was a homosexual (or, to use his son's more elegant phrase "a confirmed bachelor," whose "charming little flat" was "full . . . of photographs of young British officers" [*Speak, Memory* 60]). His brother-in-law Ruka, a frequent visitor of the family and his wife's only sibling, was also a homosexual. How very embarrassing it would have been if they had read their brother's verbose repudiation of their sexual identity. Fraternal affection was in this matter not strong enough for V. D. Nabokov to make his point with the decorum and discretion so natural to him in his many public offices.

Sergey was too young at that time to show his proclivity, but it must most likely have been far from easy to be raised by a father who considered an essential part of his personality with disgust. It is moreover unlikely that Nabokov had been particularly helpful to Sergey in overcoming his inner torments. That Nabokov's attitude was important is clear from the fact that Sergey "wanted to talk [with Nabokov] about the essential, to find out, apparently, [Nabokov's] attitude to [Sergey's] life" (*Letters to Véra* 196). This conversation was arranged by Sergey for October 26, 1932 and, as eight days later Nabokov was introduced to Sergey's partner, it might be concluded that their discussion was sufficiently satisfactory for Sergey to bring his partner to this meeting, and for another to take place on November 10.

Nabokov has been called a homophobe which, I think, is not what he was. What he certainly detested was the display of homosexual orientation. This can be done quite ostentatiously (as Prince Adulf in "Solus Rex"), or by propagandizing Greek love (as André Gide did), or defending homosexual practices without reservations (or without fear as Oscar Wilde did). All this was strongly disliked by Nabokov who could not even forgive (or forget) Virgil's tender shepherd burning with desire for another sheep tender. But less unequivocal expressions, such as an effeminate bearing, were met much more mildly. And homosexuals who refrained from affecting their disposition or even tried to hide it, were in no way criticized by Nabokov. On the contrary, he could readily sympathize with their predicament. In a note "from the time of *Pale Fire*'s composition," writes Stephen Blackwell, "Nabokov speculated about the extreme isolation of a homosexual college professor in a puritanical country, where a handshake would be the only possible erotic contact" (234).

The two meetings Nabokov had with his brother and his brother's partner correspond in some respects with the meetings V. had with his half-brother and his half-brother's partner. V.'s first meeting was in Paris, in the afternoon, in November or December, while Nabokov saw his brother with partner in Paris as well, at lunchtime, in November. The second meetings (V. with Sebastian; Nabokov with Sergey) were also in Paris, both during dinner.

When Nabokov visited his mother in Prague in the spring of 1930, Sergey showed him photographs of his partner, Hermann Thieme. "His boyfriend," writes Nabokov to Véra, "is a thickset, rather plump, forty-year-old man" (185). About three years later (November 1932) Nabokov actually met Thieme. "The husband," Nabokov writes to his wife, "I must admit, is very pleasant, *quiet*, absolutely not the pederast type, with an attractive face and manner" (208). As it has been argued that Uncle Black is in all likelihood Sebastian's unknown lover, it might be interesting to see whether the descriptions Nabokov gives of their appearances have some similarities. Sebastian writes about "the gentle old chess player Schwarz." Hermann Thieme was about forty in 1930 when Sergy was thirty years old, a substantial difference in age. The name "Schwarz," German for "black" fits well with Thieme's Austrian extraction, which might also explain the presence of Austrian money, "schillings," among Sebastian's collection of foreign coins (38).

Uncle Black's appearance and gentleness is equally recognizable. When playing chess with his cousin during V.'s visit, Uncle Black is described as "a heavy built man," which matches the "thickset, rather plump" impression Hermann Thieme made. When V. is introduced, Uncle Black courteously "bow[s]" as reciprocation. The chessman broken by Pahl Pahlich is mended "carefully" by Uncle Black. He moves his chessmen "delicately" and when during the endgame his cousin gets excited, Uncle Black remains calm.

The way in which Uncle Black entertains his nephew, a "pretty boy of four or five" (Nabokov's son Dimitri was four years old when his father composed *Sebastian Knight*) is most endearing. It can be concluded that all the features given to Uncle Black: his age, shape, quietness, gentleness and his attractive manners, are all borrowed from Sergey's lover.

VII

Nabokov concludes his short biographical sketch by saying that Sergey is entitled to more compassion and understanding than he received. As almost all the attention of their parents was devoted to Vladimir, Sergey's youth was much less fortunate. For this Nabokov could not blame himself (though he seems to have made no efforts to amend this). But Nabokov could have felt some guilt because of the injurious way he used to talk about homosexuals, and for allowing that this might have distorted a more cordial relationship with Sergey.

However, in *Sebastian Knight* Nabokov makes no attempt to suggest a close fraternity between Sebastian and his half-brother V. On the contrary, the lack of congeniality is more noticeable than between Vladimir and Sergey. In *Sebastian Knight* Nabokov chose a different way to come to terms with his feelings of remorse.

The relationship between Sebastian and Uncle Black might be the inner story of the novel, but it cannot eradicate the plain story of Sebastian's story with Nina. This latter story has been compared with Nabokov's liaison with Irina Guadanini. And Clare resembles in some ways Véra Nabokov. Stacey Schiff, who has pointed out many similarities between them, calls her the "Véra-like Clare" (98; see also annotations to chapter 9 of *Sebastian Knight*).

Sebastian met Clare in 1924, the same year that Vladimir and Véra got engaged. Irina Guadanini might have been as captivating as Nina; Schiff tells us that she was called "a siren" and "a femme fatale" (86, 87). She was a dog groomer, and in a photograph has a large dog (an Alsatian) by her side, just as Nina has her "heavy bulldog" (Grayson 72, 152). Nabokov's infatuation was very serious; he told his mother about "his perfect inability to live without" Irina (Schiff 87). Nonetheless, the affair lasted no longer than half a year in 1937 and was ended after some serious rows between Vladimir and Véra (Schiff 90). Vladimir and Irina separated in Cannes, just as V. supposes that it might have been "somewhere in Cannes" that the final break-up between Sebastian and Nina occurs (172).

In *Sebastian Knight* the novelist yields to the enchantress and leaves his devoted partner Clare. By leaving "the splendid woman he loved," writes Brian Boyd, "Nabokov has projected on to Sebastian a stylized alternative continuation of his own recent past: a writer leaves a woman obviously ideal for him to follow another who fatally attracts him, and finds his life destroyed as a consequence" (*VNRY* 501). Stacy Schiff agrees with this: "Certainly Sebastian Knight ventures where Nabokov did not, leaving his Véra-like Clare, for the other woman" (98; see also Nakata, "A Failed Reader Redeemed" 120–123).

Sebastian's life as reconstructed by V. might thus be a fictionalized future that Nabokov avoided in real life. But there is also another Sebastian whose life can be reconstructed by using the many references and clues that V. in his report offers. This life might reflect the happy but hidden life Sergey had with Hermann.

By comparing these "two modes of life," a near disastrous one and a cheerful one, the first a reflection of his own, the second of Sergey's life, Nabokov pays a great tribute to his brother.

VIII

As most critics, if not all, who wrote about *Sebastian Knight* have endorsed V.'s story that Sebastian's infatuation with Nina wrecked his life, there was not much need to investigate this reading of the novel. Priority has been given to see whether another reading, Sebastian finding a new lover in Uncle Black, is plausible too.

Many Nabokov scholars are convinced that Nabokov's novels are over-determined: they contain more information than is compatible with one reading (see, for example, Couturier, "Near-tyranny"). And for the readings that are feasible there is no hierarchy: the arguments which support one reading cannot be used to contradict another. Shakespeare's dark lady coexists with the fair youth.

In *Nikolay Gogol* Nabokov writes that Gogol's art appeals to the "secret depth of the human soul" and that only the right sort of readers will recognize this appeal: "my brother, my doubles." And he proceeds by telling: "My sister is reading. She is my aunt" (150).

Certainly Nabokov is not inviting his readers to construct an incestuous parenthood that might explain such family ties (it could be done). He is inviting his readers to be interested in human beings in such a way that the aporetic distinction between sister and aunt ceases to be of importance. In the same way it does not really matter how it can be that V.'s half-brother was in love with Nina as well as with Uncle Black, such is the secret depth of *The Real Life of Sebastian Knight*.

Works Cited

WORKS CITED BY VLADIMIR NABOKOV

(Note: Parenthetical abbreviations indicate how the works are identified in text.)

Ada, or Ardor: A Family Chronicle. New York: Vintage International, 1990. (*Ada*).
Bend Sinister. New York: Vintage International, 1990.
"Chapter Sixteen." *Speak, Memory. An Autobiography Revisited.* London: Penguin Books, 2000. 238–251.
The Defense. New York: Vintage International, 1990. (*Defense*).
Despair. New York: Vintage International, 1989.
Eugene Onegin, A Novel in Verse by Aleksandr Pushkin. Trans. and with a Commentary by Vladimir Nabokov. 4 vols. 1964. Princeton: Princeton University Press, 1975. (*Eugene Onegin*).
The Enchanter. London: Picador, 1987.
The Eye. London: Panther Books, 1972.
The Gift. New York: Vintage International, 1991. (*Gift*).
Glory. New York: Vintage International, 1991.
Invitation to a Beheading. New York: Vintage International, 1989.
King, Queen, Knave. New York: Vintage International, 1989.
Laughter in the Dark. New York: Vintage International, 1989.
Lectures on Literature. Ed. Fredson Bowers. New York: Harcourt Brace Jovanovich, 1982.
Lectures on Russian Literature. Ed. Fredson Bowers. London: Picador, 1983.
Letters to Véra. Ed. and trans. Olga Voronina and Brian Boyd. London: Penguin Classics, 2014.
Lolita (The Annotated Lolita). New York: Vintage Books, 1991.
Look at the Harlequins! New York: Vintage International, 1990.

Mary. New York: Vintage International, 1989.
Nikolai Gogol. New York: New Directions, 1961.
Pale Fire. New York: Vintage International, 1989.
Pnin. New York: Vintage International, 1989.
Poems and Problems. New York: McGraw-Hill, 1981.
The Real Life of Sebastian Knight. New York: Vintage International, 1992. (*Sebastian Knight*).
Speak, Memory: An Autobiography Revisited. New York: Vintage International, 1989. (*Speak, Memory*).
Strong Opinions. New York: Vintage International, 1990. (*SO*).
The Stories of Vladimir Nabokov. New York: Alfred A. Knopf, 1996. (*Stories*).
Transparent Things. 1972. New York: Vintage International, 1989.

OTHER WORKS CITED

(When more than one work by the same author is mentioned, one or more words from the title of the publication concerned are added to the author's name in the citations in the main text.)

Akikusa, Shun'ichiro. "The Vanished Cane and the Revised Trick: A Solution for Nabokov's 'Lips to Lips.'" *Nabokov Studies* 10 (2006): 99–120.
Alexander, Doris. *Creating Literature out of Life. The Making of Four Masterpieces.* Pennsylvania: Pennsylvania State University Press, 1996.
Alexandrov, Vladimir E. *Nabokov's Otherworld.* Princeton: Princeton UP, 1991.
———, ed. *The Garland Companion to Vladimir Nabokov.* New York and London: Garland Publishing, 1995.
Appel, Alfred, Jr. *Nabokov's Dark Cinema.* New York: Oxford UP, 1974.
———, ed. *Lolita.* By Vladimir Nabokov. *(The Annotated Lolita.)* New York: Vintage Books, 1991.
Arnold, Matthew. *Essays in Criticism.* London: Dent, 1964.
Barabtarlo, Gennady. *Aerial View: Essays on Nabokov's Art and Metaphysics.* New York: Peter Lang, 1993.
———. "The Man Is the Book." *Cycnos* 24.1 (2007): 95–104.
———. *Phantom of Fact: A Guide to Nabokov's* Pnin. Ann Arbor: Ardis, 1989.
Baer, Brian James. "The Other Russia: Re-Presenting the Gay Experience." *Kritika: Explorations in Russian and Eurasian History* 1.1 (2000): 183–194.
Baring, Maurice. "In Memoriam, A.H." *The Golden Book of English Modern Poetry.* Ed. Thomas Caldwell. London: J.M. Dent, 1935. 255–261.
———. *Landmarks in Russian Literature.* 1910. London: Methuen, 1960.
———. *The Puppet Show of Memory.* 1932. London: Cassell, 1987.
Baring-Gould, William S., and Cecil Baring-Gould. *The Annotated Mother Goose.* New York: Clarkson N. Potter / Bramhall House, 1975.

Barnstead, John. *Kuzmin: An Introductory Essay.* 2009. http://etc.dal.ca/kuzmin/intro_essay_english_uni.html.

Barolsky, Paul. "Leonardo, Satan, and the Mystery of Modern Art." *Virginia Quarterly Review* 74.3 (1998): 393–414.

Bate, Jonathan. *The Genius of Shakespeare.* London: Picador, 1998.

Baudelaire, Charles. *Les Fleurs du Mal.* Paris: Librairie Mireille Ceni, n.d.

Begnal, Michael H. "The Fledgling Fictionalist." www.libraries.psu.edu/nabokov/begnal3.htm.

Berndt de Souza Mello, Jansy. "'When a Clown Develops Wings.'" *The Nabokovian* 62 (2009): 31–37.

Bethea, David M. "Nabokov and Blok." *The Garland Companion to Vladimir Nabokov.* Ed. Vladimir E. Alexandrov. New York: Garland Publishing, 1995. 374–382.

The Bible. The King James Version. New York: Pocket Books, 1942.

Binyon, T.J. *Pushkin. A Biography.* London: HarperCollins, 2003.

Blackwell, Stephen H. *The Quill and the Scalpel: Nabokov's Art and the World of Science.* Columbus: Ohio State University Press, 2009.

Bodenstein, Jürgen. *"The Excitement of Verbal Adventure": A Study of Vladimir Nabokov's Prose.* 2 vols. Heidelberg: 1977.

Boswell, James. *The Life of Samuel Johnson.* 2 vols. London: Dent, 1952.

Bowness, Alan. *Modern European Art.* London: Thames and Hudson, 1985.

Boyd, Brian. "Annotations to *Ada*. 1. Part 1, Chapter 1." *The Nabokovian* 30 (1993): 9–48.

———. "*Lolita*: What We Know and What We Don't." *Cycnos* 24.1 (2007): 215–228.

———. *Nabokov's* Pale Fire: *The Magic of Artistic Discovery.* Princeton: Princeton UP, 1999.

———. *Stalking Nabokov.* New York: Columbia UP, 2011.

———. *Vladimir Nabokov. The American Years.* Princeton: Princeton UP, 1991. (VNAY).

———. *Vladimir Nabokov. The Russian Years.* Princeton: Princeton UP, 1990. (VNRY).

———. *Why Lyrics Last. Evolution, Cognition and Shakespeare's* Sonnets. Cambridge: Harvard UP, 2012.

———, ed. *Novels and Memoirs, 1941–1951.* By Vladimir Nabokov. New York: Library Classics of the United States, 1996.

Boyd, Brian, and Stanislav Shvabrin, eds. *Verses and Versions: Three Centuries of Russian Poetry.* Selected and translated by Vladimir Nabokov. Orlando: Harcourt, 2008.

Bradley, A.C. *Shakespearean Tragedy.* 1904. London: Macmillan, 1960.

Bradley, Rory. "*The Woman in White* as a Subtext in *The Real Life of Sebastian Knight.*" *The Nabokovian* 61 (2008): 14–23.

Breverton, Terry. *Breverton's Complete Herbal*. London: Quercus Publishing, 2011.
Brewer's Dictionary of Phrase and Fable. London: Book Club Association, 1978.
Briggs, Katherine. *A Dictionary of Fairies*. Harmondworth: Penguin Books, 1977.
Brooke, Rupert. *Poetical Works*. Ed. Geoffrey Keynes. London: Faber, 1960.
Bulfinch, Thomas. *The Golden Age of Myth and Legend*. Ware: Wordsworth Editions, *1993*.
Burgin, Diana Lewis. "Laid Out in Lavender. Perceptions of Lesbian Love in Russian Literature and Criticism of the Silver Age. 1893–1917." *Sexuality and the Body in Russian Culture*. Ed. Jane T. Costlow, Stephanie Sandler, and Judith Vowles. Stanford: Stanford University Press, 1993. 177–203.
Burnand, Sir Francis Cowley. *The Colonel*. www.xix-e_pierre-marteau.com/ed/colonel.html.
Burns, Tom. *Psychiatry: A Very Short Introduction*. Oxford: Oxford UP, 2006.
Byron, Lord. *Poetical Works*. London: Oxford UP, 1926.
Caine, William. *The Author of Trixie*. London: Herbert Jenkins, 1924.
Carey, John. *John Donne: Life, Mind and Art*. London: Faber and Faber, 1983.
Carey, John, and Alastair Fowler, eds. *The Poems*. By John Milton. London: Longmans, 1968.
Carlyle, Thomas. *The French Revolution*. New York: The Modern Library, n.d.
Carpenter, Angelica Shirley. *Lewis Carroll: Through the Looking Glass*. Minneapolis: Lerner Publications, 2003.
Carrol, Lewis. *Alice's Adventures in Wonderland*. New York: Airmont Publishing, 1965.
Caulton, Andrew. *The Absolute Solution. Nabokov's Response to Tyranny, 1938*. Bern: Peter Lang, 2013.
Caws, Mary Ann. *Marcel Proust*. Woodstock: Overlook Press, 2003.
Caws, Mary Ann, and Sarah Bird Wright. *Bloomsbury and France, Art and Friends*. Oxford: Oxford UP, 2000.
Chaucer. *Complete Works*. London: Oxford UP, 1967.
Chekhov, Anton. *The Seagull and Other Plays*. Trans. Elisaveta Fen. Harmondsworth: Penguin Books, 1954.
———. *Selected Stories*. Trans. Jessie Coulson. London: Oxford UP, 1963.
Chernowitz, Maurice E. *Proust and Painting*. New York: International University Press, 1945.
Christie, Agatha. *Murder on the Orient Express*. LondON; Fontana/Collins, 1981.
Cockburn, Claud. *Bestseller*. Harmondsworth: Penguin Books, 1975.
Coleridge, Samuel Taylor. *The Poetical Works*. London: Oxford University Press, 1957.
Collins, William Wilkie. *The Woman in White*. London: Everyman's Library, 1991.
Collins Concise Dictionary. London: Guild Publishing, 1985.
Concise Oxford Dictionary. Oxford: Clarendon Press, 1929.

Conder, Alan, ed. *Cassell's Anthology of French Poetry.* London: Cassell, 1950.

Connolly, Julian. "The Challenge of Interpreting and Decoding Nabokov: Strategies and Suggestions." *Cycnos* 24.1 (2007): 155–170.

———. "From Biography to Autobiography and Back: The Fictionalization of the Narrated Self in *The Real Life of Sebastian Knight.*" *Cycnos* 10.1 (1993): 39–46.

———, ed. *Nabokov and His Fiction: New Perspectives.* Cambridge: Cambridge UP, 1999.

Cornwell, Neil. "From Sirin to Nabokov: The Transition to English." *The Cambridge Companion to Nabokov.* Ed. Julian W. Connolly. Cambridge: Cambridge UP, 2005, 151–167.

Cottle, Basil. *The Penguin Dictionary of Surnames.* Harmondsworth: Penguin Books, 1978.

Couturier, Maurice. "Annotating vs. Interpreting Nabokov: The Author as a Helper or a Screen?" *Cycnos* 24.1 (2007): 1–13.

———. "The Near-Tyranny of the Author: *Pale Fire.*" *Nabokov and His Fiction: New Perspectives.* Ed. Julian W. Connolly. Cambridge: Cambridge UP, 1999.

———, ed. *Oeuvres romanesques completes.* By Vladimir Nabokov. Vol. II. Bibliothèque de la Pléiade. n.p.: Gallimard, 2010.

Cuddon, J. A. *The Penguin Dictionary of Literary Terms and Literary Theory.* London: Penguins Books, 1999.

da Vinci, Leonardo. *The Notebooks.* Ed. Jean Paul Richter. 2 vols. New York: Dover Publications, 1970.

Daiches, David. *Milton.* London: Arrow Books, 1963.

Davenport-Hines, Richard. *A Night at the Majestic. Proust and the Great Modernist Dinner Party of 1922.* London: Faber and Faber, 2006.

De Botton, Alain. *How Proust Can Change Your Life.* London: Picador, 1997.

Delage-Toriel, Lara. "Disclosures under Seal: Nabokov, Secrecy and the Reader." *Cycnos* 24.1 (2007): 69–79.

———. "Ultraviolet Darlings. Representaions of Women in Nabokov's Prose Fiction." Diss. University of Cambridge, 2001.

Dolinin, Alexander. *"The Gift." The Garland Companion to Vladimir Nabokov.* Ed. Vladimir E. Alexandrov. New York: Garland Publishing, 1995. 135–169.

Donne, John. *The Complete English Poems.* Ed. J. A. Smith. Harmondsworth: Penguin Books, 1981.

Douglas, Charlotte, ed. *Collected Works of Velimir Khlebnikov.* Vol. 1. *Letters and Theoretical Writings.* Trans. Paul Schmidt. Cambridge: Harvard UP, 1987.

Doyle, Sir Arthur Conan. *The Complete Sherlock Holmes Short Stories.* London: John Murray, 1971.

———. *The Hound of Baskervilles.* New York: Airmont, 1965.

Dragunoiu, Dana. *Vladimir Nabokov and the Poetics of Liberalism.* Evanston: Northwestern University Press, 2011.

Efimov, Mikhail. "Nabokov and Prince Mirsky." *The Goalkeeper*. Ed. Yuri Leving. Boston: Academic Studies Press, 2010. 218–229.

Emery, Emily. "'An Occult Resemblance': The Ripples of Chekhov in *The Real Life of Sebastian Knight*." *The Nabokovian* 20 (1988): 24–29.

Encyclopaedia Britannica. 23 vols. Chicago: William Benton, 1964.

Fischman, Zachary. "Sebastian through the Looking Glass." *The Nabokovian* 67 (2011) 28–31.

Flaubert, Gustave. *Madame Bovary*. Trans. Eleanor Marx-Aveling. New York: Pocket Books, 1949.

Fogelin, Robert J. *Wittgenstein*. London: Routledge and Kegan Paul, 1987.

Fonvizin, Denis Ivanovich. *The Infant: Four Russian Plays*. Trans. Joshua Cooper. Harmondsworth: Penguin Books, 1972.

Foster, John Burt, Jr. *Nabokov's Art of Memory and European Modernism*. Princeton: Princeton UP, 1993.

Frank, Siggy. *Nabokov's Theatrical Imagination*. Cambridge: Cambridge UP, 2012.

Freud, Sigmund. *Leonardo da Vinci: A Psychosexual Study of an Infantile Reminiscence*. Trans. A. A. Brill. The Gutenberg Project. New York: Moffat, Yard & Co., 1916.

Fuchs, R.H. *Dutch Painting*. London: Thames and Hudson, 1978.

Fussell Paul. *The Great War and Modern Memory*. London: Oxford University Press, 1977.

———. "Review of 'Notes on Prosody' by Vladimir Nabokov." *Encounter* April 1966: 76–78.

Gay, Peter. *Education of the Senses*. New York and Oxford: Oxford UP, 1984.

Gardner, Helen. "The Argument about 'The Ecstacy.'" *Elizabethan and Jacobean Studies*. Eds. Herbert Davis and Helen Gardner. Oxford: Clarendon Press, 1959. 279–306.

Gardner, Martin, ed. *The Annotated Alice: Lewis Carroll*. Harmondsworth: Penguin Books, 1977.

Gide, André. *The Counterfeiters*. Trans. Dorothy Bussy. New York: Vintage Books, 1973.

———. *If It Die*. Trans. Dorothy Bussy. New York: Vintage Books, 1963.

———. *L'immoraliste*. Paris: Mercure de France, 1902.

———. *The Notebooks of André Walter*. Trans. and Notes Wade Baskin. London: Peter Owen, 1968.

Gifford, Don. *Ulysses Annotated*. Berkeley: U of California P, 1988.

Glendinning, Victoria. *Vita: The Life of Vita Sackville-West*. London: Penguin Books, 1984.

Gogol, Nikolai. *Dead Souls*. Trans. Andrew R. MacAndrew. New York: New American Library, 1961.

Granoien, Neil. "*Wings* and 'The World of Art.'" *Russian Literature Triquarterly*. 11 (1975): 393–405.

Graves, Robert. *The Crowning Privilege*. Harmondsworth: Penguin Books, 1959.

———. *The Greek Myths*. 2 vols. Harmondsworth: Penguin Books, 1984 (vol. 1) and 1955 (vol. 2).

———. *Hercules, My Shipmate*. New York: Pyramid Books, 1966.

———. "Introduction." *Le Morte d'Arthur*. By Sir Thomas Malory. Ed. Keith Banes. New York: Bramhall House, 1952.

Gray, Camilla. *The Russian Experiment in Art, 1863–1922*. Rev. Marian Burleigh-Motley. London: Thames and Hudson, 1993.

Gray, Thomas. "Ode on a Distant Prospect of Eton College." *English Verse*. Vol. 3: *Dryden to Wordsworth*. Ed. W. Peacock. 5 vols. London: Oxford University Press, 1960.

Grayson, Jane. "The French Connection: Vladimir Nabokov and Alfred de Musset. Ideas and Practices of Translation." *Slavic and East European Review* 73.4 (1995): 613–658.

———. *Vladimir Nabokov*. London: Penguin Books, 2001.

Gregorio, Laurence A. "Sylvandre's Symposium: The Platonic and the Ambigous in *L'Astrée*." *Renaissance Quarterly* 52 (1999): 782–804.

Grigoriev, S.L. *The Diaghilev Ballet, 1919–1929*. Trans. Vera Bowen. Harmondsworth: Penguin Books, 1960.

Grossman, Lev. "The Gay Nabokov." www.salon.com/2000/05/17/nabokov_5.

Gwynn, Stephen. *Robert Louis Stevenson*. London: Macmillan and Co., 1939.

Haggerty, George E., ed. *Gay History and Cultures: An Encyclopedia*. New York: Garland Publishing, 2000.

Hall, James. *Dictionary of Subjects and Symbols in Art*. New York: Harper & Row, 1974.

Harrison, G.B., ed. *The Sonnets and A Lovers's Complaint*. By William Shakespeare. Harmondsworth: Penguin Books, 1949.

Hawthorne, Nathaniel. *Rappacini's Daughter*. London: Hesperus Press, 2003.

Higdon, David Leon. "Gay Sebastian and Cheerful Charles: Homoeroticism in Waugh's *Brideshead Revisited*." *Ariel* 25.4 (1994): 77–89.

Holland, Vyvyan. *Oscar Wilde*. London: Book Club, 1978.

Hollier, Denis, ed. *A New History of French Literature*. Cambridge: Harvard University Press, 2001.

Holloway, Mark. *Norman Douglas. A Biography*. London: Secker and Warburg, 1976.

Holmes, Richard. *The Age of Wonder*. London: HarperPress, 2009.

Homer. *The Odyssey*. Trans. E.V. Rieu. London: Penguin Books, 1991.

Hooper, Alfred. *Makers of Mathemathics*. New York: Vintage Books, 1948.

Horace. *The Complete Works*. Ed. Casper J. Kraemer Jr. New York: Modern Library, 1936.

Housman, A. E. *Collected Poems*. Harmondsworth: Penguin Books, 1961.

Hugo, Victor. "Conscience." *Cassell's Anthology of French Verse*. Ed. Alan Condor. London: Cassell, 1950. 178–180.

Huysmans, J. K. *Against Nature*. Trans. Robert Baldick. Harmondsworth: Penguin Books, 1968.

Impelluso, Lucia. *Nature and Its Symbols*. Trans. Stephen Sartarelli. Los Angeles: Getty Publications, 2004.

Jerome, Jerome K. *Three Men on the Bummel*. London: Penguin Books, 1994.

Johnson, D. Barton. "The Alpha and Omega of Nabokov's *Invitation to a Beheading*." *Nabokov's* Invitation to a Beheading. *A Critical Companion*. Ed. Julian W. Connolly. Evanston: Norhtwestern University Press, 1997. 119–138,

———. "The Books Reflected in Nabokov's *Eye*." *Slavic and East European Journal* 29.4 (1985): 393–404.

———. "Murochka, The Story of a Woman's Life." *The Nabokovian* 17 (1986): 42–45.

———. "Vladimir Nabokov and Rupert Brooke." *Nabokov and His Fiction: New Perspectives*. Ed. Julian W. Connolly. Cambridge: Cambridge UP, 1999. 177–196.

———. "Vladimir Nabokov and Walter de la Mare's 'Other World.'" *The Shape of Nabokov's World*. Vol. 1 of *Nabokov's World*. Ed. Jane Grayson, Arnold McMillin and Priscilla Meyer. Basingstoke: Palgrave, 2000. 71–87.

———. *Worlds in Regression*. Ann Arbor: Ardis, 1985.

Johnston, Robert H. *"New Mecca, New Babylon": Paris and the Russian Exiles, 1920–1945*. Kingston and Montreal: McGill-Queen's University Press, 1988.

Joyce, James. *Ulysses*. 1922. Harmondsworth: Penguin Books, 1968.

Juliar, Michael. *Vladimir Nabokov: A Descriptive Bibliography*. New York: Garland, 1986.

Karlinsky, Simon. "Death and Resurrection of Mikhail Kuzmin." *Slavic Review* 38.1 (1979): 92–96.

———. "Foreword: Who Are the Emigré Writers?" *The Bitter Air of Exile: Russian Writers in the West, 1922–1972*. Ed. Simon Karlinsky and Alfred Appel. Berkeley: University of California Press, 1977. 5–9.

———. "Russian Literature." *The Gay and Lesbian Heritage*. Ed. Claude J. Summers. New York: Routledge, 2002. 611–618.

———. ed. *Dear Bunny, Dear Volodya: The Nabokov-Wilson Letters, 1940–1971*. Berkeley: University of California Press, 2001.

Kaye, Richard. "Sexual Identity at the Fin de Siècle." *The Cambridge Companion to the Fin de Siècle*. Ed. Gail Marshall. Cambridge: Cambridge UP, 2007. 53–72.

Keats, John. *The Complete Poems*. Ed. John Barnard. Harmondsworth: Penguin Books, 1981.

Kenny, Anthony. *Wittgenstein*. Harmondsworth: Penguin Books, 1975.

Kerr, Jessica. *Shakespeare's Flowers*. Harmondsworth: Kestrel Books, 1969.

Ketchian, Sonia. *Keats and the Russian Poets*. Birmingham Slavonic Monographs. No. 33. University of Birmingham, 2001.

Keynes, Geoffrey, ed. *The Poetical Works*. By Rupert Brooke. London: Faber, 1960.

Khayyám, Omar. *Rubáiyát*. Trans. Edward Fitzgerald. Illustrations Edmund J. Sullivan. New York: Avon, n.d.

———. *Rubáiyát*. Trans. Edward Fitzgerald. Illustrations Gordon Ross. New York: Pocket Books, 1941.

Khodasevich, Vladislav. "On Sirin." Trans. Michael H. Walker. *Nabokov, Criticism, Reminiscences, Translations and Tributes*. Ed. Alfred Appel, Jr. and Charles Newman. Evanston: Northwestern University Press, 1970. 96–101.

Kipling, Rudyard. *Short Stories: Volume 1*. Harmondsworth: Penguin Books, 1984.

Knopp, Sherron E. "Vita Sackville-West." *The Gay and Lesbian Literary Heritage*. Ed. Claude J. Summers. New York: Routledge, 2002. 619–620

Kuzmin, Mikhail. *Wings: Selected Prose and Poetry*. Ed. and Trans. Michael Green. Ann Arbor: Ardis: 1980.

Langeveld, Arthur. *Russische literatuur in een notendop*. Amsterdam: Bert Bakker, 2006.

Larmour, David H.J., ed. *Discourse and Ideology in Nabokov's Prose*. London: Routledge, 2002.

Latham, Ronald. "Introduction." *The Travels*. By Marco Polo. Harmondsworth: Penguin Books, 1984. 7–29.

Laver, James. *Costume and Fashion*. London: Thames and Hudson, 1995.

Lawlor, John. Introduction. *Le Morte d'Arthur*. By Sir Thomas Malory. Ed. Janet Cowen. Vol. 1. Harmondsworth: Penguin Books, 1978

Lee, Hermione. *Biography. A Very Short Introduction*. Oxford: Oxford UP, 2009.

Lehmann, John. *Rupert Brooke: His Life and His Legend*. London: Quartet Books, 1980.

Leider, Emily. *Dark Lover: The Life and Death of Rudolph Valentino*. New York: Faber and Faber, 2004.

Léon Noel, Lucie. "Playback." *Nabokov: Criticism, Reminiscences, Translations*. Ed. Alfred Appel and Charles Newman. Evanston: Northwestern University Press, 1970. 209–219.

Lermontov, Mikhail. *A Hero of Our Time*. Trans. Vladimir and Dmitri Nabokov. Oxford: Oxford UP, 1984.

Letley, Emma. *Maurice Baring*. London: Constable, 1991.

Levi, Anthony. *Guide to French Literature. Beginnings to 1789*. Detroit: St James Press, 1994.

Leving, Yuri. *Keys to* The Gift. *A Guide to Nabokov's Novel*. Boston: Academic Studies Press, 2011.

Lindheim, Nancy. "Rethinking Sexuality and Class in *Twelfth Night*." *University of Toronto Quarterly* 76.2 (2007) 679–713.

Lippert, W., and D. Podlech. *Wild Flowers*. London: HarperCollins, 2001.

Lodge, David. *The Practice of Writing*. London: Penguin Books, 1996.

Loring, John. *Tiffany's 150 Years*. New York: Doubleday, 1987.

Livak, Leonid. *How It Was Done in Paris: Russian Émigré Literature and French Modernism*. Wisconsin: University of Wisconsin Press, 2003.

Long, Michael. *Marvell, Nabokov: Childhood and Arcadia*. Oxford: Oxford UP, 1984.

Lokrantz, Jessie Thomas. *The Underside of the Weave: Some Stylistic Devices Used by Vladimir Nabokov*. Diss. Uppsala U, 1973.

Lucie-Smith, Edward. *Symbolist Art*. London: Thames and Hudson, 1997.

The Mabinogion. Trans. Jeffrey Gantz. Harmondsworth: Penguin Books, 1976.

Maddox, Lucy. *Nabokov's Novels in English*. London: Croom Helm, 1983.

Maerz, A., and M. Rea Paul. *A Dictionary of Color*. New York: McGraw-Hill, 1930.

MacCarthy, Fiona. *Byron, Life and Legend*. London: John Murray, 2002.

Malory, Sir Thomas. *Le Morte d'Arthur*. Ed. *Keith Banes*. New York: Bramhall House, 1957.

———. *Le Morte d'Arthur*. Ed. Janet Cowen. 2 vols. Harmondsworth: Penguin Books, 1978.

Mann, Thomas. *Death in Venice*. Trans. H. T. Lowe-Porter. Harmondsworth: Penguin Books, 1955.

———. *The Magic Mountain*. Trans. H.T. Lowe-Porter. Harmondsworth: Penguin Books, 1960.

Marchand, Leslie. *Byron. A Portrait*. London: Cresset Library, 1987.

Marshall, Gail, ed. *The Cambridge Companion to the Fin de Siècle*. Cambridge: Cambridge UP, 2007.

Martin, William H., and Sandra Mason. *The Art of Omar Khayyam*. London: I.B. Tauris, 2007.

Martiny, Erik. "'Oculate Paradise': Colour Saturation in Vladimir Nabokov's *Lolita* in the Context of its Cinematographic Adaptations." *Graat,* July 10, 2011. http://www.graat.fr/6martiny.pdf.

Marvell, Andrew. *The Poems and Letters*. Ed. H.M. Margoliouth. Vol. I: *Poems*. Oxford: Oxford UP, 1971.

Mason, Bobbie Ann. *Nabokov's Garden*. Ann Arbor: Ardis, 1974.

Maturin, Charles. *Melmoth the Wanderer*. Harmondsworth: Penguin Books, 1977.

Maupassant, Guy de. *The Best Short Stories*. New York: Modern Library, 1945.

Meltzer, Françoise. "Writing and the Dance." *A New History of French Literature*. Ed. Dennis Hollier. Cambridge: Harvard University Press, 1994. 813–819.

Merkel, Stephanie. "Nabokov's *King, Queen, Knave* and the *Commedia Dell'Arte*." *Nabokov Studies* 1 (1994): 83–102.

Metropolitan Museum of Art. *Monet's Years at Giverny: Beyond Impressionism*. New York, 1978.

Meyer, Priscilla. "Anglophilia and Optimistics: Sebastian Knight's Bookshelves." *Russian Literature in the West*: A Tribute for David M. Bethea.. Ed. Alexander Dolinin, Lazar Fleishman and Leonid Livak. Stanford: Stanford Slavic Studies, 2008. 212–226.

———. "Life as Annotation: Sebastian Knight, Nathaniel Hawthorne, Vladimir Nabokov." *Cycnos* 24.1 (2007): 183–192.

Mirsky, D.S. *A History of Russian Literature*. London: Routledge and Kegan Paul, 1964.

Mochulsky, Konstantin. *Aleksandr Blok*. Trans. Doris V. Johnson. Detroit: Wayne State University Press, 1983.

Monk, Ray. *Ludwig Wittgenstein*. New York: Free Press, 1990.

Morgan, Paul B. "Nabokov and the Medieval Hunt Allegory." *Revue de la littérature comparée* 3 (1986): 321–327.

Munthe, Axel. *The Story of San Michele*. London: John Murray, 1968.

Nabokov, Dmitri, and Matthew J. Bruccoli, eds. *Vladimir Nabokov Selected Letters, 1940–1977*. San Diego: Harcourt Brace Jovanovich, 1989.

Naiman, Eric. *Nabokov, Perversely*. Ithaca and London: Cornell University Press, 2010.

Nakata, Akiko. "A Failed Reader Redeemed: 'Spring in Fialta' and *The Real Life of Sebastian Knight*." *Nabokov Studies* 11 (2007/8): 101–126.

———. "Wittgenstein Echoes in *Transparent Things*." *The Nabokovian* 45 (2000) 48–53.

Nepomnyashchy, Catherine Theimer. "Revising Nabokov Revising the Detective Novel: Vladimir, Agatha and the Terms of Engagement." *Revising Nabokov Revising*. Ed. Mitsuyoshi Numano and Tadashi Wakashima. Kyoto: The Nabokov Society of Japan, 2010. 163–168.

Nicholl, Charles. *Leonardo da Vinci*. London: Penguin Books, 2005.

Nicholson, B. E., S. Ary, and M. Gregory. *The Oxford Book of Wild Flowers*. London: Oxford UP, 1970.

Nicol, Charles. "The Mirrors of Sebastian Knight." *Nabokov: The Man and His Work*. Ed. L.S. Dembo. Madison: University of Wisconsin Press, 1967.

Norman, Will. "*The Real Life of Sebastian Knight* and the Modernist Impasse." *Nabokov Studies* 10 (2006) 67-97.

Norton Anthology of English Literature. 2 vols. New York: W.W. Norton, 1986.

Obolensky, Dmitri. *The Penguin Book of Russian Verse*. Harmondsworth: Penguin Books, 1962.

Obolensky, Valerian. *Russians in Exile: The History of a Diaspora. Part III after the Revolution.* russians.bellevueholidayrentals.com/dias9.html.

Olcott, Anthony. "The Author's Special Intention: A Study of *The Real Life of Sebastian Knight.*" *A Book of Things about Vladimir Nabokov.* Ed. Carl R. Proffer. Ann Arbor: Ardis, 1974. 104–121.

Ogrinc, Will. "Sint Sebastiaan Geschoren." *Maatstaf* 1 (1986): 39–58.

Opie, Iona, and Peter Opie. *The Oxford Dictionary of Nursery Rhymes.* Oxford: Clarendon Press, 1951.

Ovid. *Metamorphoses.* London: Penguin Books, 1955.

Oxford English Dictionary. 20 vols. Oxford: Clarendon Press, 1989.

Page, Norman. "Kipling's World of Men." *Ariel* (1979) 81–93.

———. *Nabokov. The Critical Heritage.* London: Routledge and Kegan Paul, 1982.

Paglia, Camille. *Sexual Personae.* London: Penguin Books, 1991.

Painter, George D. *Marcel Proust.* Harmondsworth: Penguin Books, 1983.

Parker, Derek. *John Donne and His World.* London: Thames and Hudson, 1975.

Pater, Walter Horatio. *The Renaissance.* London: Collins, 1961.

Pearson, Hesketh. *Oscar Wilde: His Life and Wit.* New York: Harper and Brothers, 1946.

Pegler, Martin. *Soldier's Songs and Slang of the Great War.* Oxford: Osprey Publishing, 2014.

Pequigney, Joseph. "The Two Antonio's and Same-Sex Love in *Twelfth Night* and *The Merchant of Venice.*" *English Literary Renaissance* 22 (1992): 201–221.

Peterson, Dale. "Knight's Move: Nabokov, Shlovsky and the Afterlife of Sirin." *Nabokov Studies* 11 (2007/8): 25–37.

Pitzer, Andrea. *The Secret History of Vladimir Nabokov.* New York: Pegasus Books, 2013.

Plato. *The Symposium.* Trans. W. Hamilton. Harmondsworth: Penguin, 1965.

Podlech, Dieter. *Herbs and Healing Plants.* London: HarperCollins, 1996.

Poe, Edgar Allan. *The Best Known Works.* New York: Blue Ribbon Books, 1927.

Polo, Marco. *The Travels.* Trans. Ronald Latham. Harmondsworth: Penguin Books, 1978.

Pope, Alexander. *The Poems.* Ed. John Butt. New Haven: Yale University Press, 1963.

Praz, Mario. *The Romantic Agony.* Trans. Angus Davidson. London: Fontana Library, 1966.

Proffer, Carl R. *Keys to Lolita.* Bloomington: Indiana University Press, 1968.

Proffer, Carl, and Ellendea Proffer, eds. *The Silver Age of Russian Culture.* Ann Arbor: Ardis, 1975.

Proust, Marcel. *Remembrance of Things Past.* Trans. C.K. Scott Moncrieff and Terence Kilmartin. 3 vols. London: Penguin Books, 1989.

———. *Swann's Way*. Trans. C.K. Scott Moncrieff. Harmondsworth: Penguin Books, 1957.

Quennell, Peter. *Byron: The Years of Fame*. 1935. London: Penguin Books, 1954.

Quennel, Peter, and Hamish Johnson. *Who's Who in Shakespeare*. London: Weidenfeld and Nicholson, 1973.

Quin, Dr. J. D. "Nabokov's Cardiology." *The Nabokovian* 26 (1991): 40–44.

Rampton, David. *Vladimir Nabokov*. Basingstoke: Macmillan, 1993.

Reed, Christopher. *Art and Homosexuality*. Oxford: Oxford UP, 2011.

Reynolds, Graham. *Turner*. London: Thames and Hudson, 1997.

Rimmon, Shlomith. "Problems of Voice in Nabokov's *The Real Life of Sebastian Knight*." *PTL: Journal for Descriptive Poetics and Theory* 1 (1976):498–512. Rpt. Phyllis A. Roth, ed. *Critical Essays on Vladimir Nabokov*. Boston: G.K. Hall & Co, 1984. 109–129.

Rippl, Daniela. *Vladimir Nabokov: Sein Leben im Bildern und Texten*. Berlin: Alexander Fest Verlag, 1998.

Ronen, Omry. "Emulation, Anti-Parody, Intertextuality and Annotation." *Nabokov Studies* 5 (1998/9): 63–70.

Rowe, W. W. *Nabokov's Spectral Dimension*. Ann Arbor: Ardis, 1981.

Rusinko, Elaine. "Lost in Space and Time: Gumilev's '*Zabludvsijsja Tramvaj*.'" *Slavic and East European Journal* 26.4 (1982): 383–402.

Russell, Alan. "Introduction." *Madame Bovary*. By Gustave Flaubert. Trans. Alan Russell. London: Penguin, 1950.

Rutledge, David S. *Nabokov's Permanent Mystery*. Jefferson: McFarland, 2011.

Rylkova, Galina. "Okrylyonnyy Soglyadatay—The Winged Eavesdropper: Nabokov and Kuzmin." *Discourse and Ideology in Nabokov's Prose*. Ed. David H.J. Larmour. London: Routledge, 2002. 43–58.

Sackville-West, Vita. *The Edwardians*. New York: Avon Books, 1975.

Salehar, Anna Maria. "Nabokov's *Gift*: An Apprenticeship in Creativity." *A Book of Things About Vladimir Nabokov*. Ed. Carl Proffer. Ann Arbor: Ardis, 1974. 70–83.

Sampson, George. *The Concise Cambridge History of English Literature*. Cambridge: Cambridge UP, 1970.

Schapiro, Leonard. Critical Essay. *Spring Torrents*. By Ivan Turgenev. Trans. Leonard Schapiro. London: Eyre Methuen, 1972.

Schiff, Stacy. *Véra. (Mrs. Vladimir Nabokov)*. New York: Random House, 1999.

Scheijen, Sjeng. *Sergej Diaghilev*. Amsterdam: Bert Bakker, 2011.

Schulz, Gretchen. "French Literature: Nineteenth Century." *The Gay and Lesbian Literary Heritage*. Ed. Claude J. Summers. New York: Routledge, 2002. 293–298.

Schuman, Samuel. *Nabokov's Shakespeare*. New York: Bloomsbury, 2014.

Senderovich, Savely, and Yelena Shvarts. "The Ghost in the Novel: André Chénier in Vladimir Nabokov." *Slavonic and East European Review* 78.3 (2000): 487–509.

———. "The Juice of Three Oranges. An Exploration of Nabokov's Language and World." *Nabokov's Studies* 6 (2000/2001): 75–124.

———. "Lehmann's Disease: A Comment on Nabokov's *The Real Life of Sebastian Knight*." *The Nabokovian* 63 (2009): 72–80.

Seymour, Miranda. *A Ring of Conspirators. Henry James and His Literary Circle.* London: Scribner, 2004.

———. *Otteline Morrell.* London: Sceptre, 1993.

Shakespeare, William. *The Complete Works.* London: Oxford University Press, 1955.

Shapiro, Gavriel. *The Sublime Artist's Studio.* Evanston: Northwestern University Press, 2009.

———. *The Tender Friendship and the Charm of Perfect Accord: Nabokov and His Father.* Ann Arbor: University of Michigan Press, 2014.

Shrayer, Maxim D. "Jewish Questions in Nabokov's Art and Life." *Nabokov and is Fiction: New Perspectives.* Ed. Julian W. Connolly. Cambridge: Cambridge UP, 1999. 73–91.

Shute, Jennefer. "Nabokov and Freud." *The Garland Companion to Vladimir Nabokov.* Ed Vladimir E. Alexandrov. New York: Garland Publishing, 1995. 412–420.

Shvabrin, Stanislav. *Vladimir Nabokov as Translator: The Multilingual Works of the Russian Period.* Diss. University of California, 2007. Ann Arbor: ProQuest, 2008.

———. "Vladimir Nabokov's 'La Belle Dame Sans Merci': A Study in the Ethics and Effects of Literary Adaptation." *Comparative Literature* 65.1 (2013): 101–122.

Singer, June. *Androgyny: Toward a New Theory of Sexuality.* New York: Anchor Books, 1977.

Sisson, J. B. *"The Real Life of Sebastian Knight": The Garland Companion to Vladimir Nabokov.* Ed. Vladimir E. Alexandrov. New York: Garland Publishing, 1995. 633–643.

Skonechnaia, Olga. "'People of the Moonlight': Silver Age Parodies in Nabokov's *The Eye* and *The Gift*." *Nabokov Studies* 3 (1996): 33–52.

Slivkin, Yevgeny. "The Last Stop of the Death Machine: An Attempt at a Rational Reading of 'The Runaway Streetcar' by N. Gumilev." *SEEJ* 43.1 (1999): 137–155.

Smith, A.J. "The Metaphysics of Love." *Review of English Studies. New Series* 9.36 (1958): 362–375.

———, ed. "Notes." *The Complete English Poems.* By John Donne. Harmondsworth: Penguin, 1981.

Smith, Bruce R. *Homosexual Desire in Shakespeare's England*. Chicago: U of Chicago P. 1994.

Smith, Patricia Juliana. "Marie Corelli." *The Gay and Lesbian Literary Heritage*. Ed. Claude J. Summers. New York: Routledge, 2002. 176.

Smyth, Ethel. *Maurice Baring*. London: William Heinemann, 1938.

Sologub, Fyodor. "The Poison Garden." Trans. Samuel Corian. *The Silver Age of Russian Culture*. Ed. Carl Proffer and Ellendea Proffer. Ann Arbor: Ardis, 1975. 261–275.

Stokoe, W.J. *The Observer's Book of Butterflies*. London: Frederick Warne & Co., 1958.

Southey, Robert. *Poetical Works*. London: Longman and Co., 1880.

Sparrow, John. Introduction. *Collected Poems*. By A.E. Housman. Harmondworth: Penguin, 1961.

Spenser, Edmund. *The Poetical Works*. London: Oxford UP, 1932.

Stegner, Page. *Escape into Aesthetics: The Art of Vladimir Nabokov*. London: Eyre and Spottiswoode, 1967.

Stevenson, Robert Louis. *Dr. Jekyll and Mr. Hyde and Other Stories*. Harmondsworth: Penguin, 1981.

Stewart, Philip. "Kisses, en Taille Douce." *A New History of French Literature*. Ed. Dennis Hollier. Cambridge: Harvard University Press, 1994. 507–517.

Stuart, Dabney. *Nabokov: The Dimension of Parody*. Baton Rouge: Louisiana State University Press, 1978.

Suasso, Frans. *Dichter, dame, diplomaat. Het laatste jaar van Alexander Poesjkin*. Leyden: Slavische Stichting, 1988.

Summers, Claude J., ed. *The Gay and Lesbian Literary Heritage*. New York: Routledge, 2002.

Sweeney, Susan Elizabeth. "Looking at Harlequins: Nabokov, the World of Art and the *Ballets Russes*." *Nabokov's World. Vol. 2: Reading Nabokov*. Ed. Jane Grayson, Arnold McMillan and Priscilla Meyer. Basingstoke: Palgrave, 2002. 73–95.

———. "Purloined Letters: Poe, Doyle and Nabokov." *Russian Literature Triquarterly* 24 (1991): 213–237.

———. "The Small Furious Devil: Memory in 'Scenes from the Life of a Double Monster.'" *A Small Alpine Form*. Ed. Charles Nichol and Gennady Barabtarlo. New York: Garland, 1993. 193–216.

Symons, A.J.A. *The Quest for Corvo*. Harmondsworth: Penguin Books, 1979.

Tadevosyan, Margarit, and Maxim D. Shrayer. "Thou Are Not Thou: Evelyn Waugh and Vladimir Nabokov." *The Nabokovian* 50 (2003): 24–39.

Tammi, Pekka. *Problems of Nabokov's Poetics. A Narratological Analysis*. Helsinki: Suomalainen Tiedeakatemia, 1985.

———. *Russian Subtexts in Nabokov's Fiction*. Tampere: Tampere UP, 1999.

Tolstoy, Leo. *Anna Karenina*. Trans. Rosemary Edmonds. London: Penguin, 1978.

———. *The Cossacks/ Happy Ever After/ The Death of Ivan Ilyich*. Trans. Rosemary Edmonds. Harmondsworth: Penguin Books, 1978.

———. *Master and Man*. Trans. S. Rapoport. London: Penguin Books, 1995.

———. *War and Peace*. Trans. Constance Garnett. London: Pan Books, 1972.

Toker, Leona. "'The Dead Are Good Mixers': Nabokov's Versions of Individualism." *Nabokov and His Fiction: New Perspectives*. Ed. Julian W. Connolly. Canbridge UP, 1999. 92–108.

———. *Nabokov: The Mystery of Literary Structures*. Ithaca: Cornell UP, 1989.

———. "Nabokov's Worldview." *The Cambridge Companion to Nabokov*. Ed. Julian W. Connolly. Cambridge: Cambridge UP, 2005. 232–247.

Troyat, Henri. *Pushkin*. Trans. Nancy Amphoux. New York: Minerva Press, 1975.

Urdang, Lawrence. *A Dictionary of Names and Nicknames*. Oxford: Oxford UP, 1991.

Vasari, Giorgio. *The Lives of the Artists*. Trans. Julia Bondanella and Peter Bondanella. Oxford: Oxford UP, 1998.

Vitale, Serena. *Pushkin's Button*. Trans. Ann Goldstein and Jon Rothschild. London: Fourth Estate, 1999.

Vries, Gerard de. "'Mountain, not Fountain': *Pale Fire*'s Saving Grace." *The Nabokovian* 63 (2009): 39–52.

———. "Tiaras and Triads in *Speak, Memory*." *The Nabokovian* 43 (1999): 29–35.

Vries, Gerard de, and D. Barton Johnson, with an Essay by Lisa Ashenden. *Nabokov and the Art of Painting*. Amsterdam: Amsterdam University Press, 2006.

Walton, Izaak. *The Lives of John Donne, Sir Henry Wotton, Richard Hooker, George Herbert and Robert Sanderson*.1640. London: Oxford UP, 1973.

Warner, Marina. *Joan of Arc*. Harmondsworth: Penguin Books, 1981.

Waugh, Evelyn. *Brideshead Revisited*. London: Penguin Books, 2000.

Wells H. G. *The War of the Worlds. The Invisible Man*. London: Macmillan, 1960.

Wilde, Oscar. *The Works*. London: Spring Books, 1963.

Wilder, Thornton. *The Bridge of San Luis Rey*. Harmondsworth: Penguin Books, 1959.

Wilson, Edmund. *The Triple Thinkers*. Harmondsworth: Penguin Books, 1962.

Wolff, Tatiana. *Pushkin on Literature*. London: Methuen, 1971.

Wood, Michael. *The Magician's Doubts: Nabokov and the Risks of Fiction*. London: Chatto & Windus: 1994.

Wordsworth, William. *The Poetical Works*. London: Oxford University Press, 1939.

Wright, Thomas. *Built of Books: How Reading Defined the Life of Oscar Wilde*. New York: Henry Holt, 2009.

Wyllie, Barbara. *Vladimir Nabokov*. London: Reaktion Books, 2010.

Zimmer, Dieter E. "Chinese Rhubarb and Caterpillars." 2002. www.d-e-zimmer.de.

———, ed. *Fahles Feuer*. By Vladimir Nabokov. Reinbek: Rowohlt, 2008.

———, ed. *Das wahre Leben des Sebastian Knight*. By Vladimir Nabokov. Reinbek: Rowohlt, 1996.

Zimmer, Dieter E., and Sabine Hartmann. "'The Amazing Music of Truth': Nabokov's Sources for Godunov's Central Asian Travels in *The Gift*." *Nabokov Studies* 7 (2002/2003): 33–74.

Zimmerman, Bonnie, ed. *Lesbian Histories and Cultures: An Encyclopedia*. New York: Garland, 2000.

Index

A
Abbasi, Riza 137
Adelman, Janet 152
Agostinelli, Alfred 132
Aivazovsky, Ivan 70
Akikusa, Shun'ichiro 83
Aldanov, Mark 62
Alexander, Doris 137
Alexandrov, Vladimir E. 55, 86
Andrea, Giacomo 129
Andrusov, Leonid 19
Anthès, George d' 12–13, 144
Appel, Alfred Jr. 5, 85, 106
Arc, Jeanne d' *see* Joan of Arc
Archiac, Viscount d' 13
Aristophanes 130
Arnold, Matthew 112

B
Baer, Brian James 189–190
Barabtarlo, Gennady viii, 5, 50, 56, 75
Baring, Maurice 27, 44, 110–111, 176
   "In Memoriam, A. H." 111
   Landmarks in Russian Literature 176
   The Puppet Show of Memory 110–111
Baring-Gould, William S. 152
Baring-Gould, Cecile 152
Barnstead, John 190
Barolsky, Paul 99, 105–106
Baskin, Walter 178
Bate, Jonathan 181–182
Baudelaire, Charles 60
   "*Les Metamorphoses du Vampire*" 60
Begnal, Michael H. 187–188
Berndt de Souza Mello, Jansy 44

Bethea, David M. 86
Binyon, T.J. 144
Blackwell, Stephen 191
Blake, William 164
Blok, Alexander 19, 61, 84–86
   The Puppet Show (Balaganchik) 86
   "The Strange Lady" 61
   Verses on a Beautiful Lady 19, 86
Blok, Lyubov (Mendeleeva) 86
Blum, Léon 73
Blunden, Edmund 148
Bodenstein, Jürgen 65
Boldini, Giovanni 150
Bonstetten, Charles de 112
Boswell, James 32, 95
Bowness, Alan 52
Boyd, Brian, viii, 1, 4–6, 14, 16–18, 20–21, 24–25, 27, 34, 39, 43–45, 49, 53, 56, 59, 61, 66, 69, 71, 86, 100–102, 104, 110, 112–113, 115, 118, 121, 131–132, 148, 154–155, 157, 170, 176, 182, 188, 193
Bradley, A.C. 179
Bradley, Rory 87
Breverton, Terry 34, 117
Brewer, E. Cobham 39
Briggs, Katherine 136
Brooke, Rupert 11, 17–18, 33, 87, 111–113, 148
   "The Old Vicarage, Granchester" 10, 17, 112
Bulfinch, Thomas 157
Burgin, Diana Lewis 55
Burliuk, David 20, 158
Burnand, Sir Francis 102–103, 40–41
   The Colonel 40–41

Burns, Tom   30
Bussy, Dorothy   16
Byron, Lord   18, 51, 53, 56–57, 114, 121–122, 148–150
  Childe Harold   122
  "L'Amitié est l'amour sans ailes"   18
  "The Dream"   51, 56–57, 114

C
Caine, William   141
  The Author of Trixie   26, 141
Calry, Bobby de   155
Carey, John   6, 162, 164
Carlyle, Thomas   165
Carpenter, Angelica Shirley   31
Carroll, Lewis   31, 112, 159
  Alice's Adventures in Wonderland   31, 87, 159
Caulton, Andrew   9, 18, 31, 38, 54, 57, 72, 159
Caws, Mary Ann   16, 25, 184
Chateaubriand, François-René de   119
  Mémoires d'Outre-tombe   119
Chaucer, Geoffrey   163
  Boethius   163
Chaworth, Mary   114
Chekhov, Anton   56, 94, 96–98, 107, 120, 173
  "The Black Monk"   107
  "The Lady with the Dog"   94
  The Seagull   56, 96–98, 120, 173
Chernowitz, Maurice   52
Chernyshevsky, Nikolay   3
Christie, Agatha   9, 40–41, 176
  Murder on the Orient Express   40–41
Christus, Petrus   49
Closmesnil, Léonie   184
Cockburn, Claude   106
Cocteau, Jean   25, 188
Coleridge, Samuel Taylor   143, 162
  The Rhyme of the Ancient Mariner   143
Collingwood, Stuart   31
Collins, William Wilkie   27, 42, 159–160
  The Woman in White   42–43, 159–160
Conder, Alan   73
Connolly, Julian W.   viii, 50, 164
Conrad, Joseph   87, 114
Constable, John   22
Corelli, Maria (née Mary Mackay)   31
Corelli, Arcangelo   31
Cornwell, Neil   105
Corvo, Baron *see* Rolfe, F.
Cottle, Basil   50
Couturier, Maurice   viii, 6, 10, 56, 88, 108, 121, 194
Cuddon, J.A.   30, 54

D
Da Vinci, Leonardo   41, 60, 64, 105–106, 129, 183, 185
  The Notebooks   129
Dal, Vladimir   144
Dali, Salvador   11
Daiches, David   32
Danzas, Konstantin   13–14
Daudet, Alphonse   63
  "L'Arlésienne"   63
Davenport-Hines, Richard   16, 25, 67, 150
De Botton, Alain   132
De la Mare, Walter   33, 148
Defoe, Daniel   54
  Robinson Crusoe   54
Degas, Edgar   63
Deibler, Anatole   60, 166
Delage-Toriel, Lara   viii, 31, 35, 106, 139
Demidov (family)   17
Derby, Earl of   67
Desmoulins, Camille   165
Diaghilev, Sergey   24–25, 156–157, 185, 188
Dickens, Charles   21
  A Tale of Two Cities   21
Dobrokovsky, Mechislav   158
Dolinin, Alexander   59, 86
Donne, John   21, 38, 33, 65–66, 73, 75, 161–162
  "A Valediction: Forbidding Morning"   164
  "Ecstacy"   66, 162

"Holy Sonnet X"   164
"Of the Progres of the Soul. The Second Anniversary"   33, 164
Doré, Gustave   143
Dostoevsky, Fyodor   19, 49
  The Idiot   19–20
Douglas, Alfred   113, 122
  "Two Loves"   113
Douglas, Charlotte   157–158
Douglas, Norman   25, 40, 122
  South Wind   25, 40
Doyle, Arthur Conan   9, 54–55, 140–141
  "A Scandal in Bohemia"   140
  The Complete Sherlock Holmes Short Stories   54, 61, 140–141
  The Hound of Baskervilles   60
Dragunoiu, Dana   viii, 42, 190
D'Urfé, Honoré   115
  L'Astrée   115

E
Edmunds, Jeff   viii
Efimov, Mikhail   110
Emery, Emily   97, 127
Esenin, Sergey   118
Eyck, Jan van   49

F
Faulkner, William   49
Fet, Afanasy   19, 176
Fischman, Zachary   114
Fitzgerald, Edward   112–113, 136–138
Flaubert, Gustave   56, 75, 77, 106
  Madame Bovary   56, 75, 77
Fogelin, Robert J.   74
Fonvizin, Denis Ivanovich   107
  The Infant   107
Foster, John Burt, Jr.   51–52, 151, 155–156
Fowler, Alastair   6
France, Anatole   165
  Les dieux ont soif   165
Frank, Siggy   viii, 16, 69, 85, 151
Freud, Sigmund   30, 49, 128–129

Leonardo da Vinci   129–130
Friedrich, Caspar   70
Fuchs, R.H.   22
Fussell, Paul   34, 99

G
Gardner, Helen   162
Gardner, Martin   159
Gautier, Théophile   55
  "Contralto"   55
Gay, Peter   183, 185
Gide, André   16, 41, 48–49, 133, 156, 177–178, 191
  Corydon   49
  If it Die   48–49
  Journal   49
  The Caves of the Vatican   49
  The Counterfeiters   41–42
  The Immoralist   49, 133
  The Notebooks of André Walter   48–49, 156, 177–178
Gifford, Don   152–153
Glendinning, Victoria   134
Gogol, Nikolai   58, 113, 121, 194
  Dead Souls   58, 120–122
Golding, Louis   40
  Magnolia Street   40
Goodman, Godfrey   32
  Fall of Man   32
Goodrich, Samuel   332
Gorianin, I.   69
Gozzi, Carlo   16, 85
  The Love for Three Oranges   16, 85
Granoien, Neil   185
Graves, Robert   9, 37, 65, 94, 148, 167
  Hercules, My Shipmate   37
  The Crowning Privilege   65
Gray, Camilla   157–158
Gray, Thomas   17–18, 33, 87, 111–112
  "Ode on a Distant prospect of Eton College"   112
Grayson, Jane   19, 193
Gregorio, Laurence   115
Grigoriev, S.L.   157

Grigorivich, Dmitri 19
Grimm, Jacob and Wilhelm 135
Grossman, Lev viii, 22–23, 188
Guadanini, Irina 2, 62, 65, 193
Gumilev, Nikolai 19, 32, 165–166
    "The Tram that Lost its Way" 32, 165
Gwynn, Stephen 124

H

Haggerty, George E. 128
Hall, James 47
Halle, Adam de la 44–45
    Le jeu de Robin et Marion 44
Harrison, Ernest 29
Harrison, G.B. 182
Hartmann, Sabine 171
Hathaway, Anne 181
Hawthorne, Nathan 19, 32
    Rappaccini's Daughter 19
Herbert, Auberon 111
Herder, Johann Gottfried 97
Higdon, David Leon 124
Holland, Vyvyan 102
Holloway, Mark 122
Holmes, Richard 55
Homer 8, 62, 167, 183
    Iliad 8–9, 183
    Odyssey 62, 183
Hooper, Alfred 15, 40
Hopkins, Gerard Manley 112
Horace 8, 20, 33
    The Art of Poetry 8, 20, 33
Housman, A.E. 17–18, 33, 111–113
    "Ask me no more, for fear I should reply" 113
    "Oh who is that young sinner with the handcuffs on his wrists?" 113
    "XL" (*A Shropshire Lad*) 17
Hugo, Victor 73
    "La conscience" 73
Hull, E.M. 106
    The Sheik 106
Huxley, Aldous 40
    Crome Yellow 40
Huysmans, J.-K. 184–185
    Against Nature 184

I

Il'in, Sergei 69

J

Jack, P.M. 99
James, Henry 51–52
Jerome, Jerome K. 32
    Three Men on the Bummel 32
Joan of Arc 70, 125, 144, 170–172
Johnson, D. Barton viii, 33, 50, 116–117, 126, 148
Johnson, Hamish 152
Johnson, Samuel 32, 95, 112
Johnston, Robert H. 176
Joyce, James 30, 32, 90, 132, 148, 151
    Ulysses 26, 28, 40, 67, 90, 150–152
Juliar, Michael 1

K

Kanaris, Konstantinos 121
Karlinsky, Simon 2, 18, 41, 86, 99, 110, 127, 148, 153, 185, 189
Kaye, Richard 183–184
Keats, John 18–19, 52, 98
    "La Belle Dame Sans Merci" 18–19, 52, 98
Kenny, Anthony 74
Kerr, Jessica 136
Ketchian, Sonia 19
Keynes, Geoffrey 112
Khayyám, Omar 136–138
    Rubáiyát 136–138
Khodasevich, Vladislav 30, 66
Kilmartin, Terence 133
Kipling, Rudyard 16, 18, 33, 67, 111–114, 131
    "Mrs. Bathurst" 67, 131
Knopp, Sherron E. 134
Kolokotronis, Theodoros 121
Koltsov, Aleksei 19
Kruchenykh, Aleksei 18
Kutepov, Alexander 121
Kuzmin, Mikhail 133, 190
    Wings 133, 190

L

Langeveld, Arthur viii, 20
Larmour, David H. J. 54
Latham, Ronald 45
Laver, James 34
Le Carré, John 9
Lee, Hermione 3
Lehmann, John 46, 113
Leider, Emily 106
Léon Noel, Lucie 4, 85
Leonardo *see* Da Vinci
  Lermontov, Mikhail 62
  "The Dream" 62
Letley, Emma 111
Levi, Anthony 115
Leving, Yuri viii, 73, 137
Lindheim, Nancy 152
Lippert, W. 38
Livak, Leonid 30, 42, 49
Lodge, David 50
Lokrantz, Jessie 176
Long, Michael 46
Loring, John 22
Lorrain, Jean 185
  Très Russe 185
Loukas (Chalandritsanos) 122
Lucie-Smith, Edward 183, 185

M

Mabinogion, The 100
Maddox, Lucy 53, 96
Maerz, A. 22
Maeterlinck, Maurice 97
MacCarthy, Fiona 18
Mackay, Mary *see* Marie Corelli
Malory, Sir Thomas 94
  Le Morte d'Arthur 94
Mann, Thomas 30–31, 40, 44, 49, 55, 127–128
  Death in Venice 127
  The Magic Mountain 40, 55, 127–128
Mansfield, Katherine 16
Marchand, Leslie 53, 114, 122
Martin, William H. 136–137
Martiny, Erik 116
Marvell, Andrew 28
  "On a Drop of Dew" 28
  "The Mower's Song" 28
Mason, Bobbie Ann 123
Mason, Sandra 136–137
Mata Hari *see* Zelle
Matsys, Quentin 49
Maturin, Charles 145
  Melmoth the Wanderer 145
Maugham, W. Somerset 9
Maupassant, Guy de 64, 101
  "That Pig of a Morin" 64, 101–102
Maurois, André 3
Mavrocordatos, Alexandros 121
Mayakovsky, Vladimir 157
Meilakh, M. 69
Memling, Hans 49
Melnikov-Papoushek, Nadezhda 51
Meltzer, Françoise 183
Merkel, Stephanie 85
Meyer, Priscilla viii, 19, 32
Miaulis, A.V. 121
Milton, John 5–6, 32
Mirsky, D.S. 86, 110, 157–158
Mochulsky, Konstantin 19, 86
Möller, Reimer 188
Monet, Claude 52
Montesquiou, Robert de 150, 185
Montezuma 165
Moreau, Gustave 183–185
Monk, Ray 74
Morgan, Paul B. 101
Morrell, Otteline 114
Morton, Thomas 31
Munthe, Axel 56–57, 61, 77–78
  The Story of San Michele 56, 61, 77–78

N

Nabokov, Dmitri 1, 192
Nabokov, Elena Ivanova 2, 22, 71, 188–189, 192–193
Nabokov, Konstantin 191
Nabokov, Sergey 1–2, 22, 62, 145, 187–189, 191–194
Nabokov, V.D. 14–15, 27, 110, 190–191
Nabokov, Véra 1–2, 37, 40, 43, 122, 162, 189, 192–194

Index

Nabokov, Vladimir 1–3, 5–7, 9, 11–13, 15–16, 18–44, 48–52, 56, 61–62, 65–75, 83–86, 88, 92, 94, 96–97, 100, 106, 110–113, 115–124, 127, 129–134, 137–141, 143–145, 148, 151, 153–158, 161–162, 169–172, 176, 181–182, 186–188, 191–194
  Ada 5, 25–26, 118, 123, 156
  Bend Sinister 22, 43, 92–93
  "Chapter Sixteen" 42, 170
  Defense, The 35, 49, 83
  Despair 41, 83, 129, 139
  Eugene Onegin, A Novel in Verse by Alexander Pushkin 14, 121, 123
  The Enchanter 1, 135
  The Eye 83, 135, 139, 149
  The Gift 1, 3, 42–43, 46, 49, 59, 65, 72–73, 84, 118, 120, 130, 137, 139, 144, 161, 170–172
  Glory 11, 27–28, 53–54, 130, 139, 154
  Invitation to a Beheading 126, 140, 166, 170
  Lectures on Literature 6, 38, 62, 119, 123–124, 132–133
  Lectures on Russian Literature 13, 97, 120
  Letters to Véra 29, 35, 40, 49, 51, 110, 189, 191
  Lolita 5, 7, 40–41, 49, 60, 85, 90, 100, 122, 138, 170, 176
  Look at the Harlequins! 9, 43, 53, 58, 96, 113, 118, 143, 165
  Mary 51, 56, 120, 130, 139
  Nikolay Gogol 121, 194
  Pale Fire 49, 73, 83, 118, 120, 130, 144, 164, 168–170, 191
  Pnin 5, 28, 49, 83, 117, 130, 170
  Poems and Problems 10
  Speak, Memory 2, 4–5, 10–11, 14–15, 17–18, 20, 24–27, 36, 38–39, 42, 55, 57, 61–62, 86, 116–117, 131, 144–145, 148, 154–156, 162, 170, 187–188, 191
  Strong Opinions 70, 85, 138
  Stories 14, 25, 44, 94
  Transparent Things 74, 130, 172
Nakata, Akiko 65, 74, 194
Naiman, Eric viii, 26, 130
Nepomnyashchy, Catherine Theimer 41
Nicholas II 189
Nicholl, Charles 64, 129, 183
Nicholson, B.E. 117
Nicholson, Harold 134
  Some People 134
Nicol, Charles 4
Nijinska, Bronislava 25
Nijinsky, Vaslav 25
Norman, Will 29
Nussbaum (monsieur Noyer) 155

O

Obolensky, Dmitri 32
Obolensky, Valerian 176
Ogrinc, Will 145
Olcott, Anthony 4, 75
Opie, Iona 34, 64
Opie, Peter 34, 64
Orczy, Baroness 9
Ovid 100
  Metamorphoses 100
Owen, Wilfred 148
Oxford Companion to English Literature, The 127

P

Page, Norman 3, 99, 113
Paglia, Camille 145, 185
Painter, George 132, 150, 184
Parker, Derek 164
Parker, Stephen Jan viii
Pater, Walter Horatio 60, 112–113, 183, 185
  The Renaissance 183
Peacock, Thomas Love 40
Pearson, Hesketh 102, 113, 122
Pegler, Martin 34
Pequigney, Joseph 153
Peterson, Dale 174
Pilorge, Maurice 166
Pitzer, Andrea 56, 61, 73, 188

Plato   130
   Symposium   130
Platonov, Andrei   91
   The Return   91
Podlech, Dieter   12, 38
Poe, Edgar Allan   141–142
   "The Purloined Letter"   141–142
Polo, Marco   45, 157
   The Travels   45, 157
Ponomareva, Tatiana   viii
Pope, Alexander   37
   Essay on Criticism   37
Praz, Mario   184–184
Prévost, l'Abbé   62, 100
   Manon Lescaut   62, 100
Proffer, Carl R.   5
Proffer, Ellendea   5
Proust, Marcel   10–11, 23, 25–26, 30, 49, 51–52, 67, 104, 119, 123, 132–133, 148–150, 155–156, 183–185
   Jean Santeuil   184
   A l'ombre de jeunes filles en fleurs (In the Shade of Blooming Young Girls)   133
   Remembrance of Things Past   11, 23, 119, 123, 132–133, 148–150, 156, 183–184
   Swann's Way   10, 123, 133, 156
   Le Temps Retrouvé   104, 132, 183
Pushkin, Alexander   12–14, 29, 49, 82, 121, 144, 158, 162, 171–172, 181
   Eugene Onegin   29, 46, 67, 162
   "The Last of the Relatives of Joan of Arc"   144
   "The Prophet"   171
Pythagoras   15

Q
Quennell, Peter   122, 152
Quin, J.D.   12

R
Racine, Jean   55
Rampton, David   3
Razin, Stenka   55
Reed, Christopher   184
Remigius (Saint Remy)   171

Reynolds, Graham   70
Rimmon, Shlomith   58
Ripon, Lady (Constance Gwladys Robinson)   25
Robinson, Jack   54
Roelofs, Willem   22
Rolfe, Fr.   99
   Hadrian the VII   99
Romanov, Konstantin   189
Rondeaux, Madeleine   48
Ronen, Omry   18
Ross, Gordon   136
Rowe, W. W.   12
Rukavishnikov, Vasily Ivanovich *see* Uncle Ruka.
Rusinko, Elaine   165
Russell, Alan   75
Rutledge, David S.   114
Rylkova, Galina   viii, 49

S
Sackville-West, Vita   134
   The Edwardians   134
Salehar, Anna Maria   171
Sampson, George
Samain, Albert   54
Sand, George   156
   François le Champi   156
Sappho   119
Sassoon, Siegfried   148
Schapiro, Leonard   120
Scheijen, Sjeng   25
Schiff, Stacy   37, 62, 106, 145, 162, 193–194
Schiff, Sydney   16
Schulz, Gretchen   176
Schuman, Samuel   151
Scott Moncrieff, C.K.   133
Ségur, Comtesse de   156
   Les Malheurs de Sophie   156
Senderovich, Savely   12, 16, 64, 85–86
Settembrini, Luigi   128
   I Neoplatonici   128
Seymour, Miranda   52, 114
Shakespeare, William   24, 48–49, 57, 92–93, 130, 132, 136, 151–153, 179–182, 194
   As You Like It   130

Hamlet 6, 18, 20–21, 25, 33, 45–46, 48, 92–93, 179, 181
Julius Caesar 57
King Lear 26, 48, 93–94, 181
Macbeth 31, 48, 181
Midsummer-Night's Dream 136, 181
Othello 28, 34, 45, 98, 181
The Merchant of Venice 152–153, 181
The Tempest 48, 151, 181
Twelfth Night 48, 151–153, 181
Sonnets 24, 179, 181–182
Shapiro, Gavriel 21, 190
Sheldon, Victoria 44
Shrayer, Maxim D. 124, 145, 158
Shvabrin, Stanislav viii, 18–20, 61, 86, 144
Shvarts, Yelena 12, 16, 64, 85–86
Sisson, Jonathan B. 23, 28
Skonechnaia, Olga 130
Slivkin, Yevgeny 165
Smith, A. J. 162–164
Smith, Bruce R. 152, 181
Smith, Patricia Juliana 31
Smyth, Ethel 110–111
Socrates 28, 170
Sologub, Fyodor 19
    "The Poison Garden" 19
Somov, Konstantin 21, 85
Southey, Robert 88, 146
    "The Old Man's Comforts" 88, 146
Steele, Richard 67
Stokoe, W.J. 26
Sparrow, John 112
Spenser, Edmund 123
    The Faerie Queen 123
Stegner, Page 3
Stevenson, Robert Louis 25, 124
    Strange Case of Dr. Jekyll and Mr. Hyde 25, 124
Stewart, Philip 144
Strachey, Lytton 16
Stuck, Franz 185
Suasso, Frans 13
Sullivan, Edmund J. 136
Suvorin, Mikhail 14

Sweeney, Susan Elizabeth viii, 21, 75, 85, 141–142
Symons, A.J.A. 99–100

T

Tadevosyan, Margerit 124, 145
Tammi, Pekka viii, 7, 28
Tasso, Torquato 123
    Gerusalemme liberata 123
Tchaikovsky, Peter Ilyich 190
Tchelitchew, Pavel 188
Tennyson, Alfred 111
    In Memoriam A.H.H. 111
Thiébaux, Marcelle 101
Thieme, Hermann 22, 188, 192
Tolstoy, Leo 11, 47, 75, 97
    Anna Karenina 11
    Master and Man 75
    The Cossacks, 47
    War and Peace 47, 97
Toker, Leona viii, 75, 168–169
Troyes, Chrétien de 42
    Perceval ou le Conte du Graal 42
Turgenev, Ivan 11, 19, 120
    Smoke 11, 120
    Spring Torrents 19
Turner, J.W.M. 22, 70

U

Uncle Ruka 20, 26, 35, 39, 47, 54, 65, 67, 73, 117, 144, 153–155, 191
Urdang, Lawrence 30

V

Valentino, Rudolph 38, 106
Vasari, Giorgio 105, 129
Vielgorsky, Iosif 121
Virgil 191
Vitale, Serena 13–14, 144
Vogüé, E.M. de 184
    Le roman Russe 184
Voltaire 144
    La Pucelle 144
Vries, Gerard de 116, 168, 190
Vyazemsky, P.A. 13

W

Walton, Isaac 164
Warner, Marina 125

Waugh, Evelyn   123–124
   Brideshead Revisited   123–124
Weemes, J.   162
   A Treatise of the Four Degenerate Sons   162
Wells, H.G.   9, 25–27, 51–52, 110
   Boon   52
   The Invisible Man   25–26
Whistler, James   150
Wilde, Oscar   102, 113, 122, 133, 145, 156, 183–185, 191
   Salomé   184
   The Decay of Lying   102
   The Portrait of Dorian Gray   133
Wilder, Thornton   25, 107, 110
   The Bridge of San Luis Rey   25, 107
   The Ides of March   110
Wilson, Edmund   99, 110, 112, 153, 155, 186
Wittgenstein, Ludwig   74
   Philosophische Grammatik   74
   Tractatus Logico–Philosophicus   74
Wolff, Tatiana   121
Wood, Michael   21
Woolf, Virginia   16
Wordsworth, William   10, 112
   The Prelude   10
Wright, Sarah Bird   16
Wright, Thomas   113, 122, 145
Wriothesley, Henry   182
Wyllie, Barbara   viii, 5, 116

Y
Yeats, William Butler   16

Z
Zelle, Margarete Gertrude   17, 59, 108
Zimmer, Dieter   6, 63, 71, 119, 121, 138, 171
Zimmerman, Bonnie   127

www.ingramcontent.com/pod-product-compliance
Lightning Source LLC
Chambersburg PA
CBHW071740150426
43191CB00010B/1642